COLLEGE CLASSICS IN ENGLISH

General Editor

NORTHROP FRYE

THREE RESTORATION COMEDIES

The Country Wife
BY WILLIAM WYCHERLEY

The Way of the World
BY WILLIAM CONGREVE

The Rehearsal
BY GEORGE VILLIERS
SECOND DUKE OF BUCKINGHAM

Edited by G. G. Falle
Trinity College, University of Toronto

MACMILLAN OF CANADA—TORONTO

Contents

Contents

Three Restoration Comedies

Introduction

The three comedies contained in this volume serve as an illustration of Socrates' argument, in the *Symposium* of Plato, that the genius of comedy is the same as that of tragedy, and that the true artist in tragedy is an artist in comedy too. *The Country Wife* and *The Way of the World* are almost universally regarded as high points in the history of English dramatic comedy, while *The Rehearsal* is a farce (that is, another form of comedy) that consciously parodies and burlesques the art of the heroic play, the major contribution of the Restoration and the eighteenth century to the noble tradition of English tragedy. In its preoccupation with man as a social animal, with what is universal in human experience, with the problems inherent in any attempt to establish a lasting social order, comedy, it may be argued, is a more pervasive human condition than tragedy; there the focus is upon the individual soul, upon a metaphysical rather than a social action, and upon the regeneration and redemption of the human spirit. Since one of the aims of comedy has always been to examine man as an essentially social phenomenon and to explore means by which a stable society may be constructed, and since it is a perennial interest of man to live in a world of order and value, comedy has generally been regarded as an art of reconciliation. The comic artist attempts to reconcile those disparities and contrarieties in our human experience that man's finite intelligence cannot explain.

Henri Bergson and George Meredith, the nineteenth century's most distinguished comic theorists, agree that comedy is a civilizing and humanizing agent: a means to moral freedom, a deliverance from anarchy, a step in the direction of culture. It emerges from what Meredith calls "our united social intelligence"; unlike satire, it is related to a broad conception of nature (nothing human is alien to the comic spirit); it allows for an intensification of insight into the human situation; it pleads for tolerance of, and sympathy for, human frailty; its ultimate appeal is for freedom from illusion, for the courage to absent ourselves from felicity a while and to look with hope into the realities of experience. Despite its demand for participation, it does not, as tragedy does, demand our total involvement, an involvement that can easily blur or obscure valid judgment. It insists upon a decorous degree of personal and aesthetic detachment which, while it engages sensibility and mind, guarantees none the less freedom of evaluation. Finally, it is an instrument of rehabilitation and redemption; for it is through enlightenment and "thoughtful" laughter that man is redeemed from pride, vanity, and complacency.

The social action of which comedy may be defined as an "imitation" is one in which a new order, generally associated with youth and regeneration, displaces an old one, associated with age and disintegration. In *The Way of the World* the social order presided over by Lady Wishfort gives way, in the course of the action, to one represented by Mirabell and Millamant. The movement is away from illusion, in the direction of an acceptance that reconciles illusion and reality. The degree of irony employed by the comic artist will vary according to his purpose, and it is suggested here that the most intensive use of irony will result in the profoundest comic action; in other words, so-called "dark comedy" is the most intense form that comedy can take. The protagonists of the greatest comedy are the agents of a gradually intensifying action that in its denouement highlights the ironies in the human condition. In terms of the "happy ending", the boy-gets-girl resolution, the displacement of the old by the new will reveal differing levels of irony. Sometimes the change is complete as in romantic comedy, but in deeper forms of comedy we are aware that little has changed – indeed, that, given the frailty of human nature, little *can* be changed. The comic artist concerned with these deeper forms seems to ask that we make a conscious distinction between illusion and reality, learn to accept illusion for what it is, and with that acceptance, which is a form of knowledge of ourselves and of our condition, see into the true nature of reality. In this sense, comedy is both a civilizing and a moral agent, the degree of its moral agency being dependent upon the degree of its humanizing effect.

As Aristotle tells us in the *Poetics*, a unified plot is

> ... that which has a beginning, a middle, and an end. A beginning is that which does not itself follow anything by causal necessity, but after which something naturally is or comes to be. An end, on the contrary, is that which itself naturally follows some other thing, either by necessity, or as a rule, but has nothing following it. A middle is that which follows something as some other thing follows it.

The comic action usually begins with an established social structure that suffers from disorder, disintegration, and a falling-away from positive social and moral values. Society is governed by middle-aged figures, who in their growing complacency have allowed, consciously or unconsciously, the displacement of justice by injustice, honour by self-interest, truth by hypocrisy and affectation, reality by illusion, love by sexual appetite. The characteristics of the old order are made clear by the personages of the action, by their follies and frailties, by the rational (and irrational) nature of their moral choices. (The greater the author's emphasis upon human folly as distinguished from human frailty, the greater the incidence of satire in the action.) *Satire* In *The Way of the World* Lady Wishfort is in control of the social world depicted in the play; she is the symbol of a disintegrating social order.

The general movement of the action is in the direction of social reconstruction, of attempts on the part of the young protagonists to replace the old order by a new that will reflect positive values and the health and vigour of youth. The "middle" of the plot intensifies the action, and it is in terms of this process of intensification that the resolution (or "end") is determined. This deepening process affects both action and character alike. In the former we find it in the sequence of scenes of the play. The early scenes are trivial in relation to those that precede the denouement: little more than correct

Plot.

observance of social propriety and decorum is involved. But the culminating scenes in the process are fraught with dangers and consequences of considerable gravity. In *The Way of the World* the incidents of the action move from the glib and affectedly cynical repartee of the opening acts, through the plan devised by Mirabell to present Lady Wishfort with a new suitor (and consequently to force her hand), to the complexity of the final act, where Lady Wishfort is threatened with financial ruin, Mrs. Fainall with dishonour, and the young protagonists, Mirabell and Millamant, with the destruction of their mutual love and happiness. In the case of character, intensification focuses upon an educative process involving the youthful protagonists, by which they become more fully aware of the problems inherent in the social condition, and learn to distinguish between the illusory and the real. In the famous *"proviso* scene" in the fourth act of the Congreve play the lovers dispel any illusory view of marriage and come to recognize the reality of their mutual responsibilities. It is a scene of recognition and discovery.

The Aristotelian "end" of the action is in the denouement, the reconciliation of all the seeming contradictions that the incidents of the play and the responses of the characters have exemplified. The tangles of the plot are unravelled, a system of suitable rewards and punishments is implemented; and one feels that, once the agents of the action have recovered from the shock of discovery and recognition, the natural course of life will be resumed. A new order is usually suggested as the youthful protagonists assume the authority that, at the outset of the play, was in the hands of the older generation, and the drama concludes with a ritual symbolic of order – usually a dance or a wedding, or both. To what degree the moral characteristics of the new order will differ from those of the old will depend largely upon the degree of irony inherent in the author's view of the world. It is only in the most idealistic comedy that any total change is effected. More often the author suggests, as Congreve does at the end of *The Way of the World*, that by exorcising an evil lodged within the structure of their society, Mirabell and Millamant give us hope of a brighter future.

Wycherley's irony is deeper at the same point in the action of *The Country Wife*. Little, in truth, has been concluded. Life will go on much as usual: the new has not displaced the old; the Pinchwifes, Fidgets, and Squeamishes are still victims of their foolish illusions; Sparkish remains untouched by the turn of events; and the wit of Horner and the game of cuckoldry will continue quite unabated. It is true that the series of amorous chases has ended in the marriage of Alithea and Harcourt, but the irony in the nature of that situation leaves us but small comfort. Perhaps the most hopeful sign in the denouement is the experience of Mrs. Pinchwife. She has, at least, been through the educative process, and she emerges at the end of the play, not with illusion dispelled (Wycherley seems to suggest that it would be unreasonable and unreal to expect so much) but with a fuller knowledge of the ways of the world.

As comedy is concerned with investigating the reason, that faculty that distinguishes man from animal, so it is concerned with the sexual impulse, which human nature shares with animal nature. Since ancient times, when comedy was associated with the phallic rites, Eros has been the presiding genius of comedy; and, as Professor Frye has observed, Eros "has to adapt himself to the moral facts of society". Again it is a question of reconciliation: of reconciling sexual drives with intellectual and moral standards, of squaring such natural impulses with the nobler aspirations of the human spirit. The price of repression is dehumanization, as the Houyhnhnms in the fourth book of Swift's *Gulliver's Travels* so aptly illustrate. But since the sexual impulses of man relate him to the animal world, sex is of the very nature of comedy in measuring the distance between man at his worst and man at his best. In art the use of the obscene word or gesture in order to portray character will serve to underline a self-gratifying sexuality, as in the case of Lady Fidget. Indecency for the sake of indecency is a mark of the vulgar and the uncivilized; but in art indecency may be used structurally as an appropriate symbol for human depravity, as a means of emphasizing a failure to reach commonly accepted standards of human civility and morality.

The so-called "comedy of manners", a form of comedy that flourished during the literary age known as the Restoration (1660-1700), had its origins in Elizabethan comedy, but the Jonsonian "comedy of humours" of the earlier seventeenth century did much to disturb the continuity of the tradition, and also to modify it when it reappeared in the work of Etherege, Wycherley, and Congreve. This particular order of comedy aims to examine critically the manners, that is, the social and moral standards, that regulate an entire society; more generally, comedy is an anatomy of social *mores*. Its most distinguishing feature is, perhaps, its language which, at its best, results in the highly artificial and polished rhetoric of *The Way of the World*. The characters of the comedy of manners are frequently as representative of universal types as they are individuals, and in this respect the genre owes much to Ben Jonson's theory of humours. According to Jonson, men are distinguishable one from another by certain predominant humours, that is, states of mind or sensibility by which their responses to given situations may be predicted with a considerable degree of accuracy. As in Jonsonian comedy, so in the comedy of the Restoration the clue to a character's true nature is often revealed in his name. In the plays under discussion here, Lady Wishfort as the woman of sensual appetite, Witwoud as the would-be wit, Petulant, Fainall as the deceiver, Pinchwife, Sparkish, and Fidget are examples.

The comedy of manners found its most eloquent expression between about 1668 and 1700 in the plays of Etherege, Wycherley, and Congreve. The tradition survived early-eighteenth-century sentimental comedy and was later modified by Sheridan, who modelled *The School for Scandal* upon *The Way of the World* with what must be generally conceded as only moderate success. In the late years of the nineteenth century Oscar Wilde subscribed to the tradition and made further modifications, and, more recently, there have been evidences of manners comedy in parts of T. S. Eliot's dramatic comedy, notably in *The Cocktail Party*; but the peak of the tradition was reached by the Restoration dramatists.

The Country Wife

There are two major lines of dramatic action in Wycherley's play: the device of Horner, who announces to the town that he is sexually impotent as the result of a disease contracted during a recent visit to France, and the age-old tale of the old man married to the young wife. Mr. Horner's device is, of course, a hoax; the gentlemen of the town give him easy access to their wives, and the ladies, once let in upon "the dear secret", admit him as their lover without fear of damaging their reputations. This main theme of *The Country Wife* was probably suggested to Wycherley by the *Eunuchus* of Terence, a Roman dramatist of the second century B.C., who in turn had borrowed it from the Greek comic writer Menander. The marriage of Mr. and Mrs. Pinchwife recalls Chaucer's treatment of the January and May theme in *The Merchant's Tale*. It is fairly obvious that Wycherley took certain details of plot from Molière's *L'Ecole des Femmes* and *L'Ecole des Maris*. Such incidental borrowings must be acknowledged, but *The Country Wife* is very much English Restoration comedy and bears the indelible mark of Wycherley's dramatic genius.

The major conflict in the play is between the old social order (represented by Sir Jaspar Fidget, Mr. Pinchwife, and, in a minor way, Old Lady Squeamish), which is corroded by deceit, affectation, and the most arrant hypocrisy, and young Harry Horner, whose major aim is to capitalize to his own advantage upon the corruptions of society. Mistress Margery Pinchwife, the country wife, is the link between the two sides of the conflict: she is married to a rakish and debauched member of the old order, and is simultaneously the more-than-willing victim of Horner's nefarious stratagem. The fact that she provides the title for the play is a mark of her significance in terms of the total dramatic action. A certain intensification develops in the course of the action as we learn of the successes of Horner's scheme, which ultimately threatens the theme of "true love" in the sub-plot involving Alithea, Mr. Pinchwife's sister, and Harcourt, Horner's friend. The resolution does not result in the

Outcome

displacement of the old by the new (despite the happy outcome of the Alithea-Harcourt sub-plot) but more satirically, not
to say cynically, upon the prolongation of a lie. At a moment
when Horner is about to be unmasked, the ladies (Lady Fidget,
Mistress Dainty, and Mistress Squeamish), to save what little is
left of their reputations, swear to the truth of his impotence,
and Mistress Pinchwife, against her better knowledge and
judgment, is prevailed upon to acquiesce. The resolution is a
stalemate, and this would appear to be at the heart of Wycherley's satiric purpose. Given the self-interest and natural appetites
of human nature, little can be changed; such is the way of the
world. There is little felicity for the audience in the Alithea-
Harcourt affair, for the corruptness of the men, the hypocrisy of
the women, and the deceit of Horner proceed uninterrupted,
and Mistress Margery's naïve directness and honest dealing go
Honesty wasted for naught in a world where illusion prevails to camouflage a
shameless reality. It is fitting that the play should conclude
with a dance of cuckolds, for the dishonour of cuckoldom ironically inverts the order symbolized by the dance.

In our understanding of the play's characters, the major
problem rests in the figure of Harry Horner. Bonamy Dobrée
sees him as a villain, a "grim, nightmare" figure, "dominating
the helpless, hopeless apes who call themselves civilized men".
But Horner does not victimize the innocent; the men he cuckolds and the women who willingly gratify his pleasures are no
less villainous than he; and in the case of Mistress Margery, the
scheming wit and ingenuity displayed in her letter to Horner
and in her tricking of her husband to deliver her to her lover
are indications that she is far from "helpless" in her situation.
Horner is, rather, the libertine, a man willing to flout the false
mores of his society in order to satisfy his own desires. He is not
without certain recognizable virtues, if Wycherley chooses more
often to depict them negatively than positively. As a man of wit
he is shown to be vastly superior to the would-be wits of the
play, Sir Jaspar, Pinchwife, and the insufferable Sparkish; and
as a friend, he has occasion to indicate his hopes for Harcourt's
happiness with Alithea, although in the final scene he is forced

Horner

momentarily to betray his friend in order not to betray his mistress. He is not without honour, but his wit and his integrity are always at the service of self-interest; if there is any hope for the social order, that hope lies with Harcourt and Alithea, for Horner, with his superior intelligence, is satisfied to prey upon the weaknesses of the old, rather than be instrumental in formulating positive standards to govern the new.

Of the women, Mistress Margery is the most engaging figure in the play. Hazlitt saw in her a curious blend of "self-will, curiosity, art, and ignorance", but there is a degree of pathos in her situation and character as well. Guarded under lock and key by a jealous huband, she commands our sympathy as when, in the postscript of her letter to Horner, she pleads with him to keep their secret from her husband "lest he should come home and pinch me, or kill my squirrel". From her country home she has brought lively natural impulses, which are more fully stimulated by the intrigues of the town and the obsessive fears of her husband that she will make him a cuckold. She is not entirely innocent of the ways of love as she admits with charming *naïveté* in her letter to Horner: "...I'm sure if you and I were in the country at cards together, I could not help treading on your toe under the table, or rubbing knees with you, and staring in your face, till you saw me, and then looking down, and blushing for an hour together." She lacks the sophistication of Alithea, who is fully aware of the crooked ways of a corrupt world, which Margery learns in the course of the action. As Alithea must break down certain barriers of a false social propriety and decorum before she can be free of Sparkish and honourably married to Harcourt, so Margery must learn to come to terms with the ineluctable appearances that obscure the truth at the heart of a debased society.

The crowd of Fidgets and Squeamishes that Wycherley has drawn with such brilliance and acute perception are, in the absence of any mutual enjoyments, dedicated to the pursuit of their own selfish interests. The self-importance of Sir Jaspar and the glaring coxcombry of Sparkish are matched by the mincing depravity of Mistress Dainty and the overt sensuality of Lady Fidget, who is a superb match in wit and self-interest for Horner. Each character creates for himself an image of his own nature, an appearance, that serves as a disguise for the sordid truth that lies beneath. As Norman Holland has observed, they are given to two kinds of deception: the deception of others and of themselves. Associated with the former is "a certain cynical wisdom about human nature" that endows them with a power to control, by means of the consistent pretence, the progress of the artificial game of life in which they are engaged. As the resolution of the play suggests, there is no cure for self-deception; survival depends upon the maintenance of the deception, and those who are not fools are knaves. There is a glimmer of hope in the honesty of Harcourt and the congeniality of Alithea, two people whose experience has culminated in an ability to distinguish between the apparent and the real, and whose love remains their precarious stay against confusion.

Finally, the language of the play calls for brief comment. *The Country Wife* has not the highly controlled rhetoric that provides the brilliant verbal structure and poetic effectiveness of *The Way of the World*. With few exceptions, Wycherley's language is the language of practical reality. Apart from the romantic dialogue of Harcourt and Alithea, which is dotted with religious and spiritual image and metaphor, the general tone of the dialogue is in keeping with the utilitarian and self-gratifying aims and purposes of the characters. By means of a reductive verbal technique, Wycherley diminishes abstract virtues and even people to physical facts or objects: love is "the London disease" or "that worse distemper"; to Mr. Pinchwife marriage is a matter of giving Sparkish "five thousand pounds to lie with my sister"; honour has a kind of cash-surrender value, or in the simple language of Alithea's maid is merely "a disease in the head, like the megrim or falling-sickness"; sisters and daughters become equivalents to the money of usury, "safest, when put out"; a masked woman is "like a covered dish"; and a rival, says Sparkish, is "as good sauce for a married man to a wife, as an orange to veal". Some of Wycherley's best verbal effects are in his mastery of the bawdy *double entendre*, which is seen to best advantage in the famous "china" scene of the fourth act. The opening lines of the play – "A quack is as fit for a pimp, as a midwife for a bawd; they are still but in their way both helpers of nature" – set the general tone of Horner's repartee, while in Lady Fidget's observance of all the outward formal niceties of speech Wycherley ironically highlights her true character. She is scandalized by Sir Jaspar's use of the word "naked" in her presence; and at the moment she is about to give herself to Horner, she prattles of her "dear honour" and appeals to her lover with the unforgettable "Nay, fy! let us not be smutty." Like Lady Wishfort in *The Way of the World* she is one of the master-strokes of the play, and her dialogue is superbly tailored to fit her licentious character.

The Way of the World

The complexity of family relationships in Congreve's great play demands brief explanation before one looks at the more important complexity of emotional relationships. Lady Wishfort is the governing figure of the decadent social order that, in the course of the dramatic action, is displaced by a new and vital society, of which Mirabell and Millamant, the youthful protagonists, are symbols. Mistress Arabella Fainall, Lady Wishfort's daughter, was first married to Mr. Languish. Upon his death she became mistress to Mirabell (to whom she secretly entrusted the disposition of her fortune) and later, upon Mirabell's advice, married Mr. Fainall. Mistress Millamant is the niece and ward of Lady Wishfort, who controls half of her estate; it is understood that that portion will revert to Millamant upon her marriage to a man of whom Lady Wishfort approves. Sir Wilfull Witwoud is Lady Wishfort's nephew; young Tony Witwoud is Sir Wilfull's half-brother. Mistress Fainall, Mistress Millamant, and Sir Wilfull are all, then, first cousins. That Congreve took delight in the confusion is fairly evident in a speech of Mr. Fainall in the first act: "[Sir Wilfull] is half brother to this Witwoud by a former wife, who was sister to my Lady Wishfort, my wife's mother. If you [Mirabell] marry Millamant, you must call cousins too." Outside the family circle are Mirabell, the former lover of Mrs. Fainall and (to gain access to Millamant) pretended admirer of Lady Wishfort herself; and Mistress Marwood, mistress to Fainall, and victim of a sexual passion for Mirabell that is corroded by an insane jealousy.

The main action of the play concerns two attempts (one made by Mirabell, the other by Fainall) to wrest the social power from Lady Wishfort, who controls the fortune and destiny of the major participants in the action. Whereas Fainall's attempt is motivated by lust for money and, consequently, for power, Mirabell's is motivated by his honourable desire to win the hand of Millamant, to protect Mrs. Fainall from the machinations of her villainous husband, and to safeguard Lady Wishfort from Fainall's blackmailing stratagems. Lady Wishfort blocks Mirabell's primary purpose because of the humiliation and indignation she has suffered as a result of his ironic advances to her. He must then resort to a scheme that will put her in his power, and to achieve this end he adopts the rather cruel device of disguising his servant Waitwell as his uncle (Sir Rowland) and presenting him as an ardent suitor to Lady Wishfort. Just as Lady Wishfort is being threatened with bankruptcy by Fainall's villainous plot, by which he aims to gain control of the estates of his mother-in-law, his wife, and Mistress Millamant, Mirabell rescues her by removing Waitwell's disguise and publicly acknowledging his trusteeship of Mrs. Fainall's fortune. Fainall and his mistress (Marwood) are consequently thwarted in their avaricious designs, the condition of the pathetic Mrs. Fainall is eased by the exposure of her treacherous husband, and Lady Wishfort gives her approval to the marriage of Mirabell and Millamant.

The contrast between the apparent and the real, which is at the heart of all great comedy, is central to the action and the characters of *The Way of the World*; and it is objictified by means of an irony that is much more subtly pervasive than the deliberate and overt ironies of *The Country Wife*. In her desperate attempts to maintain the ardour and vigour of youth in middle age and to present herself as a most desirable object of amorous passion, the aging Lady Wishfort fails to distinguish between her true nature and the artifice she creates. Her gullibility is as evident as her gross sensuality and her inability to see that the personal eminence and social power she once enjoyed are no longer hers to command. As she prepares to receive her most recent admirer, Mirabell's "uncle", she can think only of creating the right social impression:

> Will he be importunate, Foible, and push? For if he should not be importunate, I shall never break decorums. I shall die with confusion, if I am forced to advance. Oh no, I can never advance! I shall swoon if he should expect advances. No, I hope Sir Rowland is better bred than to put a lady to the necessity of breaking her forms. I won't be too coy neither. I won't give him despair; but a little disdain is not amiss, a little scorn is alluring.

In a passage of matchless rhetoric she excitedly dwells upon appearance:

> Well, and how shall I receive him? In what figure shall I give his heart the first impression? There is a great deal in the first impression. Shall I sit? No, I won't sit, I'll walk; aye, I'll walk from the door upon his entrance; and then turn full upon him. No, that will be too sudden. I'll lie, aye, I'll lie down. I'll receive him in my little dressing-room; there's a couch. Yes, yes, I'll give the first impression on a couch. I won't lie neither, but loll and lean upon one elbow; with one foot a little dangling off, jogging in a thoughtful way. Yes, and then as soon as he appears, start, aye, start and be surprised, and rise to meet him in a pretty disorder. Yes, oh, nothing is more alluring than a levee from a couch, in some confusion; it shows the foot to advantage, and furnishes with blushes and recomposing airs beyond comparison.

In the final act, after Mirabell's scheme has been revealed, she indicates her total blindness to the ridiculous truth of the Sir Rowland episode as she takes the false Marwood to her heart and suggests that they retire from "the bad world" to a pastoral Arcadia: "I would retire to deserts and solitudes, and feed harmless sheep by groves and purling streams. Dear Marwood, let us leave the world, and retire by ourselves and be shepherdesses."

Mr. Fainall is the evil genius of the play. Like Mirabell, he possesses intelligence and wit, and in the opening scene of the play the two men appear as typical Restoration gallants, with an urbanity and a degree of libertinism appropriate to their social position; but their similarities are only apparent as the development of the dramatic action shows. Despite his trickery of Lady Wishfort, Mirabell's intentions in the play are related to a convention of honour; Fainall, on the other hand, deliberately rejects natural honour in favour of an artificial code based exclusively on self-interest. He has married Lady Wishfort's widowed daughter only for her fortune, and the abject failure of their marriage, due largely to his illicit affair with Mistress Marwood, disrupts the natural order symbolized by the marriage bond. His inability to secure control of his wife's estate (secretly entrusted to Mirabell) and the information he acquires (through the vindictive offices of Marwood) of his wife's former liaison with Mirabell have so embittered him that he is committed to a course of action by which he may take revenge upon the society that has "wronged" him. As an instrument of intensification in the total dramatic action, he turns to blackmail, fraud, and finally to physical violence when, in the final scene, he threatens to attack his wife. In a moment of passion Marwood describes Fainall a "bankrupt in honour, as indigent of wealth", and in the great scene of the third act in which Fainall learns from Marwood of his wife's former infidelities, his true character is revealed through the cold, callous, and soulless rhetoric that Congreve reserves for him. "Scurvy wedlock", jealousy, bitterness, the stakes one puts up in the game of marriage – these are all part of "the way of the world" as Fainall sees it; and as he seals the malice of Marwood's plot with a kiss, he commits himself to appearance, even though it be false, and to a subversion of the good:

> Let husbands be jealous; but let the lover still believe. Or
> if he doubt, let it be only to endear his pleasure, and pre-

Central theme : apparent / real.

pare the joy that follows, when he proves his mistress true.
But let husbands' doubts convert to endless jealousy; or if
they have belief, let it corrupt to superstition and blind
credulity. I am single, and will herd no more with 'em.
True, I wear the badge, but I'll disown the order. And since
I take my leave of 'em, I care not if I leave 'em a common
motto to their common crest.

>   All husbands must or pain or shame endure;
>   The wise too jealous are, fools too secure.

The experience of the true wits and true lovers of the play,
Millamant (_mille amants_) and Mirabell (_mirabilis_: wonderful),
issues in a definition of the true marriage and at the same time
provides illumination of the central theme that contrasts the
apparent and the real. Of the two, Millamant's character is the
more difficult to understand since we are not certain of the
condition of her heart's affections until the end of the _proviso_
scene in the fourth act, whereas the truth of Mirabell's heart is
clear to us from the beginning. Early in the play Millamant
chooses to refer to him as "sententious Mirabell", and his demand for constant "plain-dealing and sincerity" is a mark of
his sententiousness. What he must learn in the course of his
experience is to put aside his air of solemn gravity, "that violent
and inflexible wise face, like Solomon at the dividing of the
child in an old tapestry hanging", and to accommodate the little
frivolities and ironically amusing paradoxes that inhere in all
social experience. The most enchanting of comic heroines,
Millamant, upon her first entrance ironically equated with Milton's Dalila, is the perfect image of the Restoration coquette.
But with all her tantalizing feminine charm, her capriciousness
and changeability, and her "whirlwind" nature, she has a true
wit, even if it seem fanciful or whimsical. It is her silent plea
that Mirabell recognize her surface appearances for what they
are and discover the depth of her feeling that is her true character. It is no less a mark of the soundness of Mirabell's character
that he accepts Millamant's faults as part of her complex nature:

> ... I like her with all her faults, nay, like her for her faults.
> Her follies are so natural, or so artful, that they become

N.B. Art / Nature.

her; and those affectations which in another woman would be odious, serve but to make her more agreeable.

Her purpose is to discover the truth of her own heart, to be certain that she entrusts it to the right person in marriage, and to safeguard a proper degree of independence. The famous bargaining scene of the fourth act marks the point in the dramatic action at which the educative process of the young lovers is completed. At its conclusion, all illusion has been dispelled and for the first time the lovers can admit to themselves the truth of their innermost affections.

The *proviso* scene begins with a rhymed couplet from a Suckling lyric that Millamant has been reflecting upon. It is most fitting that she speak the first line and Mirabell the second, since the division of the lines prefigures an ultimate unity of which the couplet was considered the perfect poetic symbol. Millamant's conditions are all in terms of social conventions, and, as Paul and Miriam Mueschke have pointed out, they are "the result of her desire to prolong and increase the prenuptial glamour". First, she demands that she continue to maintain her own individual identity and liberty: "Positively, Mirabell, I'll lie abed in a morning as long as I please." Then she insists that they scrupulously and decorously observe all the right social appearances: "Let us never visit together, nor go to a play together. But let us be very strange and well-bred; let us be as strange as if we had been married a great while, and as well-bred as if we were not married at all." With her final condition that she be free to exercise her own will and taste in certain areas of social intercourse, she agrees that, "These articles subscribed, if I continue to endure you a little longer, I may by degrees dwindle into a wife." Where Millamant's "articles" are concerned with social amenities, Mirabell's contain particular instructions and injunctions:

> ...I covenant...that you admit no sworn confidante, or intimate of your own sex; no she-friend....No decoy-duck to wheedle you a fop, scrambling to the play....I article that you continue to like your own face....To which end,

together with all vizards for the day, I prohibit all masks for the night. ... *Item*, I shut my doors against all bawds. ...

His judicial wit turns then to certain sexual conditions, which are the more dramatically effective because of Millamant's reaction to them, one of pretended disgust:

MIR. ... *Item*, when you shall be breeding —
MRS. MIL. Ah! name it not.
MIR. Which may be presumed, with a blessing on our endeavours —
MRS. MIL. Odious endeavours!
MIR. I denounce against all strait-lacing, squeezing for a shape, till you mould my boy's head like a sugar-loaf, and instead of a man child, make me father to a crooked billet.

And finally, after banishing spiritous liquors from the tea-table and refusing her the right "to drink healths, or toast fellows", he concludes that, "These *provisos* admitted, in other things I may prove a tractable and complying husband."

In the course of this great dramatic scene, Mirabell's "sententiousness" has been wittily converted to a fuller understanding of Millamant's nature; and through Mirabell's honest dealing Millamant's coquetry has been dispelled and her maturity revealed. But she has not yet completely capitulated. Upon the entry of Mrs. Fainall, she carries on the witty pretence for a few lines, agrees to "endure" him ("Well, you ridiculous thing you, I'll have you"), and then dismisses him with the assurance, "I suppose you have said something to please me." It is not until Mirabell has left the room that she surrenders. In the midst of Mrs. Fainall's unheeded prattle of Sir Rowland, Sir Wilfull, and Petulant, Millamant has become all fire and air, and in a moment of ecstasy she reveals herself: "Well, if Mirabell should not make a good husband, I am a lost thing; for I find I love him violently." Like Wycherley's famous "china" scene and Sheridan's "screen" scene in *The School for Scandal*, Congreve's *proviso* scene occurs in the fourth act, and marks the great climax of the total dramatic action. The remainder of the play is given over to the unravelling of the twisted strands of the plot and to the denouement.

Dance

The closing scene of *The Way of the World*, with the appearance of the "black box" containing the papers that will rout Fainall and the forces of evil, concludes with a dance. It is not the ironic dance of *The Country Wife*, but rather a symbol of the transference of social order and control from Lady Wishfort to Mirabell and his now-fully-won Millamant. Exhausted, Lady Wishfort withdraws from the dance, and her physical bankruptcy is another mark that the old order has passed away. Norman Holland wisely cautions his readers against any misinterpretation of Lady Wishfort as a farcical figure. The dramatic situations Congreve has devised for her guarantee an appropriate degree of ridiculousness and absurdity. She is an important blocking figure in the total action and consequently must display a kind of authority in keeping with her dramatic responsibilities. Mr. Holland concludes that, "at the end, she should appear deflated and awry, and for that effect, she must first have a substantial, authoritarian personality to deteriorate".

Language

Enough has perhaps been said of the superbly contrived rhetoric of Congreve's great play, but since it is the language of the play that is in large part responsible for the poetic character of *The Way of the World*, a further note may be justified. Congreve uses language in such a way as to solidify dramatic structure and to delineate character. Witwoud's irrepressibly affected similes, Petulant's trifling and crotchety chatter, Sir Wilfull's "lingo", Fainall's steely-cold and stinging wit – these are of great importance both in defining character and in providing a variety of rhetorical fare that is difficult to match in the history of English comic writing. The diaphanous charm and caprice of Millamant are reflected in the clipped clauses and phrases that mark her dialogue. She pins up her hair with letters, but "Only with those in verse, Mr. Witwoud. I never pin up my hair with prose." The scattered rhythms and contrived repetitions are affined to her flights of fancy and to her coquettish nature:

Mirabell, did you take exceptions last night? Oh, aye, and
went away. Now I think on't, I'm angry. No, now I think
on't, I'm pleased; for I believe I gave you some pain.

Lord, what is a lover, that it can give? Why, one makes
lovers as fast as one pleases, and they live as long as one
pleases, and they die as soon as one pleases; and then, if
one pleases, one makes more.

But it is Lady Wishfort's rhetorical range that is the most
striking single linguistic feature of the play. In her moments of
raging excitement, she is a fund of vulgar image and diction.
To Peg, who feebly attempts to repair the ravages of time, Lady
Wishfort shouts with impatience and confusion:

Ratafia, fool! No, fool! Not the ratafia, fool. Grant me
patience! I mean the Spanish paper, idiot; complexion,
darling. Paint, paint, paint; dost thou understand that,
changeling, dangling thy hands like bobbins before thee?
Why dost thou not stir, puppet? thou wooden thing upon
wires!

And she dismisses her waiting-woman Foible, who has betrayed
her, in a passage that is remarkable for its superb rhythmical
construction no less than for its torrent of abusive images:

Out of my house, out of my house, thou viper! thou serpent,
that I have fostered! thou bosom traitress, that I raised from
nothing! Begone! begone! begone! go! go! That I took
from washing of old gauze and weaving of dead hair, with
a bleak blue nose, over a chafing-dish of starved embers,
and dining behind a traverse rag, in a shop no bigger than
a birdcage! Go, go! starve again, do, do! ... Go set up for
yourself again! Do, drive a trade, do, with your three-
pennyworth of small ware flaunting upon a packthread,
under a brandy-seller's bulk, or against a dead wall by a
ballad-monger! Go, hang out an old frisoneer-gorget, with
a yard of yellow colberteen again. Do; an old gnawed mask,
two rows of pins, and a child's fiddle; a glass necklace with
the beads broken, and a quilted nightcap with one ear. Go,
go, drive a trade!

But when she plays the amorous lady of quality to Sir Rowland, she is mistress of all the "elegant" and hypocritical cant of her depraved society:

> But as I am a person, Sir Rowland, you must not attribute my yielding to any sinister appetite, or indigestion of widowhood; nor impute my complacency to any lethargy of continence. I hope you do not think me prone to any iteration of nuptials. . . . If you do, I protest I must recede, or think that I have made a prostitution of decorums. . . . If you think the least scruple of carnality was an ingredient —

To such cascading eloquence "Sir Rowland" makes the brilliant and appropriate reply: "Dear madam, no. You are all camphire and frankincense, all chastity and odour." The success of *The Way of the World* is ultimately dependent upon the range of its poetic expression, for such mastery of language as Congreve displays is the hallmark of the play's greatness.

The Rehearsal

The Country Wife and *The Way of the World* belong to the high order of comedy of manners. *The Rehearsal* is farce, parody, and burlesque, all lower forms of the comic genre; and the kind of laughter it evokes is not "thoughtful" but rather full-bodied, raucous, and broad. As a play it is not related to the subtly ironic manners comedy of Congreve nor does it constitute a judgment upon social *mores* in the manner of Wycherley. It is rather a spoof upon a predominant fashion in the serious drama of the time: it ridicules what is most solemnly revered in heroic tragedy; it trivializes what is most serious and grave, and renders serious what is obviously trivial. For its effect it depends upon what is readily recognizable as ridiculous and absurd, and in its emphasis upon a norm of common sense and probability it cuts man down to size by making nonsense of foolishly high-flown aspirations, pretensions, and ideals. It teaches that "The proper study of mankind is man." Although *The Rehearsal* does not explore the distinctions between the apparent and the real with the same degree of penetration as we have seen in the Congreve and Wycherley plays, the contrast is none the less present as a complete appraisal of the play will suggest.

It has been generally agreed that in the writing of the play Buckingham received help from Thomas Sprat, the Duke's chaplain and historian of the Royal Society, "Matt" Clifford, one of the literati of the age, and Samuel Butler, author of the greatest of Restoration burlesque poems, *Hudibras*; but it would seem evident that the original idea and its execution were mainly Buckingham's. *The Rehearsal* has a long history. According to several reports a first draft, ready for production as early as 1665 but delayed owing to the closing of the theatres in the year of the plague, aimed to burlesque Sir William Davenant's *The Siege of Rhodes* (1656), probably the first of the great rhymed heroic plays destined to become the staple tragic fare of the Restoration theatre and of a good part of that of the eighteenth century. (In his first draft Buckingham doubtless included among the objects of his satire the plays of Sir Robert Howard, Dryden's brother-in-law and one of the most eminent writers for the contemporary stage.) By 1670 Davenant was dead, and his successor in the art of the heroic play was the laureate, John Dryden. It was obvious to Buckingham and his collaborators that, under the circumstances, *The Rehearsal* should be revised, and in the second draft, first produced in 1671 and published in 1672, the hero, Mr. Bayes, was immediately and universally recognized as a satiric portrait of Dryden. But Buckingham's satiric thrusts were not directed against the laureate so much as against the whole cult of heroic tragedy of which Dryden was the grand master. There is no question that his rhymed plays figure largely among those so mercilessly parodied in Buckingham's farce, but of the seventeen plays named in Briscoe's *Key* of 1704 as objects of burlesque in *The Rehearsal* only six are by Dryden.

The heroic play is derived from two quite different dramatic traditions: the tradition of Marlowe inherited by the late Elizabethan and Jacobean dramatists; and the tradition of the French theatre, best exemplified in the work of Pierre Corneille. From the French master English authors took as the major dramatic action a conflict of love and honour; and the rhymed penta-metric couplets of the English heroic drama were modelled upon the rhymed hexameters of the French school. The extra-vagantly excessive action, the violence, the bombast and rant and rhetorical tearing of a passion to tatters – these elements of the heroic play derive from the English plays of the earlier seventeenth century, especially those of Ford and Webster. Heroic tragedy is, then, a curious blend of the naturalistic elements of the native tradition and the artificial conventions of the French. Whatever its merits as a tragic form, it enjoyed a tremendous vogue throughout the Restoration and much of the eighteenth century, and, despite the success of Buckingham's wonderful burlesque, its popularity continued with unabated vigour. Perhaps it is a mark of the cultivation of the age that its taste could accommodate the heroic character of the epic poem and of its serious drama and, at the same time, the essentially anti-heroic features of the best of its comedy.

The Restoration's admiration of the heroic or epic poem goes far towards explaining its admiration of heroic tragedy. In the minds of men of taste and cultivation the epic poem was the greatest of literary forms, and that predilection is reflected in the ways the heroic dramatist attempted to translate the range, magnificence, and elevated language typical of the epic poem into the more confined structure of the five-act tragedy. Accord-ing to Aristotle, epic and tragedy belong to the same genre of heroic poetry, and consequently Dryden felt justified in model-ling his dramatic action, characterization, and rhetoric upon epic originals. In his essay *Of Heroic Plays*, for example, he tells us that the character of Almanzor, the hero of his elaborate two-part ten-act play *The Conquest of Granada* (and the model for the Drawcansir of *The Rehearsal*), was based on Homer's Achilles. But where the vast scope of the epic is sufficient to accommodate a far-ranging action, figures of the greatest nobil-ity and valour, and a poetry appropriate to these in eloquence and passion, the more restricted limits of the dramatic form are not sufficient; rather, scenes become overcrowded, characters seem excessively artificial, and eloquence gives way to bombast and rant. It was these very discrepancies that Buckingham sought to exploit in his parody of the heroic play.

A rehearsal of Mr. Bayes's most recent heroic tragedy provides the general framework of the play. Mr. Bayes has invited two friends, Johnson and Smith, to be present as he directs the rehearsal and coaches the members of the cast in the speaking of their lines. In Mr. Bayes Buckingham has drawn a brilliantly satiric portrait of Dryden, but the major interest lies in the play within the play, the burlesque upon heroic tragedy in general. The action is one of cumulative confusions that include the usurpation of the sovereignty of two kings of Brentford, who in the final act reclaim their rightful place by descending "in the clouds, singing, in white garments"; a conflict between love and fate in the plight of Cloris and Prince Prettyman ("Sometimes a fisher's son, sometimes a prince"), who falls asleep in what should be the most ardent of his love-scenes; the major conten-tion between love and honour in the heart of Prince Volscius, who, impregnable to Amaryllis's darts of love, is smitten by Parthenope, whose mother "sells ale by the town-walls", and is ultimately accorded a soliloquy that fails to solve the love-honour conflict as he departs from the scene "with one boot on, and the other off"; and the magnificent heroics of the perfect conquering hero, Drawcansir, who, after waging a mighty battle "between foot and great hobby-horses" and killing everybody on both sides, manages to speak in mock-Achillean fashion an heroic soliloquy:

> Others may boast a single man to kill,
> But I the blood of thousands daily spill.
> Let petty kings the names of parties know;
> Where'er I come, I slay both friend and foe.

The elements of the action are totally disparate; nothing fits with anything else, and the argument of the unrehearsed fifth act, read out by one of the players, leaves the plot in hilariously hopeless disorder.

Cloris at length, being sensible of Prince Prettyman's pas-

sion, consents to marry him; but just as they are going to
church, Prince Prettyman meeting by chance with old Joan,
the chandler's widow, and remembering it was she that first
brought him acquainted with Cloris, out of a high point of
honour breaks off his match with Cloris and marries old
Joan. Upon which, Cloris, in despair, drowns herself, and
Prince Prettyman discontentedly walks by the riverside.

The rehearsal terminates as Johnson and Smith make a hasty
retreat and the players break off for dinner. Deserted, Mr. Bayes
determines to be revenged upon them all in satire and lampoon.

Heroic tragedy was no less noted for its rhetorical magnilo-
quence than for its elaborate staging, its great "machines" for
achieving supernatural effects, and its music and ballet. Buckingham makes capital use of strained metaphor and the complex
epic simile in the dialogue of the principals; most of these have
been noted in the footnotes and their parallels in the heroic
plays of the time cited. The stage effects call for additional
comment. To depict a fitting terror Mr. Bayes decides to cast
his prologue in the form of a dialogue between Thunder and
Lightning; and to heighten the passion he chooses to make "an
allusion to love" in the form of a simile, which begins:

So boar and sow, when any storm is nigh,
Snuff up, and smell it gath'ring in the sky; ...

In this he strives "to oblige the auditors by civility, by good
nature, good language, and all that". Later he provides on the
stage simultaneous eclipses of the sun and the moon. This representation takes the form of a dance performed by Luna,
Orbis, and Sol, who, by adopting appropriate positions with
respect to one another, represent the heavenly and earthly
phenomena against a musical accompaniment of a popular
country dance. The pagan gods play their supernatural part in
the affairs of men when Pallas (Athena) stays the hands of the
usurping monarchs from a double suicide for the death of their
mutually beloved Lardella, and pronounces in goddesslike tones
"Lardella lives" as "the coffin opens, and a banquet is discovered". There is, finally, a battle fought *"in recitativo"*, and an

epic marshalling of the hosts of war which include the Acton Musketeers, the Chelsea Cuirassiers, the Chiswickians, the Mortlake boys, and the Hammersmith Brigade. All the epic paraphernalia are represented in Buckingham's riotous exposé of the absurd formlessness of the extravagant action, the "excessive and overboiling" characterization, the empty moralizing, and the prodigious verbal rant of the heroic play.

As the play in the process of rehearsal is an outrageous caricature of the best of the heroic tragedy of the time (and plays such as Dryden's *Tyrannic Love* and the elaborately conceived *Conquest of Granada* have much to recommend them), so Mr. Bayes is a caricature of the popular heroic dramatist in general, and an even more extravagant caricature of John Dryden. Mr. Bayes is presented as an advocate of "the new way of writing", a method that in its formulation of plot, character, and language totally contravenes the laws of reason and good sense. According to Mr. Johnson he belongs to "the new kind of wits" whose plays aim "to elevate and surprise ..., a phrase they have got amongst them, to express their no-meaning by. ...'tis fighting, loving, sleeping, rhyming, dying, dancing, singing, crying, and every thing but thinking and sense." In an age when dramatic theory emphasized the value of imitating what was best in the dramatic tradition, Mr. Bayes's spiderlike dependence upon his stock of native wit is shockingly reprehensible. He relies exclusively upon his own luxuriant (and ridiculous) fancy: "I tread upon no man's heels; but make my flight with my own wings"; and he contemns Jonson and Beaumont, the most respected dramatists of the preceding age, because they "borrowed all they writ from nature: I am for fetching it purely out of my own fancy, I."

Mr. Bayes's practice in the writing of the rehearsed play is a constant reminder of the artificial way in which the heroic play was ostensibly contrived. It is written according to a certain recipe, like the making of a pudding, and the ingredients are an exaggeratedly heroic plot, including "a combat betwixt love and honour", superhuman characters who touch the heights and depths of forced passion, rational (but mainly irrational) ethical choices, a full-flown rhetoric to give the appropriate elevation of style, and, finally, all the trappings of supernatural stage effects, dance, and music. According to Mr. Bayes, "you must ever interlard your plays with songs, ghosts, and idols" as "you must ever make a simile when you are surprised"; you must have the required number of antitheses, and clothe a most valorous action with "forced conceit, smooth verse, and a rant"; and in the exposition a "whispering scene" can be used to great advantage as the details of the plot are communicated by means of stage-whispers inaudible to the audience. *The Rehearsal* may be considered an ironic essay in literary criticism that calls attention to the ridiculous claptrap of the dramatic illusion of which authors like Bayes are such absurdly innocent victims.

As the arrogant, self-opinionated practitioner of the art of heroic tragedy, Mr. Bayes is ridiculous enough; and as the protagonist of the major action he is a figure of the most riotous farce. In a scene in the second act he demonstrates to four players how they should rise from the dead to music "in *Effaut flat*", and in the process breaks his nose, which he attempts to repair with a wet piece of brown paper. And later, in the midst of a passage that is "true spirit and flame all through, egad", he loses his wig. Mr. Bayes is a ludicrously ironic illustration of the perennial discrepancy in the artist between "the man who suffers and the mind which creates". Side by side with the overblown rhetorical passion of the dialogue of the rehearsed play is Mr. Bayes's private jargon – the interminable "egads", "i'faiths", "gadzookers", and "'sdeaths" of his common speech and the sometimes crude and always inelegant cant of his trade. That his personal language should be so consistently predictable and at the same time so at odds with the artificial dialogue of his play is one of the most comic configurations of his character. He is at once the arrogant, self-assured poetic craftsman reduced to absurdity by the ill-fated flights of his own sublime fancy, and the pettishly vain, affected, and pretentious bourgeois who writes for "fame and reputation" and keeps a weather eye on the box-office.

The laughter provoked by "His Grace of Bucks's farce" is far from Meredith's "thoughtful" laughter; rather it is the full-bodied laughter we accord to persons and objects we immediately recognize as ridiculous. In *The Rehearsal* our common-sense awareness of what constitutes a good play is outraged by the obvious excesses of Mr. Bayes's eccentric dramatic practice: by the extravagant complexities of the action; by methods of characterization that deliberately ignore reality, reasonableness, and plausibility; by peripheral theatrical effects that defy probability; and by an overblown language that can be described only as fustian. In short, Mr. Bayes has chosen to dismiss nature as "the source, and end, and test of Art", and, instead, to adhere to artificial rules and conventions that, when unscrupulously amplified, can issue only in overt burlesque and caricature. "This new way of wit" provides "Plays without head or tail" and only reflects a "prodigious way of writing" that travesties "reason, nature, art, and wit". The more Mr. Bayes rejects nature and reason and the more he allows himself to be victimized by the excesses of his own inventiveness and "poetic" enthusiasm, the more ridiculous he becomes; as the audience, we acknowledge our reaction to what is patently absurd in judgment and taste by the uproarious laughter appropriate to farce. Buckingham's high-spirited play is, then, among other things, an essay in dramatic criticism. Paradoxically enough, it is of a piece with the major critical premises of the most distinguished literary critic of the age, John Dryden. Our recognition of the irony inherent in that paradox induces another kind of laughter.

The Country Wife

WILLIAM WYCHERLEY

Indignor quicquam reprehendi, non quia crasse
Compositum illepideve putetur, sed quia nuper:
Nec veniam Antiquis, sed honorem et praemia posci.

HORAT.[1]

---

[1]The epigraph is taken from Horace, *Epist.*, II, i, lines 76-78. In Alexander
Pope's translation it reads:

> I lose my patience, and I own it too,
> When works are censur'd, not as bad, but new;
> While if our Elders break all Reason's laws,
> These fools demand not Pardon, but Applause.

— *Imitations of Horace*:
The First Epistle of the Second Book, lines 115-18.

William Wycherley

BIOGRAPHICAL DATA

1641 Born at Clive, near Shrewsbury, Shropshire.

1656 Sent to France for his education. Learned the arts of the gentleman in the *précieuses* society of the Duchesse de Montausier, a daughter of the famous Rambouillet family.

1659 Returned to London. Admitted to the Inner Temple where he acquired some little knowledge of the law.

1660 Entered in the Bodleian Library, Oxford, as *Philosophiae Studiosus*, residing in the Provost's lodgings of Queen's College. It does not appear that he ever took a degree. Shortly afterwards he returned to the legal offices of the Inner Temple.

1672 *Published* Love in a Wood, *a comedy, his first play. Probably performed in the previous year.*

Won the favour of the King's mistress, the notorious Duchess of Cleveland, who secured for him a commission in the regiment of the Duke of Buckingham, author of *The Rehearsal*, to whom he was appointed equerry.

1673 *Published* The Gentleman Dancing Master, *a comedy. It was probably produced earlier, in 1672.*

1675 *Published* The Country Wife, *a comedy. It may have been produced as early as 1673. The play was in part derived from Terence's* Eunuchus; *certain incidents and scenes were derived from Molière's* L'Ecole des Femmes *and* L'Ecole des Maris.

1676 *Published* The Plain Dealer, *a comedy, produced in the same year. The play has as its source Molière's* Le Misanthrope.

1678 Serious illness. Visited in his lodgings by Charles II, who advised that the dramatist go to the south of France to recuperate, and provided him with a purse of five hundred pounds.

1679 Returned from France to England. Highly favoured by the King, who wished to engage him as private tutor to his natural son the Duke of Richmond at the handsome annual salary of fifteen hundred pounds.

1680 Married the widowed Countess of Drogheda, an "ill-tempered, imperious, and extravagantly jealous" woman. His marriage incurred the displeasure of the King, who immediately withdrew his royal patronage.

1681 Death of his wife. Deeply involved in debt and litigation. Committed to Fleet Prison for debt; remained there three or four years.

1685 *The Plain Dealer* praised by King James II, who befriended him by securing his release from prison, discharging his debts, and providing him with a pension of two hundred pounds a year.

1688 Retired to his country estate in Shropshire: "the humble hermit at Clive" (Dennis).

1697 Death of his father, and return to London. Ill health and further legal and financial difficulties.

1704 Published Miscellany Poems, *which won him the admiration and friendship of the young Alexander Pope.*

1715 Death on December 31. Eleven days before he died he married Elizabeth Jackson. The purpose was to defeat hostile attempts of a disagreeable nephew to secure his estate. Buried in the vault of the church of St. Paul, Covent Garden.

Prologue

SPOKEN BY MR. HART [MR. HORNER]

Poets, like cudgel'd bullies, never do
At first or second blow submit to you;
But will provoke you still, and ne'er have done,
Till you are weary first with laying on.
The late so baffled scribbler of this day,[1]   5
Though he stands trembling, bids me boldly say,
What we before most plays are us'd to do,
For poets out of fear first draw on you;
In a fierce prologue the still pit defy,
And, ere you speak, like Castril,[2] give the lie.   10
But though our Bayes's[3] battles oft I've fought,
And with bruis'd knuckles their dear conquests bought;
Nay, never yet fear'd odds upon the stage,
In prologue dare not hector with the age;
But would take quarter from your saving hands,   15
Though Bayes within all yielding countermands,
Says, you confed'rate wits no quarter give,
Therefore his play shan't ask your leave to live.
Well, let the vain rash fop, by huffing so,
Think to obtain the better terms of you;   20
But we, the actors, humbly will submit,
Now, and at any time, to a full pit;

[1] a reference to Wycherley's earlier play *The Gentleman Dancing Master* (1673), which had had but little success. baffled: dishonoured.

[2] Kastrill: the "angry boy" in Ben Jonson's play *The Alchemist*.

[3] "Mr. Bayes" was the name given Dryden in Buckingham's *The Rehearsal* (1672); it remained his nickname to the end of his career. Later it became the sobriquet for any author, and here "Mr. Bayes" refers to Wycherley as well as Dryden. Mr. Hart, who created the part of Horner and speaks the Prologue, suggests in this line the many times he had played the hero in Dryden's heroic tragedies.

Nay, often we anticipate your rage,
And murder poets for you, on our stage:
We set no guards upon our tiring-room,[4]   25
But when with flying colours there you come,
We patiently, you see, give up to you
Our poets, virgins, nay, our matrons too.

[4] the actors' dressing-room.

Dramatis Personae

Men

MR. HORNER
MR. HARCOURT
MR. DORILANT
MR. PINCHWIFE
MR. SPARKISH
SIR JASPAR FIDGET
DR. QUACK
A BOY
A BOOKSELLER
A PARSON

Women

MRS. MARGERY PINCHWIFE
MRS. ALITHEA, sister to PINCHWIFE
MY LADY FIDGET
MRS. DAINTY FIDGET, sister to SIR JASPAR
MRS. SQUEAMISH
OLD LADY SQUEAMISH
LUCY, ALITHEA's maid
Waiters, servants, and attendants

SCENE: *London*

THE COUNTRY WIFE

Act I

HORNER's *Lodging*

Enter HORNER, *and* QUACK *following him at a distance*

HORN. *(aside)* A quack is as fit for a pimp, as a midwife for a
bawd; they are still but in their way both helpers of nature.–
(aloud) Well, my dear doctor, hast thou done what I desired?

QUACK. I have undone you for ever with the women, and reported you throughout the whole town as bad as an eunuch,
with as much trouble as if I had made you one in earnest.

HORN. But have you told all the midwives you know, the orange-
wenches at the playhouses, the city husbands, and old fumbling keepers of this end of the town? for they'll be the
readiest to report it.

QUACK. I have told all the chambermaids, waiting-women, tire-
women, and old women of my acquaintance; nay, and whispered it as a secret to 'em, and to the whisperers of Whitehall,[1] so that you need not doubt 'twill spread, and you will
be as odious to the handsome young women as —

HORN. As the small-pox. Well —

QUACK. And to the married women of this end of the town, as —

HORN. As the great ones;[2] nay, as their own husbands.

QUACK. And to the city dames, as aniseed Robin,[3] of filthy and
contemptible memory; and they will frighten their children
with your name, especially their females.

---

[1] the royal Palace of Charles II, and
the centre of governmental business.
It was noted for its "whisperers", or
rumour-mongers, gossips.

[2] the pox (i.e., venereal disease), in
contrast to the *small* pox. See Act II,

p. 52, lines 14-16.

[3] a famous hermaphrodite, renowned
for his obscenity. He may have received the name "aniseed" because
he peddled aniseed-water about the
streets.

HORN. And cry, Horner's coming to carry you away. I am only afraid 'twill not be believed. You told 'em 'twas by an English-French disaster, and an English-French chirurgeon,[4] who has given me at once not only a cure, but an antidote for the future against that damned malady, and that worse distemper, love, and all other women's evils?

QUACK. Your late journey into France has made it the more credible, and your being here a fortnight before you appeared in public, looks as if you apprehended the shame, which I wonder you do not. Well, I have been hired by young gallants to belie 'em t'other way; but you are the first would be thought a man unfit for women.

HORN. Dear Mr. Doctor, let vain rogues be contented only to be thought abler men than they are, generally 'tis all the pleasure they have; but mine lies another way.

QUACK. You take, methinks, a very preposterous way to it, and as ridiculous as if we operators in physic[5] should put forth bills to disparage our medicaments, with hopes to gain customers.

HORN. Doctor, there are quacks in love as well as physic, who get but the fewer and worse patients for their boasting; a good name is seldom got by giving it one's self; and women, no more than honour, are compassed by bragging. Come, come, Doctor, the wisest lawyer never discovers the merits of his cause till the trial; the wealthiest man conceals his riches, and the cunning gamester his play. Shy husbands and keepers, like old rooks, are not to be cheated but by a new unpractised trick: false friendship will pass now no more than false dice upon 'em; no, not in the city.

Enter BOY

BOY. There are two ladies and a gentleman coming up. *(Exit.)*
HORN. A pox![6] some unbelieving sisters of my former acquaintance, who, I am afraid, expect their sense should be satisfied of the falsity of the report. No—this formal fool and women!

---

[4] surgeon.   [6] a mild oath.
[5] medicine.

Enter SIR JASPAR FIDGET, LADY FIDGET, *and* MRS. DAINTY
FIDGET

QUACK. His wife and sister.

SIR JASP. My coach breaking just now before your door, sir,
I look upon as an occasional[7] reprimand to me, sir, for
not kissing your hands, sir, since your coming out of France,
sir; and so my disaster, sir, has been my good fortune, sir;
and this is my wife and sister, sir.

HORN. What then, sir?

SIR JASP. My lady, and sister, sir. – Wife, this is Master Horner.

LADY FID. Master Horner, husband!

SIR JASP. My lady, my Lady Fidget, sir.

HORN. So, sir.

SIR JASP. Won't you be acquainted with her, sir? – *(aside)* So,
the report is true, I find, by his coldness or aversion to the
sex; but I'll play the wag with him. – *(aloud)* Pray salute my
wife, my lady, sir.[8]

HORN. I will kiss no man's wife, sir, for him, sir; I have taken
my eternal leave, sir, of the sex already, sir.

SIR JASP. *(aside)* Ha! ha! ha! I'll plague him yet. – *(aloud)* Not
know my wife, sir?

HORN. I do know your wife, sir; she's a woman, sir, and consequently a monster, sir, a greater monster than a husband,
sir.

SIR JASP. A husband! how, sir?

HORN. So, sir; but I make no more cuckolds, sir. *(Makes horns.[9])*

SIR JASP. Ha! ha! ha! Mercury! Mercury![10]

LADY FID. Pray, Sir Jaspar, let us be gone from this rude fellow.

MRS. DAIN. Who, by his breeding, would think he had ever been
in France?

LADY FID. Foh! he's but too much a French fellow,[11] such as hate

---

[7] caused by a special occurrence, i.e.,
his coach's breaking down.

[8] It was customary for a gentleman to
"salute" a lady to whom he was in-
troduced by kissing her.

[9] Horns on the forehead were the
proverbial mark of the cuckold.

[10] a mild oath; but ironic in the context since mercury was used in the
treatment of venereal disease.

[11] The English were very critical of
French manners, which they considered loose and insufficiently decorous.

women of quality and virtue for their love to their husbands, Sir Jaspar. A woman is hated by 'em as much for loving her husband as for loving their money. But pray let's be gone.

HORN. You do well, madam; for I have nothing that you came for. I have brought over not so much as a bawdy picture, new postures,[12] nor the second part of the *Ecole des Filles*;[13] nor —

QUACK. *(apart to* HORNER*)* Hold, for shame, sir! what d'ye mean? you'll ruin yourself for ever with the sex —

SIR JASP. Ha! ha! ha! he hates women perfectly, I find.

MRS. DAIN. What pity 'tis he should!

LADY FID. Ay, he's a base rude fellow for't. But affectation makes not a woman more odious to them than virtue.

HORN. Because your virtue is your greatest affectation, madam.

LADY FID. How, you saucy fellow! would you wrong my honour?

HORN. If I could.

LADY FID. How d'ye mean, sir?

SIR JASP. Ha! ha! ha! no, he can't wrong your ladyship's honour, upon my honour. He, poor man – hark you in your ear – *(whispers)* a mere eunuch.

LADY FID. O filthy French beast! foh! foh! why do we stay? let's be gone: I can't endure the sight of him.

SIR JASP. Stay but till the chairs come; they'll be here presently.

LADY FID. No, no.

SIR JASP. Nor can I stay longer. 'Tis, let me see, a quarter and half quarter of a minute past eleven. The council will be sat; I must away. Business must be preferred always before love and ceremony with the wise, Mr. Horner.

HORN. And the impotent, Sir Jaspar.

SIR JASP. Ay, ay, the impotent, Master Horner; hah! hah! hah!

LADY FID. What, leave us with a filthy man alone in his lodgings?

SIR JASP. He's an innocent man now, you know. Pray stay, I'll

---

[12] pornographic pictures.

[13] a most obscene and licentious book published in France in 1655. Pepys (13 January 1668) described it as "the most bawdy, lewd book that ever I saw"; but he bought it none the less "to inform himself in the villainy of the world". (9 February 1668 – Lord's Day!)

hasten the chairs to you. — Mr. Horner, your servant; I should be glad to see you at my house. Pray come and dine with me, and play at cards with my wife after dinner; you are fit for women at that game yet, ha! ha! — *(aside)* 'Tis as much a husband's prudence to provide innocent diversion for a wife as to hinder her unlawful pleasures; and he had better employ her than let her employ herself. — *(aloud)* Farewell.

HORN. Your servant, Sir Jaspar.   *(Exit SIR JASPAR.)*

LADY FID. I will not stay with him, foh! —

HORN. Nay, madam, I beseech you stay, if it be but to see I can be as civil to ladies yet as they would desire.

LADY FID. No, no, foh! you cannot be civil to ladies.

MRS. DAIN. You as civil as ladies would desire?

LADY FID. No, no, no, foh! foh! foh!

(Exeunt LADY FIDGET and MRS. DAINTY FIDGET.)

QUACK. Now, I think, I, or you yourself, rather, have done your business with the women.

HORN. Thou art an ass. Don't you see already, upon the report, and my carriage, this grave man of business leaves his wife in my lodgings, invites me to his house and wife, who before would not be acquainted with me out of jealousy?

QUACK. Nay, by this means you may be the more acquainted with the husbands, but the less with the wives.

HORN. Let me alone; if I can but abuse the husbands, I'll soon disabuse the wives. Stay — I'll reckon you up the advantages I am like to have by my stratagem. First, I shall be rid of all my old acquaintances, the most insatiable sorts of duns, that invade our lodgings in a morning; and next to the pleasure of making a new mistress is that of being rid of an old one, and of all old debts. Love, when it comes to be so, is paid the most unwillingly.

QUACK. Well, you may be so rid of your old acquaintances; but how will you get any new ones?

HORN. Doctor, thou wilt never make a good chemist, thou art so incredulous and impatient. Ask but all the young fellows of the town if they do not lose more time, like huntsmen, in starting the game, than in running it down. One knows not where to find 'em; who will or will not. Women of quality are so civil, you can hardly distinguish love from good breeding, and a man is often mistaken: but now I can be sure she that shows an aversion to me loves the sport, as those women that are gone, whom I warrant to be right.[14] And then the next thing is, your women of honour, as you call 'em, are only chary of their reputations, not their persons; and 'tis scandal they would avoid, not men. Now may I have, by the reputation of an eunuch, the privileges of one, and be seen in a lady's chamber in a morning as early as her husband; kiss virgins before their parents or lovers; and may be, in short, the *passe-partout* of the town. Now, doctor.

QUACK. Nay, now you shall be the doctor; and your process is so new that we do not know but it may succeed.

HORN. Not so new neither; *probatum est,*[15] doctor.

QUACK. Well, I wish you luck, and many patients, whilst I go to mine. *(Exit.)*

Enter HARCOURT *and* DORILANT *to* HORNER

HAR. Come, your appearance at the play yesterday has, I hope, hardened you for the future against the women's contempt, and the men's raillery; and now you'll abroad as you were wont.

HORN. Did I not bear it bravely?

DOR. With a most theatrical impudence, nay, more than the orange-wenches show there, or a drunken vizard-mask,[16] or a great-bellied actress; nay, or the most impudent of creatures, an ill poet; or what is yet more impudent, a second-hand critic.

HORN. But what say the ladies? have they no pity?

---

[14] loose, of easy virtue.

[15] "It has been tried before." In another sense Wycherley wittily points to the similarities of plot (especially Horner's device) in *The Country Wife* and Terence's *Eunuchus.*

[16] a woman of questionable reputation. Such ladies, masked, frequented the theatres in search of assignations; and the men of the town were regular theatre-goers.

HAR. What ladies? The vizard-masks, you know, never pity a man when all's gone, though in their service.

DOR. And for the women in the boxes, you'd never pity them when 'twas in your power.

HAR. They say 'tis pity but all that deal with common women should be served so.

DOR. Nay, I dare swear they won't admit you to play at cards with them, go to plays with 'em, or do the little duties which other shadows of men are wont to do for 'em.

HORN. Who do you call shadows of men?

DOR. Half-men.

HORN. What, boys?

DOR. Ay, your old boys, old *beaux garçons*,[17] who, like superannuated stallions, are suffered to run, feed, and whinny with the mares as long as they live, though they can do nothing else.

HORN. Well, a pox on love and wenching! Women serve but to keep a man from better company. Though I can't enjoy them, I shall you the more. Good fellowship and friendship are lasting, rational and manly pleasures.

HAR. For all that, give me some of those pleasures you call effeminate too; they help to relish one another.

HORN. They disturb one another.

HAR. No, mistresses are like books; if you pore upon them too much, they doze you, and make you unfit for company; but if used discreetly, you are the fitter for conversation by 'em.

DOR. A mistress should be like a little country retreat near the town; not to dwell in constantly, but only for a night and away, to taste the town the better when a man returns.

HORN. I tell you, 'tis as hard to be a good fellow, a good friend, and a lover of women, as 'tis to be a good fellow, a good friend, and a lover of money. You cannot follow both, then choose your side. Wine gives you liberty, love takes it away.

DOR. Gad, he's in the right on't.

HORN. Wine gives you joy; love, grief and tortures, besides the

---

[17] men who squire married ladies about; sometimes kept men; gigolos.

chirurgeon's.[18] Wine makes us witty; love, only sots. Wine
makes us sleep; love breaks it.

DOR. By the world he has reason, Harcourt.

HORN. Wine makes —

DOR. Ay, wine makes us – makes us princes; love makes us beg-
gars, poor rogues, egad – and wine —

HORN. So, there's one converted. – No, no, love and wine, oil
and vinegar.

HAR. I grant it; love will still be uppermost.[19]

HORN. Come, for my part, I will have only those glorious manly
pleasures of being very drunk and very slovenly.

Enter BOY

BOY. Mr. Sparkish is below, sir.   *(Exit.)*

HAR. What, my dear friend! a rogue that is fond of me, only, I
think, for abusing him.

DOR. No, he can no more think the men laugh at him than that
women jilt him; his opinion of himself is so good.

HORN. Well, there's another pleasure by drinking I thought not
of, – I shall lose his acquaintance, because he cannot drink:
and you know 'tis a very hard thing to be rid of him; for
he's one of those nauseous offerers at wit, who, like the
worst fiddlers, run themselves into all companies.

HAR. One that, by being in the company of men of sense, would
pass for one.

HORN. And may so to the short-sighted world; as a false jewel
amongst true ones is not discerned at a distance. His company is as troublesome to us as a cuckold's when you have a
mind to his wife's.

HAR. No, the rogue will not let us enjoy one another, but
ravishes our conversation; though he signifies no more to't
than Sir Martin Mar-all's gaping,[20] and awkward thrum-

---

[18] The sense is that the "grief and
tortures" of love itself are augmented
by those of the surgeon in his treatment of venereal disease.

[19] i.e., love will always be above wine,
as oil remains above vinegar.

[20] a reference to Dryden's comedy *Sir
Martin Mar-all* (1667), in one scene
of which the awkward Sir Martin
blunderingly serenades his mistress
on the lute, while his concealed servant actually provides the music and
song.

ming upon the lute, does to his man's voice and music.

DOR. And to pass for a wit in town shows himself a fool every night to us, that are guilty of the plot.

HORN. Such wits as he are, to a company of reasonable men, like rooks to the gamesters; who only fill a room at the table, but are so far from contributing to the play, that they only serve to spoil the fancy of those that do.

DOR. Nay, they are used like rooks too, snubbed, checked, and abused; yet the rogues will hang on.

HORN. A pox on 'em, and all that force nature, and would be still what she forbids 'em! Affectation is her greatest monster.

HAR. Most men are the contraries to that they would seem. Your bully, you see, is a coward with a long sword; the little humbly-fawning physician, with his ebony cane, is he that destroys men.

DOR. The usurer, a poor rogue, possessed of mouldy bonds and mortgages; and we they call spendthrifts, are only wealthy, who lay out his money upon daily new purchases of pleasure.

HORN. Ay, your arrantest cheat is your trustee or executor; your jealous man, the greatest cuckold; your churchman the greatest atheist; and your noisy pert rogue of a wit, the greatest fop, dullest ass, and worst company, as you shall see; for here he comes.

Enter SPARKISH *to them*

SPARK. How is't, sparks? how is't? Well, faith, Harry, I must rally[21] thee a little, ha! ha! ha! upon the report in town of thee, ha! ha! ha! I can't hold i'faith; shall I speak?

HORN. Yes; but you'll be so bitter then.

SPARK. Honest Dick and Frank here shall answer for me; I will not be extreme bitter, by the universe.

[21] a word derived from the noun "raillery", meaning a mild form of ridicule or mockery.

HAR. We will be bound in a ten-thousand-pound bond, he shall not be bitter at all.

DOR. Nor sharp, nor sweet.

HORN. What, not downright insipid?

SPARK. Nay then, since you are so brisk, and provoke me, take what follows. You must know, I was discoursing and rallying with some ladies yesterday, and they happened to talk of the fine new signs in town —

HORN. Very fine ladies, I believe.

SPARK. Said I, I know where the best new sign is. – Where? says one of the ladies. – In Covent Garden, I replied. – Said another, In what street? – In Russel Street, answered I. – Lord, says another, I'm sure there was ne'er a fine new sign there yesterday. – Yes, but there was, said I again; and it came out of France, and has been there a fortnight.

DOR. A pox! I can hear no more, prithee.

HORN. No, hear him out; let him tune his crowd²² a while.

HAR. The worst music, the greatest preparation.

SPARK. Nay, faith, I'll make you laugh. – It cannot be, says a third lady. – Yes, yes, quoth I again. – Says a fourth lady. —

HORN. Look to't, we'll have no more ladies.

SPARK. No – then mark, mark, now. Said I to the fourth, Did you never see Mr. Horner? he lodges in Russel Street, and he's a sign of a man, you know, since he came out of France; heh! ha! he!

HORN. But the devil take me if thine be the sign of a jest.

SPARK. With that they all fell a-laughing, till they bepissed themselves. What, but it does not move you, methinks? Well, I see one had as good go to law without a witness, as break a jest without a laugher on one's side. – Come, come, sparks, but where do we dine? I have left at Whitehall an earl, to dine with you.

DOR. Why, I thought thou hadst loved a man with a title better than a suit with a French trimming to't.

HAR. Go to him again.

²² an ancient form of the fiddle. The whole phrase means, "Let him have his fun with preliminaries before he gets to the point."

SPARK. No, sir, a wit to me is the greatest title in the world.

HORN. But go dine with your earl, sir; he may be exceptious.[23] We are your friends, and will not take it ill to be left, I do assure you.

HAR. Nay, faith, he shall go to him.

SPARK. Nay, pray, gentlemen.

DOR. We'll thrust you out, if you won't; what, disappoint anybody for us?

SPARK. Nay, dear gentlemen, hear me.

HORN. No, no, sir, by no means; pray go, sir.

SPARK. Why, dear rogues —

DOR. No, no.

(They all thrust him out of the room.)

ALL. Ha! ha! ha!

Re-enter SPARKISH

SPARK. But, sparks, pray hear me. What, d'ye think I'll eat then with gay, shallow fops and silent coxcombs? I think wit as necessary at dinner as a glass of good wine; and that's the reason I never have any stomach when I eat alone. – Come, but where do we dine?

HORN. Even where you will.

SPARK. At *Chateline's*?[24]

DOR. Yes, if you will.

SPARK. Or at the *Cock*?[25]

DOR. Yes, if you please.

SPARK. Or at the *Dog and Partridge*?[26]

HORN. Ay, if you have a mind to't; for we shall dine at neither.

SPARK. Pshaw! with your fooling we shall lose the new play; and I would no more miss seeing a new play the first day, than I would miss setting in the wits' row. Therefore I'll go fetch my mistress, and away.   *(Exit.)*

Enter PINCHWIFE *to them*

[23] vexed (that Sparkish has not kept the engagement).

[24] *Chatelain's*: a fashionable ordinary (restaurant) in Covent Garden, popular with the town wits. See Pepys (13 March 1668).

[25] a public house in Covent Garden.

[26] another eating-house, in Fleet Street. See Shadwell, *The Sullen Lovers*, II, iii.

HORN. Who have we here? Pinchwife?

PINCH. Gentlemen, your humble servant.

HORN. Well, Jack, by thy long absence from the town, the grumness of thy countenance, and the slovenliness of thy habit, I should give thee joy, should I not, of marriage?

PINCH. *(aside)* Death! does he know I'm married too? I thought to have concealed it from him at least. – *(aloud)* My long stay in the country will excuse my dress; and I have a suit of law that brings me up to town, that puts me out of humour. Besides, I must give Sparkish to-morrow five thousand pounds to lie with my sister.

HORN. Nay, you country gentlemen, rather than not purchase, will buy anything; and he is a cracked title, if we may quibble. Well, but am I to give thee joy? I heard thou wert married.

PINCH. What then?

HORN. Why, the next thing that is to be heard is, thou'rt a cuckold.

PINCH. *(aside)* Insupportable name!

HORN. But I did not expect marriage from such a whoremaster as you; one that knew the town so much, and women so well.

PINCH. Why, I have married no London wife.

HORN. Pshaw! that's all one. That grave circumspection in marrying a country wife, is like refusing a deceitful pampered Smithfield jade,[27] to go and be cheated by a friend in the country.

PINCH. *(aside)* A pox on him and his simile! – *(aloud)* At least we are a little surer of the breed there, know what her keeping has been, whether foiled[28] or unsound.

---

[27] a worthless horse. Smithfield was famous as a horse-market where people were cheated in "bargains". Cf. Dryden, Epilogue to *Mr. Limberham* (1678):

This Town two Bargains has, not worth one farthing,

A *Smithfield* Horse, and Wife of *Covent-Garden*.
Cf. Pope's "Smithfield Muses", *The Dunciad*, I, line 2.

[28] dishonoured, deflowered. Also a term in horse-breeding meaning injured (lamed) by foundering.

HORN. Come, come, I have known a clap gotten in Wales;[29] and there are cousins, justices' clerks, and chaplains in the country, I won't say coachmen. But she's handsome and young?

PINCH. *(aside)* I'll answer as I should do. – *(aloud)* No, no; she has no beauty but her youth, no attraction but her modesty: wholesome, homely, and housewifely; that's all.

DOR. He talks as like a grazier as he looks.

PINCH. She's too awkward, ill-favoured, and silly to bring to town.

HAR. Then methinks you should bring her to be taught breeding.[30]

PINCH. To be taught! no, sir, I thank you. Good wives and private soldiers should be ignorant. *(aside)* I'll keep her from your instructions, I warrant you.

HAR. *(aside)* The rogue is as jealous as if his wife were not ignorant.

HORN. Why, if she be ill-favoured, there will be less danger here for you than by leaving her in the country. We have such variety of dainties that we are seldom hungry.

DOR. But they have always coarse, constant, swingeing[31] stomachs in the country.

HAR. Foul feeders indeed!

DOR. And your hospitality is great there.

HAR. Open house; every man's welcome.

PINCH. So, so, gentlemen.

HORN. But prithee, why would'st thou marry her? If she be ugly, ill-bred, and silly, she must be rich then.

PINCH. As rich as if she brought me twenty thousand pound out of this town; for she'll be as sure not to spend her moderate portion, as a London baggage would be to spend hers, let it be what it would: so 'tis all one. Then, because she's ugly, she's the likelier to be my own; and being ill-bred, she'll hate conversation; and since silly and innocent, will not

---

[29] a case of venereal disease. The inference is that such cases are as common in the provinces ("in Wales") as in the cities.

[30] A pun is obviously intended.
[31] huge.

know the difference betwixt a man of one-and-twenty and one of forty.

HORN. Nine — to my knowledge.[82] But if she be silly, she'll expect as much from a man of forty-nine, as from him of one-and-twenty. But methinks wit is more necessary than beauty; and I think no young woman ugly that has it, and no handsome woman agreeable without it.

PINCH. 'Tis my maxim, he's a fool that marries; but he's a greater that does not marry a fool.[83] What is wit in a wife good for, but to make a man a cuckold?

HORN. Yes, to keep it from his knowledge.

PINCH. A fool cannot contrive to make her husband a cuckold.

HORN. No; but she'll club with a man that can: and what is worse, if she cannot make her husband a cuckold, she'll make him jealous, and pass for one: and then 'tis all one.

PINCH. Well, well, I'll take care, for one, my wife shall make me no cuckold, though she had your help, Mr. Horner. I understand the town, sir.

DOR. *(aside)* His help!

HAR. *(aside)* He's come newly to town, it seems, and has not heard how things are with him.

HORN. But tell me, has marriage cured thee of whoring, which it seldom does?

HAR. 'Tis more than age can do.

HORN. No, the word is, I'll marry and live honest: but a marriage vow is like a penitent gamester's oath, and entering into bonds and penalties to stint himself to such a particular small sum at play for the future, which makes him but the more eager; and not being able to hold out, loses his money again, and his forfeit to boot.

DOR. Ay, ay, a gamester will be a gamester whilst his money lasts; and a whoremaster whilst his vigour.

HAR. Nay, I have known 'em, when they are broke, and can lose

---

[82] Horner teases Pinchwife, who has given his age as forty, rather than forty-nine.

[83] Cf. Molière, *L'Ecole des Femmes*, I, i, 82: "Epouser une sotte est pour n'être point sot."

no more, keep a fumbling with the box in their hands to fool with only, and hinder other gamesters.

DOR. That had wherewithal to make lusty stakes.

PINCH. Well, gentlemen, you may laugh at me; but you shall never lie with my wife: I know the town.

HORN. But prithee, was not the way you were in better? is not keeping better than marriage?

PINCH. A pox on't! the jades would jilt me, I could never keep a whore to myself.

HORN. So, then you only married to keep a whore to yourself. Well, but let me tell you, women, as you say, are like soldiers, made constant and loyal by good pay, rather than by oaths and covenants. Therefore I'd advise my friends to keep rather than marry, since too I find, by your example, it does not serve one's turn; for I saw you yesterday in the eighteenpenny place[34] with a pretty country-wench.

PINCH. (aside) How the devil! did he see my wife then? I sat there that she might not be seen. But she shall never go to a play again.

HORN. What! dost thou blush, at nine-and-forty, for having been seen with a wench?

DOR. No, faith, I warrant 'twas his wife, which he seated there out of sight; for he's a cunning rogue, and understands the town.

HAR. He blushes. Then 'twas his wife; for men are now more ashamed to be seen with them in public than with a wench.

PINCH. (aside) Hell and damnation! I'm undone, since Horner has seen her, and they know 'twas she.

HORN. But prithee, was it thy wife? She was exceeding pretty. I was in love with her at that distance.

PINCH. You are like never to be nearer to her. Your servant, gentlemen.   (Offers to go.)

HORN. Nay, prithee stay.

[34] The eighteenpenny seats were in the middle gallery, that part of the theatre frequented by ladies of the town, "vizard-masks". Gentlemen of quality (especially when accompanied by their ladies) and unaccompanied ladies of fashion would normally sit in the more expensive boxes, or in the pit. See beginning of Act II.

PINCH. I cannot; I will not.

HORN. Come, you shall dine with us.

PINCH. I have dined already.

HORN. Come, I know thou hast not: I'll treat thee, dear rogue; thou sha't spend none of thy Hampshire money[35] to-day.

PINCH. *(aside)* Treat me! So, he uses me already like his cuckold.

HORN. Nay, you shall not go.

PINCH. I must; I have business at home.   *(Exit.)*

HAR. To beat his wife. He's as jealous of her as a Cheapside husband of a Covent Garden wife.[36]

HORN. Why, 'tis as hard to find an old whoremaster without jealousy and the gout, as a young one without fear, or the pox: —

   As gout in age from pox in youth proceeds,
   So wenching past, then jealousy succeeds;
   The worst disease that love and wenching breeds.[37]

          (Exeunt.)

[35] perhaps a chaffing reference to Mrs. Pinchwife's dowry; in addition, a reference to Mr. Pinchwife's purchase of "cheap seats" in the theatre the day before.

[36] i.e., as a London businessman who has married into well-to-do Covent Garden society would be jealous of his pleasure-loving wife.
Covent Garden: originally the "convent garden" of the Benedictine monks, Covent Garden, in the mid-seventeenth century a fine square designed by Inigo Jones, became a fashionable residential district. The Piazza was an area of exclusive lodgings above the arcades of Covent Garden. See page 115 — SPARKISH. I keep my wedding at my aunt's in the Piazza.

[37] It was the custom among dramatists of the day to close an act with a rhymed couplet or two, or (as here) with a rhymed triplet. Cf. *The Way of the World.*

Act II

A Room in PINCHWIFE's House

MRS. MARGERY PINCHWIFE *and* ALITHEA. PINCHWIFE
peeping behind at the door

MRS. PINCH. Pray, sister, where are the best fields and woods to walk in, in London?

ALITH. A pretty question! – Why, sister, Mulberry Garden[1] and St. James's Park;[2] and, for close walks, the New Exchange.[3]

MRS. PINCH. Pray, sister, tell me why my husband looks so grum here in town, and keeps me up so close, and will not let me go a-walking, nor let me wear my best gown yesterday.

ALITH. O, he's jealous, sister.

MRS. PINCH. Jealous! what's that?

ALITH. He's afraid you should love another man.

MRS. PINCH. How should he be afraid of my loving another man, when he will not let me see any but himself?

ALITH. Did he not carry you yesterday to a play?

MRS. PINCH. Ay; but we sat amongst ugly people. He would not let me come near the gentry, who sat under us, so that I could not see 'em. He told me, none but naughty women sat there, whom they toused and moused.[4] But I would have ventured, for all that.

---

[1] a public park famous for its mulberry trees, near the present location of Buckingham Palace. During the Restoration it was famous as a place of intrigue and rendezvous, and was closed about the date of Wycherley's play.

[2] another public park, which included Rosamonda's Lake. See Pope, *The Rape of the Lock*, V, 133-6.

[3] an exclusive area of milliners', dressmakers', and perfumers' shops, and a favourite resort of ladies and gentlemen of pleasure. It acquired such a bad name that it lost its vogue in the reign of Queen Anne, and was taken down in 1737.

[4] used roughly, rudely, or indecently.

ALITH. But how did you like the play?

MRS. PINCH. Indeed I was aweary of the play; but I liked huge-
ously the actors. They are the goodliest, properest men,
sister!

ALITH. O, but you must not like the actors, sister.

MRS. PINCH. Ay, how should I help it, sister? Pray, sister, when
my husband comes in, will you ask leave for me to go
a-walking?

ALITH. *(aside)* A-walking! ha! ha! Lord, a country-gentlewoman's
pleasure is the drudgery of a footpost; and she requires as
much airing as her husband's horses. – *(aloud)* But here
comes your husband: I'll ask, though I'm sure he'll not
grant it.

MRS. PINCH. He says he won't let me go abroad for fear of catching the pox.

ALITH. Fy! the small-pox, you should say.

Enter PINCHWIFE *to them*

MRS. PINCH. O my dear, dear bud,[5] welcome home! Why dost
thou look so fropish?[6] who has nangered[7] thee?

PINCH. You're a fool.

(MRS. PINCHWIFE *goes aside, and cries.*)

ALITH. Faith, so she is, for crying for no fault, poor tender
creature!

PINCH. What, you would have her as impudent as yourself, as
arrant a jilflirt, a gadder, a magpie,[8] and to say all, a mere
notorious town-woman?

ALITH. Brother, you are my only censurer; and the honour of
your family will sooner suffer in your wife there than in me,
though I take the innocent liberty of the town.

PINCH. Hark you, mistress, do not talk so before my wife. – The
innocent liberty of the town!

ALITH. Why, pray, who boasts of any intrigue with me? what

---

[5] honey-bud, a provincial term of
endearment.

[6] peevish.

[7] angered (a provincialism).

[8] jilflirt: a giddy or silly woman.
gadder: a gadabout. magpie: a
chatterer.

lampoon has made my name notorious? what ill women frequent my lodgings? I keep no company with any women of scandalous reputations.

PINCH. No, you keep the men of scandalous reputations company.

ALITH. Where? would you not have me civil? answer 'em in a box at the plays? in the drawing-room at Whitehall? in St. James's Park? Mulberry Garden? or —

PINCH. Hold, hold! Do not teach my wife where the men are to be found: I believe she's the worse for your town-documents already. I bid you keep her in ignorance, as I do.

MRS. PINCH. Indeed, be not angry with her, bud, she will tell me nothing of the town, though I ask her a thousand times a day.

PINCH. Then you are very inquisitive to know, I find?

MRS. PINCH. Not I indeed, dear; I hate London. Our place-house[9] in the country is worth a thousand of't: would I were there again!

PINCH. So you shall, I warrant. But were you not talking of plays and players when I came in? – *(to* ALITHEA*)* You are her encourager in such discourses.

MRS. PINCH. No, indeed, dear; she chid me just now for liking the playermen.

PINCH. *(aside)* Nay, if she be so innocent as to own to me her liking them, there is no hurt in't. – *(aloud)* Come, my poor rogue, but thou likest none better than me?

MRS. PINCH. Yes, indeed, but I do. The playermen are finer folks.

PINCH. But you love none better than me?

MRS. PINCH. You are my own dear bud, and I know you. I hate a stranger.

PINCH. Ay, my dear, you must love me only; and not be like the naughty town-women, who only hate their husbands, and love every man else; love plays, visits, fine coaches, fine clothes, fiddles, balls, treats, and so lead a wicked town-life.

[9] manor-house.

MRS. PINCH. Nay, if to enjoy all these things be a town-life, London is not so bad a place, dear.

PINCH. How! if you love me, you must hate London.

ALITH. *(aside)* The fool has forbid me discovering to her the pleasures of the town, and he is now setting her agog upon them himself.

MRS. PINCH. But, husband, do the town-women love the playermen too?

PINCH. Yes, I warrant you.

MRS. PINCH. Ay, I warrant you.

PINCH. Why, you do not, I hope?

MRS. PINCH. No, no, bud. But why have we no playermen in the country?

PINCH. Ha! – Mrs. Minx, ask me no more to go to a play.

MRS. PINCH. Nay, why, love? I did not care for going: but when you forbid me, you make me, as 'twere, desire it.

ALITH. *(aside)* So 'twill be in other things, I warrant.

MRS. PINCH. Pray let me go to a play, dear.

PINCH. Hold your peace, I wo' not.

MRS. PINCH. Why, love?

PINCH. Why, I'll tell you.

ALITH. *(aside)* Nay, if he tell her, she'll give him more cause to forbid her that place.

MRS. PINCH. Pray why, dear?

PINCH. First, you like the actors; and the gallants may like you.

MRS. PINCH. What, a homely country girl! No, bud, nobody will like me.

PINCH. I tell you yes, they may.

MRS. PINCH. No, no, you jest – I won't believe you: I will go.

PINCH. I tell you then, that one of the lewdest fellows in town, who saw you there, told me he was in love with you.

MRS. PINCH. Indeed! who, who, pray who was't?

PINCH. *(aside)* I've gone too far, and slipped before I was aware; how overjoyed she is!

MRS. PINCH. Was it any Hampshire gallant, any of our neighbours? I promise you, I am beholding to him.

PINCH. I promise you, you lie; for he would but ruin you, as he has done hundreds. He has no other love for women but that; such as he look upon women, like basilisks, but to destroy 'em.

MRS. PINCH. Ay, but if he loves me, why should he ruin me? answer me to that. Methinks he should not, I would do him no harm.

ALITH. Ha! ha! ha!

PINCH. 'Tis very well; but I'll keep him from doing you any harm, or me either. But here comes company; get you in, get you in.

MRS. PINCH. But, pray, husband, is he a pretty gentleman that loves me?

PINCH. In, baggage, in.   *(Thrusts her in, and shuts the door.)*

Enter SPARKISH *and* HARCOURT

What, all the lewd libertines of the town brought to my lodging by this easy coxcomb! 'sdeath, I'll not suffer it.

SPARK. Here, Harcourt, do you approve my choice? – *(to* ALITHEA*)* Dear little rogue, I told you I'd bring you acquainted with all my friends, the wits and —

                              *(*HARCOURT *salutes her.)*

PINCH. Ay, they shall know her, as well as you yourself will, I warrant you.

SPARK. This is one of those, my pretty rogue, that are to dance at your wedding to-morrow; and him you must bid welcome ever, to what you and I have.

PINCH. *(aside)* Monstrous!

SPARK. Harcourt, how dost thou like her, faith? Nay, dear, do not look down; I should hate to have a wife of mine out of countenance at anything.

PINCH. *(aside)* Wonderful!

SPARK. Tell me, I say, Harcourt, how dost thou like her? Thou hast stared upon her enough, to resolve me.

HAR. So infinitely well, that I could wish I had a mistress too, that might differ from her in nothing but her love and engagement to you.

ALITH. Sir, Master Sparkish has often told me that his acquaintance were all wits and raillieurs, and now I find it.

SPARK. No, by the universe, madam, he does not rally now; you may believe him. I do assure you, he is the honestest, worthiest, true-hearted gentleman – a man of such perfect honour, he would say nothing to a lady he does not mean.

PINCH. *(aside)* Praising another man to his mistress!

HAR. Sir, you are so beyond expectation obliging, that —

SPARK. Nay, egad, I am sure you do admire her extremely; I see't in your eyes. – He does admire you, madam. – By the world, don't you?

HAR. Yes, above the world, or the most glorious part of it, her whole sex: and till now I never thought I should have envied you, or any man about to marry, but you have the best excuse for marriage I ever knew.

ALITH. Nay, now, sir, I'm satisfied you are of the society of the wits and raillieurs, since you cannot spare your friend, even when he is but too civil to you; but the surest sign is, since you are an enemy to marriage, – for that I hear you hate as much as business or bad wine.

HAR. Truly, madam, I was never an enemy to marriage till now, because marriage was never an enemy to me before.

ALITH. But why, sir, is marriage an enemy to you now? because it robs you of your friend here? for you look upon a friend married, as one gone into a monastery, that is, dead to the world.

HAR. 'Tis indeed, because you marry him; I see, madam, you can guess my meaning. I do confess heartily and openly, I wish it were in my power to break the match; by Heavens I would.

SPARK. Poor Frank!

ALITH. Would you be so unkind to me?

HAR. No, no, 'tis not because I would be unkind to you.

SPARK. Poor Frank! no, gad, 'tis only his kindness to me.

PINCH. *(aside)* Great kindness to you indeed! Insensible fop, let a man make love to his wife to his face!

SPARK. Come, dear Frank, for all my wife there, that shall be, thou shalt enjoy me sometimes, dear rogue. By my honour, we men of wit condole for our deceased brother in marriage, as much as for one dead in earnest: I think that was prettily said of me, ha, Harcourt? – But come, Frank, be not melancholy for me.

HAR. No, I assure you, I am not melancholy for you.

SPARK. Prithee, Frank, dost think my wife that shall be there, a fine person?

HAR. I could gaze upon her till I became as blind as you are.

SPARK. How as I am? how?

HAR. Because you are a lover, and true lovers are blind, stock blind.

SPARK. True, true; but by the world she has wit too, as well as beauty: go, go with her into a corner, and try if she has wit; talk to her anything, she's bashful before me.

HAR. Indeed, if a woman wants wit in a corner, she has it nowhere.

ALITH. *(aside to SPARKISH)* Sir, you dispose of me a little before your time —

SPARK. Nay, nay, madam, let me have an earnest[10] of your obedience, or – go, go, madam —

(HARCOURT courts ALITHEA aside.)

PINCH. How, sir! if you are not concerned for the honour of a wife, I am for that of a sister; he shall not debauch her. Be a pander to your own wife! bring men to her! let 'em make love before your face! thrust 'em into a corner together, then leave 'em in private! is this your town wit and conduct?

SPARK. Ha! ha! ha! a silly wise rogue would make one laugh more than a stark fool, ha! ha! I shall burst. Nay, you shall not disturb 'em; I'll vex thee, by the world.

(Struggles with PINCHWIFE to keep
him from HARCOURT and ALITHEA.)

ALITH. The writings are drawn, sir, settlements made; 'tis too late, sir, and past all revocation.

HAR. Then so is my death.

ALITH. I would not be unjust to him.

---

[10] token, or pledge.

HAR. Then why to me so?

ALITH. I have no obligation to you.

HAR. My love.

ALITH. I had his before.

HAR. You never had it; he wants, you see, jealousy, the only in-
fallible sign of it.

ALITH. Love proceeds from esteem; he cannot distrust my virtue: besides, he loves me, or he would not marry me.

HAR. Marrying you is no more sign of his love than bribing your
woman,[11] that he may marry you, is a sign of his generosity.
Marriage is rather a sign of interest than love; and he that
marries a fortune covets a mistress, not loves her. But if you
take marriage for a sign of love, take it from me immediately.

ALITH. No, now you have put a scruple in my head; but in short,
sir, to end our dispute, I must marry him, my reputation
would suffer in the world else.

HAR. No; if you do marry him, with your pardon, madam, your
reputation suffers in the world, and you would be thought
in necessity for a cloak.

ALITH. Nay, now you are rude, sir. – Mr. Sparkish, pray come
hither, your friend here is very troublesome, and very loving.

HAR. *(aside to* ALITHEA*)* Hold! hold! —

PINCH. D'ye hear that?

SPARK. Why, d'ye think I'll seem to be jealous, like a country
bumpkin?

PINCH. No, rather be a cuckold, like a credulous cit.[12]

HAR. Madam, you would not have been so little generous as to
have told him.

ALITH. Yes, since you could be so little generous as to wrong him.

HAR. Wrong him! no man can do't, he's beneath an injury: a
bubble,[13] a coward, a senseless idiot, a wretch so contemptible to all the world but you, that —

---

[11] servant, or maid.

[12] a city-fellow; often a term of con-

tempt. (Origin: citizen.)

[13] a gullible fellow, a dupe.

ALITH. Hold, do not rail at him, for since he is like to be my husband, I am resolved to like him: nay, I think I am obliged to tell him you are not his friend. – Master Sparkish, Master Sparkish!

SPARK. What, what? – *(to HARCOURT)* Now, dear rogue, has not she wit?

HAR. *(surlily)* Not so much as I thought, and hoped she had.

ALITH. Mr. Sparkish, do you bring people to rail at you?

HAR. Madam —

SPARK. How! no; but if he does rail at me, 'tis but in jest, I warrant: what we wits do for one another, and never take any notice of it.

ALITH. He spoke so scurrilously of you, I had no patience to hear him; besides, he has been making love to me.

HAR. *(aside)* True, damned tell-tale woman!

SPARK. Pshaw! to show his parts – we wits rail and make love often, but to show our parts: as we have no affections, so we have no malice, we —

ALITH. He said you were a wretch below an injury —

SPARK. Pshaw!

HAR. *(aside)* Damned, senseless, impudent, virtuous jade! Well, since she won't let me have her, she'll do as good, she'll make me hate her.

ALITH. A common bubble —

SPARK. Pshaw!

ALITH. A coward —

SPARK. Pshaw, pshaw!

ALITH. A senseless, drivelling idiot —

SPARK. How! did he disparage my parts? Nay, then, my honour's concerned, I can't put up that, sir; by the world, brother, help me to kill him – *(aside)* I may draw now, since we have the odds of him: – 'tis a good occasion, too, before my mistress — *(Offers to draw.)*

ALITH. Hold, hold!

SPARK. What, what?

ALITH. *(aside)* I must not let 'em kill the gentleman neither, for his kindness to me: I am so far from hating him, that I wish my gallant had his person and understanding. Nay, if my honour —

SPARK. I'll be thy death.

ALITH. Hold, hold! Indeed, to tell the truth, the gentleman said after all, that what he spoke was but out of friendship to you.

SPARK. How! say I am, I am a fool, that is, no wit, out of friendship to me?

ALITH. Yes, to try whether I was concerned enough for you; and made love to me only to be satisfied of my virtue, for your sake.

HAR. *(aside)* Kind, however.

SPARK. Nay, if it were so, my dear rogue, I ask thee pardon; but why would not you tell me so, faith?

HAR. Because I did not think on't, faith.

SPARK. Come, Horner does not come; Harcourt, let's be gone to the new play. – Come, madam.

ALITH. I will not go, if you intend to leave me alone in the box, and run into the pit, as you use to do.[14]

SPARK. Pshaw! I'll leave Harcourt with you in the box to entertain you, and that's as good; if I sat in the box, I should be thought no judge but of trimmings. – Come away, Harcourt, lead her down.

(Exeunt SPARKISH, HARCOURT, *and* ALITHEA.*)*

PINCH. Well, go thy ways, for the flower of the true town fops, such as spend their estates before they come to 'em, and are cuckolds before they're married. But let me go look to my own freehold.[15] – How!

Enter LADY FIDGET, MISTRESS[16] DAINTY FIDGET, *and* MISTRESS SQUEAMISH

LADY FID. Your servant, sir: where is your lady? We are come to wait upon her to the new play.

PINCH. New play!

[14] are in the habit of doing.
[15] i.e., Margery.
[16] "Mistress" was a polite form of address for both unmarried and married women.

LADY FID. And my husband will wait upon you presently.

PINCH. *(aside)* Damn your civility. – *(aloud)* Madam, by no means; I will not see Sir Jaspar here, till I have waited upon him at home; nor shall my wife see you till she has waited upon your ladyship at your lodgings.[17]

LADY FID. Now we are here, sir?

PINCH. No, Madam.

MRS. DAIN. Pray, let us see her.

MRS. SQUEAM. We will not stir till we see her.

PINCH. *(aside)* A pox on you all! – *(Goes to the door, and returns.)* She has locked the door, and is gone abroad.

LADY FID. No, you have locked the door, and she's within.

MRS. DAIN. They told us below she was here.

PINCH. *(aside)* Will nothing do? – *(aloud)* Well, it must out then. To tell you the truth, ladies, which I was afraid to let you know before, lest it might endanger your lives, my wife has just now the small-pox come out upon her; do not be frightened; but pray be gone, ladies; you shall not stay here in danger of your lives; pray get you gone, ladies.

LADY FID. No, no, we have all had 'em.

MRS. SQUEAM. Alack, alack!

MRS. DAIN. Come, come, we must see how it goes with her; I understand the disease.

LADY FID. Come!

PINCH. *(aside)* Well, there is no being too hard for women at their own weapon, lying, therefore I'll quit the field. *(Exit.)*

MRS. SQUEAM. Here's an example of jealousy!

LADY FID. Indeed, as the world goes, I wonder there are no more jealous, since wives are so neglected.

MRS. DAIN. Pshaw! as the world goes, to what end should they be jealous?

LADY FID. Foh! 'tis a nasty world.

MRS. SQUEAM. That men of parts, great acquaintance, and qual-

[17] Mr. Pinchwife uses conventions of social decorum as an excuse for his refusal to introduce his wife to what he considers such undesirable acquaintance.

ity, should take up with and spend themselves and fortunes in keeping little playhouse creatures, foh!

LADY FID. Nay, that women of understanding, great acquaintance, and good quality, should fall a-keeping too of little creatures, foh!

MRS. SQUEAM. Why, 'tis the men of quality's fault; they never visit women of honour and reputation as they used to do; and have not so much as common civility for ladies of our rank, but use us with the same indifference and ill-breeding as if we were all married to 'em.

LADY FID. She says true; 'tis an arrant shame women of quality should be so slighted; methinks birth – birth should go for something; I have known men admired, courted, and followed for their titles only.

MRS. SQUEAM. Ay, one would think men of honour should not love, no more than marry, out of their own rank.

MRS. DAIN. Fy, fy, upon 'em! they are come to think cross-breeding for themselves best, as well as for their dogs and horses.

LADY FID. They are dogs and horses for't.

MRS. SQUEAM. One would think, if not for love, for vanity a little.

MRS. DAIN. Nay, they do satisfy their vanity upon us sometimes; and are kind to us in their report, tell all the world they lie with us.

LADY FID. Damned rascals, that we should be only wronged by 'em! To report a man has had a person, when he has not had a person, is the greatest wrong in the whole world that can be done to a person.

MRS. SQUEAM. Well, 'tis an arrant shame noble persons should be so wronged and neglected.

LADY FID. But still 'tis an arranter shame for a noble person to neglect her own honour, and defame her own noble person with little inconsiderable fellows, foh!

MRS. DAIN. I suppose the crime against our honour is the same with a man of quality as with another.

LADY FID. How! no, sure, the man of quality is likest one's husband, and therefore the fault should be the less.

MRS. DAIN. But then the pleasure should be the less.

LADY FID. Fy, fy, fy, for shame, sister! whither shall we ramble? Be continent in your discourse, or I shall hate you.

MRS. DAIN. Besides, an intrigue is so much the more notorious for the man's quality.

MRS. SQUEAM. 'Tis true, nobody takes notice of a private man, and therefore with him 'tis more secret; and the crime's the less when 'tis not known.[18]

LADY FID. You say true; i'faith, I think you are in the right on't: 'tis not an injury to a husband, till it be an injury to our honours; so that a woman of honour loses no honour with a private person; and to say truth —

MRS. DAIN. *(apart to MRS. SQUEAMISH)* So, the little fellow is grown a private person – with her —

LADY FID. But still my dear, dear honour —

Enter SIR JASPAR FIDGET, HORNER, and DORILANT

SIR JASP. Ay, my dear, dear of honour, thou hast still so much honour in thy mouth —

HORN. *(aside)* That she has none elsewhere.

LADY FID. Oh, what d'ye mean to bring in these upon us?

MRS. DAIN. Foh! these are as bad as wits.

MRS. SQUEAM. Foh!

LADY FID. Let us leave the room.

SIR JASP. Stay, stay; faith, to tell you the naked truth —

LADY FID. Fy, Sir Jaspar! do not use that word naked.

SIR JASP. Well, well, in short I have business at Whitehall, and cannot go to the play with you, therefore would have you go —

LADY FID. With those two to a play?

SIR JASP. No, not with t'other, but with Mr. Horner; there can be no more scandal to go with him than with Mr. Tattle, or Master Limberham.[19]

---

[18] Possibly an echo of Molière, *Tartuffe*, IV, v, 118-20.

[19] Mr. Tattle, or Master Limberham: names in common use to denote a harmless fellow, fond of ladies' company, in whose care a lady's virtue would be perfectly safe. The Mr. Tattle of Congreve's comedy *Love for Love* (1695) is described in the *dramatis personae* as "a half-witted Beau, vain of his amours, yet valuing himself for secrecy". Dryden's Master Limberham of *The Kind Keeper* (1678) is a "tame, foolish" man.

LADY FID. With that nasty fellow! no – no.

SIR JASP. Nay, prithee, dear, hear me.

(Whispers to LADY FIDGET.)

HORN. Ladies —

*(*HORNER *and* DORILANT *draw near* MRS.
SQUEAMISH *and* MRS. DAINTY FIDGET.)*

MRS. DAIN. Stand off.

MRS. SQUEAM. Do not approach us.

MRS. DAIN. You herd with the wits, you are obscenity all over.

MRS. SQUEAM. And I would as soon look upon a picture of Adam
and Eve, without fig-leaves, as any of you, if I could help it;
therefore keep off, and do not make us sick.

DOR. What a devil are these?

HORN. Why, these are pretenders to honour, as critics to wit,
only by censuring others; and as every raw, peevish, out-of-
humoured, affected, dull, tea-drinking, arithmetical fop, sets
up for a wit by railing at men of sense, so these for honour,
by railing at the court, and ladies of as great honour as
quality.

SIR JASP. Come, Mr. Horner, I must desire you to go with these
ladies to the play, sir.

HORN. I, sir?

SIR JASP. Ay, ay, come, sir.

HORN. I must beg your pardon, sir, and theirs; I will not be seen
in women's company in public again for the world.

SIR JASP. Ha, ha, strange aversion!

MRS. SQUEAM. No, he's for women's company in private.

SIR. JASP. He – poor man – he – ha! ha! ha!

MRS. DAIN. 'Tis a greater shame amongst lewd fellows to be seen
in virtuous women's company, than for the women to be
seen with them.

HORN. Indeed, madam, the time was I only hated virtuous
women, but now I hate the other too; I beg your pardon,
ladies.

LADY FID. You are very obliging, sir, because we would not be
troubled with you.

SIR JASP. In sober sadness, he shall go.

DOR. Nay, if he wo' not, I am ready to wait upon the ladies, and I think I am the fitter man.

SIR JASP. You, sir! no, I thank you for that. Master Horner is a privileged man amongst the virtuous ladies, 'twill be a great while before you are so; heh! he! he! he's my wife's gallant; heh! he! he! No, pray withdraw, sir, for as I take it, the virtuous ladies have no business with you.

DOR. And I am sure he can have none with them. 'Tis strange a man can't come amongst virtuous women now, but upon the same terms as men are admitted into the Great Turk's seraglio.[20] But heavens keep me from being an ombre[21] player with 'em – But where is Pinchwife?   *(Exit.)*

SIR JASP. Come, come, man; what, avoid the sweet society of womankind? that sweet, soft, gentle, tame, noble creature, woman, made for man's companion —

HORN. So is that soft, gentle, tame, and more noble creature, a spaniel, and has all their tricks; can fawn, lie down, suffer beating, and fawn the more; barks at your friends when they come to see you, makes your bed hard, gives you fleas, and the mange sometimes. And all the difference is, the spaniel's the more faithful animal, and fawns but upon one master.

SIR JASP. Heh! he! he!

MRS. SQUEAM. O the rude beast!

MRS. DAIN. Insolent brute!

LADY FID. Brute! stinking, mortified, rotten French wether,[22] to dare —

SIR JASP. Hold, an't please your ladyship. – For shame, Master Horner! Your mother was a woman – *(aside)* Now I shall never reconcile 'em. – *(aside to* LADY FIDGET*)* Hark you, madam, take my advice in your anger. You know you often want one to make up your drolling pack of ombre players,

---

[20] Only eunuchs were admitted to the seraglio of the sultan of Turkey.

[21] a card game. The seventeenth-century spelling was "hombre" (Spanish for "man"), and it is obviously that Wycherley intended a pun. Cf. Pope, *The Rape of the Lock,* Canto III.

[22] a castrated sheep.

and you may cheat him easily; for he's an ill gamester, and consequently loves play. Besides, you know, you have but two old civil gentlemen (with stinking breaths too) to wait upon you abroad; take in the third into your service. The other are but crazy; and a lady should have a supernumerary gentleman-usher[23] as a supernumerary coachhorse, lest sometimes you should be forced to stay at home.

LADY FID. But are you sure he loves play, and has money?

SIR JASP. He loves play as much as you, and has money as much as I.

LADY FID. Then I am contented to make him pay for his scurrility. Money makes up in a measure all other wants in men – *(aside)* Those whom we cannot make hold for gallants, we make fine.[24]

SIR JASP. *(aside)* So, so; now to mollify, to wheedle him. – *(aside to* HORNER*)* Master Horner, will you never keep civil company? methinks 'tis time now, since you are only fit for them. Come, come, man, you must e'en fall to visiting our wives, eating at our tables, drinking tea with our virtuous relations after dinner, dealing cards to 'em, reading plays and gazettes to 'em, picking fleas out of their shocks[25] for 'em, collecting receipts, new songs, women, pages, and footmen for 'em.

HORN. I hope they'll afford me better employment, sir.

SIR JASP. Heh! he! he! 'tis fit you know your work before you come into your place. And since you are unprovided of a lady to flatter, and a good house to eat at, pray frequent mine, and call my wife mistress, and she shall call you gallant, according to the custom.

HORN. Who, I?

SIR JASP. Faith, thou sha't for my sake; come, for my sake only.

HORN. For your sake —

SIR JASP. *(to* LADY FIDGET*)* Come, come, here's a gamester for you;

---

[23] an attendant escort to wait upon a lady and her pleasures.

[24] force to pay a fine.

[25] lap-dogs. Cf. Belinda's "Shock",

Pope, *The Rape of the Lock*, I, and *passim*. Some editions of Wycherley's play misprint "smocks"!

let him be a little familiar sometimes; nay, what if a little rude? Gamesters may be rude with ladies, you know.

LADY FID. Yes; losing gamesters have a privilege with women.

HORN. I always thought the contrary, that the winning gamester had most privilege with women; for when you have lost your money to a man, you'll lose anything you have, all you have, they say, and he may use you as he pleases.[26]

SIR JASP. Heh! he! he! well, win or lose, you shall have your liberty with her.

LADY FID. As he behaves himself; and for your sake I'll give him admittance and freedom.

HORN. All sorts of freedom, madam?

SIR JASP. Ay, ay, ay, all sorts of freedom thou canst take. And so go to her, begin thy new employment; wheedle her, jest with her, and be better acquainted one with another.

HORN. *(aside)* I think I know her already; therefore may venture with her my secret for hers.

(HORNER and LADY FIDGET whisper.)

SIR JASP. *(to MRS. DAINTY FIDGET and MRS. SQUEAMISH)* Sister, cuz, I have provided an innocent playfellow for you there.

MRS. DAIN. Who, he?

MRS. SQUEAM. There's a playfellow, indeed!

SIR JASP. Yes sure. – What, he is good enough to play at cards, blindman's-buff, or the fool with, sometimes!

MRS. SQUEAM. Foh! we'll have no such playfellows.

MRS. DAIN. No, sir; you shan't choose playfellows for us, we thank you.

SIR JASP. Nay, pray hear me.   *(Whispering to them.)*

LADY FID. But, poor gentleman, could you be so generous, so truly a man of honour, as for the sakes of us women of honour, to cause yourself to be reported no man? No man! and to suffer yourself the greatest shame that could fall upon a man, that none might fall upon us women by your conversation? but, indeed, sir, as perfectly, perfectly the

[26] an echo of Molière, *L'Ecole des Femmes*, III, ii, 119-21:
    Car ce jeu décevant,
    Pousse une femme souvent
    A jouer de tout son reste.

same man as before your going into France, sir? as perfectly,
perfectly, sir?

HORN. As perfectly, perfectly, madam. Nay, I scorn you should
take my word; I desire to be tried only, madam.

LADY FID. Well, that's spoken again like a man of honour: all
men of honour desire to come to the test. But, indeed,
generally you men report such things of yourselves, one does
not know how or whom to believe; and it is come to that
pass, we dare not take your words no more than your
tailor's, without some staid servant of yours be bound with
you. But I have so strong a faith in your honour, dear, dear,
noble sir, that I'd forfeit mine for yours, at any time, dear
sir.

HORN. No, madam, you should not need to forfeit it for me; I
have given you security already to save you harmless, my
late reputation being so well known in the world, madam.

LADY FID. But if upon any future falling-out, or upon a suspicion of my taking the trust out of your hands, to employ
some other, you yourself should betray your trust, dear sir?
I mean, if you'll give me leave to speak obscenely, you might
tell, dear sir.

HORN. If I did, nobody would believe me. The reputation of
impotency is as hardly recovered again in the world as that
of cowardice, dear madam.

LADY FID. Nay, then, as one may say, you may do your worst,
dear, dear sir.

SIR JASP. Come, is your ladyship reconciled to him yet? have you
agreed on matters? for I must be gone to Whitehall.

LADY FID. Why, indeed, Sir Jaspar, Master Horner is a thousand,
thousand times a better man than I thought him. Cousin
Squeamish, Sister Dainty, I can name him now. Truly, not
long ago, you know, I thought his very name obscenity; and
I would as soon have lain with him as have named him.

SIR JASP. Very likely, poor madam.

MRS. DAIN. I believe it.

MRS. SQUEAM. No doubt on't.

SIR JASP. Well, well – that your ladyship is as virtuous as any

she, I know, and him all the town knows – heh! he! he!
therefore now you like him, get you gone to your business
together, go, go to your business, I say, pleasure, whilst I go
to my pleasure, business.

LADY FID. Come, then, dear gallant.

HORN. Come away, my dearest mistress.

SIR JASP. So, so; why, 'tis as I'd have it.   *(Exit.)*

HORN. And as I'd have it.

LADY FID. Who for his business from his wife will run,
       Takes the best care to have her business done.

                                (Exeunt.)

Act III

SCENE I – *A Room in* PINCHWIFE'*s House*

ALITHEA *and* MRS. PINCHWIFE

ALITH. Sister, what ails you? you are grown melancholy.

MRS. PINCH. Would it not make any one melancholy to see you go every day fluttering about abroad, whilst I must stay at home like a poor, lonely, sullen bird in a cage?

ALITH. Ay, sister; but you came young, and just from the nest to your cage: so that I thought you liked it, and could be as cheerful in't as others that took their flight themselves early, and are hopping abroad in the open air.

MRS. PINCH. Nay, I confess I was quiet enough till my husband told me what pure lives the London ladies live abroad, with their dancing, meetings, and junketings, and dressed every day in their best gowns; and I warrant you, play at nine-pins every day of the week, so they do.

Enter PINCHWIFE

PINCH. Come, what's here to do? you are putting the town-pleasures in her head, and setting her a-longing.

ALITH. Yes, after nine-pins. You suffer none to give her those longings you mean but yourself.

PINCH. I tell her of the vanities of the town like a confessor.

ALITH. A confessor! just such a confessor as he that, by forbidding a silly ostler to grease the horse's teeth, taught him to do't.

PINCH. Come, Mistress Flippant, good precepts are lost when bad examples are still before us: the liberty you take abroad makes her hanker after it, and out of humour at home. Poor wretch! she desired not to come to London; I would bring her.

ALITH. Very well.

PINCH. She has been this week in town, and never desired till this afternoon to go abroad.

ALITH. Was she not at a play yesterday?

PINCH. Yes; but she ne'er asked me; I was myself the cause of her going.

ALITH. Then if she ask you again, you are the cause of her asking, and not my example.

PINCH. Well, to-morrow night I shall be rid of you; and the next day, before 'tis light, she and I'll be rid of the town, and my dreadful apprehensions. – (to MRS. PINCHWIFE) Come, be not melancholy; for thou sha't go into the country after to-morrow, dearest.

ALITH. Great comfort!

MRS. PINCH. Pish! what d'ye tell me of the country for?

PINCH. How's this! what, pish at the country?

MRS. PINCH. Let me alone; I am not well.

PINCH. O, if that be all – what ails my dearest?

MRS. PINCH. Truly, I don't know: but I have not been well since you told me there was a gallant at the play in love with me.

PINCH. Ha! —

ALITH. That's by my example too!

PINCH. Nay, if you are not well, but are so concerned, because a lewd fellow chanced to lie, and say he liked you, you'll make me sick too.

MRS. PINCH. Of what sickness?

PINCH. O, of that which is worse than the plague, jealousy.

MRS. PINCH. Pish, you jeer! I'm sure there's no such disease in our receipt-book at home.

PINCH. (aside) No, thou never met'st with it, poor innocent. – Well, if thou cuckold me, 'twill be my own fault – for cuckolds and bastards are generally makers of their own fortune.

MRS. PINCH. Well, but pray, bud, let's go to a play to-night.

PINCH. 'Tis just done, she comes from it.[1] But why are you so eager to see a play?

MRS. PINCH. Faith, dear, not that I care one pin for their talk there; but I like to look upon the player-men, and would see, if I could, the gallant you say loves me: that's all, dear bud.

PINCH. Is that all, dear bud?

ALITH. This proceeds from my example!

MRS. PINCH. But if the play be done, let's go abroad, however, dear bud.

PINCH. Come, have a little patience and thou shalt go into the country on Friday.

MRS. PINCH. Therefore I would see first some sights to tell my neighbours of. Nay, I will go abroad, that's once.

ALITH. I'm the cause of this desire too!

PINCH. But now I think on't, who was the cause of Horner's coming to my lodgings to-day? That was you.

ALITH. No, you, because you would not let him see your handsome wife out of your lodging.

MRS. PINCH. Why, O Lord! did the gentleman come hither to see me indeed?

PINCH. No, no. – You are not the cause of that damned question too, Mistress Alithea? – *(aside)* Well, she's in the right of it. He is in love with my wife – and comes after her – 'tis so – but I'll nip his love in the bud; lest he should follow us into the country, and break his chariot-wheel near our house, on purpose for an excuse to come to't. But I think I know the town.

MRS. PINCH. Come, pray, bud, let's go abroad before 'tis late; for I will go, that's flat and plain.

PINCH. *(aside)* So! the obstinacy already of a town-wife; and I must, whilst she's here, humour her like one. – *(aloud)* Sister, how shall we do, that she may not be seen or known?

ALITH. Let her put on her mask.

PINCH. Pshaw! a mask makes people but the more inquisitive,

---

[1] Alithea has just returned from the theatre.

and is as ridiculous a disguise as a stage-beard: her shape, stature, habit will be known. And if we should meet with Horner, he would be sure to take acquaintance with us, must wish her joy, kiss her, talk to her, leer upon her, and the devil and all. No, I'll not use her to a mask, 'tis dangerous; for masks have made more cuckolds than the best faces that ever were known.

ALITH. How will you do then?

MRS. PINCH. Nay, shall we go? The Exchange will be shut, and I have a mind to see that.

PINCH. So – I have it – I'll dress her up in the suit we are to carry down to her brother, little Sir James; nay, I understand the town-tricks. Come, let's go dress her. A mask! no – a woman masked, like a covered dish, gives a man curiosity and appetite; when, it may be, uncovered, 'twould turn his stomach: no, no.

ALITH. Indeed your comparison is something a greasy one: but I had a gentle gallant used to say, a beauty masked, like the sun in eclipse, gathers together more gazers than if it shined out. *(Exeunt.)*

SCENE II – *The New Exchange*

Enter HORNER, HARCOURT, *and* DORILANT

DOR. Engaged to women, and not sup with us?

HORN. Ay, a pox on 'em all!

HAR. You were much a more reasonable man in the morning, and had as noble resolutions against 'em as a widower of a week's liberty.

DOR. Did I ever think to see you keep company with women in vain?

HORN. In vain: no – 'tis since I can't love 'em, to be revenged on 'em.

HAR. Now your sting is gone, you looked in the box amongst all those women like a drone in the hive; all upon you, shoved and ill-used by 'em all, and thrust from one side to t'other.

DOR. Yet he must be buzzing amongst 'em still, like other old beetle-headed liquorish drones. Avoid 'em, and hate 'em, as they hate you.

HORN. Because I do hate 'em, and would hate 'em yet more, I'll frequent 'em. You may see by marriage, nothing makes a man hate a woman more than her constant conversation. In short, I converse with 'em, as you do with rich fools, to laugh at 'em and use 'em ill.

DOR. But I would no more sup with women, unless I could lie with 'em, than sup with a rich coxcomb, unless I could cheat him.

HORN. Yes, I have known thee sup with a fool for his drinking; if he could set out your hand that way only, you were satisfied, and if he were a wine-swallowing mouth, 'twas enough.[2]

HAR. Yes, a man drinks often with a fool, as he tosses with a marker, only to keep his hand in ure.[3] But do the ladies drink?

HORN. Yes, sir; and I shall have the pleasure at least of laying 'em flat with a bottle, and bring as much scandal that way upon 'em as formerly t'other.

HAR. Perhaps you may prove as weak a brother amongst 'em that way as t'other.

DOR. Foh! drinking with women is as unnatural as scolding with 'em. But 'tis a pleasure of decayed fornicators, and the basest way of quenching love.

HAR. Nay, 'tis drowning love, instead of quenching it. But leave us for civil women too!

DOR. Ay, when he can't be the better for 'em. We hardly pardon a man that leaves his friend for a wench, and that's a pretty lawful call.

HORN. Faith, I would not leave you for 'em, if they would not drink.

DOR. Who would disappoint his company at Lewis's for a gossiping?

HAR. Foh! Wine and women, good apart, together as nauseous

---

[2] The sense is: "If he put a glass in your hand, you were satisfied; if he was a drinker himself, nothing mattered."

[3] use, practice

as sack and sugar. But hark you, sir, before you go, a little of your advice; an old maimed general, when unfit for action, is fittest for counsel. I have other designs upon women than eating and drinking with them; I am in love with Sparkish's mistress, whom he is to marry to-morrow: now how shall I get her?

Enter SPARKISH, *looking about*

HORN. Why, here comes one will help you to her.

HAR. He! he, I tell you, is my rival, and will hinder my love.

HORN. No; a foolish rival and a jealous husband assist their rival's designs; for they are sure to make their women hate them, which is the first step to their love for another man.

HAR. But I cannot come near his mistress but in his company.

HORN. Still the better for you; for fools are most easily cheated when they themselves are accessaries: and he is to be bub-bled[4] of his mistress as of his money, the common mistress, by keeping him company.

SPARK. Who is that that is to be bubbled? Faith, let me snack;[5] I han't met with a bubble since Christmas. 'Gad, I think bubbles are like their brother woodcocks,[6] go out with the cold weather.

HAR. *(apart to* HORNER*)* A pox! he did not hear all, I hope.

SPARK. Come, you bubbling rogues you, where do we sup? – Oh, Harcourt, my mistress tells me you have been making fierce love to her all the play long: ha! ha! – But I —

HAR. I make love to her!

SPARK. Nay, I forgive thee, for I think I know thee, and I know her; but I am sure I know myself.

HAR. Did she tell you so? I see all women are like these of the Exchange;[7] who, to enhance the price of their commodities, report to their fond customers offers which were never made 'em.

HORN. Ay, women are as apt to tell before the intrigue, as men

---

[4] deceived, cheated, cozened.
[5] share the secret.
[6] dupes, foolish fellows. (The wood-cock is proverbially a stupid bird because it is easily netted.)
[7] women of easy virtue.

after it, and so show themselves the vainer sex. But hast thou a mistress, Sparkish? 'Tis as hard for me to believe it, as that thou ever hadst a bubble, as you bragged just now.

SPARK. O, your servant, sir: are you at your raillery, sir? But we were some of us beforehand with you to-day at the play. The wits were something bold with you, sir; did you not hear us laugh?

HORN. Yes; but I thought you had gone to plays to laugh at the poet's wit, not at your own.

SPARK. Your servant, sir: no, I thank you. 'Gad, I go to a play as to a country treat; I carry my own wine to one, and my own wit to t'other, or else I'm sure I should not be merry at either. And the reason why we are so often louder than the players, is, because we think we speak more wit, and so become the poet's rivals in his audience: for to tell you the truth, we hate the silly rogues; nay, so much, that we find fault even with their bawdy upon the stage, whilst we talk nothing else in the pit as loud.

HORN. But why shouldst thou hate the silly poets? Thou hast too much wit to be one; and they, like whores, are only hated by each other: and thou dost scorn writing, I'm sure.

SPARK. Yes; I'd have you to know I scorn writing: but women, women, that make men do all foolish things, make 'em write songs too. Everybody does it. 'Tis even as common with lovers, as playing with fans; and you can no more help rhyming to your Phyllis, than drinking to your Phyllis.

HAR. Nay, poetry in love is no more to be avoided than jealousy.

DOR. But the poets damned your songs, did they?

SPARK. Damn the poets! they have turned 'em into burlesque, as they call it. That burlesque is a hocus-pocus trick they have got, which, by the virtue of *Hictius doctius topsy turvy*,[8] they make a wise and witty man in the world, a fool upon the stage, you know not how: and 'tis therefore I hate 'em too, for I know not but it may be my own case; for they'll

---

[8] the gibberish or nonsensical jargon used by the juggler or magician before he performs his trick. It may derive from *hic est doctus*: "here is the doctor (or master)".

put a man into a play for looking asquint. Their predecessors were contented to make serving-men only their stage-fools: but these rogues must have gentlemen, with a pox to 'em, nay, knights; and, indeed, you shall hardly see a fool upon the stage but he's a knight.[9] And to tell you the truth, they have kept me these six years from being a knight in earnest, for fear of being knighted in a play, and dubbed a fool.

DOR. Blame 'em not, they must follow their copy, the age.

HAR. But why shouldst thou be afraid of being in a play, who expose yourself every day in the play-houses, and at public places?

HORN. 'Tis but being on the stage, instead of standing on a bench in the pit.

DOR. Don't you give money to painters to draw you like? and are you afraid of your pictures at length in a playhouse, where all your mistresses may see you?

SPARK. A pox! painters don't draw the small-pox or pimples in one's face.[10] Come, damn all your silly authors whatever, all books and booksellers, by the world; and all readers, courteous or uncourteous!

HAR. But who comes here, Sparkish?

Enter PINCHWIFE *and* MRS. PINCHWIFE *in man's clothes,* ALITHEA, *and* LUCY, *her maid*

SPARK. Oh, hide me! There's my mistress too.

(SPARKISH *hides himself behind* HARCOURT.)

HAR. She sees you.

SPARK. But I will not see her. 'Tis time to go to Whitehall, and I must not fail the drawing-room.

[9] The ridiculous characters in Restoration comedy are frequently knights: for example, Sir Humphry Noddy (Shadwell's *Bury Fair*), Sir Formal Trifle (Shadwell's *The Virtuoso*), Sir Fopling Flutter (Etherege's *The Man of Mode*), Sir Wilfull Witwoud (Congreve's *The Way of the World*). Cf. Molière, *L'Impromptu de Versailles*, part i: "Le marquis aujourd'hui est le plaisant de la comédie." Jeremy Collier (*A Short View of the Immorality and Profaneness of the English Stage*, Chapter 4, 1698) was to reprove Restoration dramatists for such disrespectful practice.

[10] a central argument in Restoration and eighteenth-century critical and aesthetic theory.

HAR. Pray, first carry me, and reconcile me to her.

SPARK. Another time. Faith, the king will have supped.

HAR. Not with the worse stomach for thy absence. Thou art one of those fools that think their attendance at the king's meals as necessary as his physicians', when you are more troublesome to him than his doctors or his dogs.

SPARK. Pshaw! I know my interest, sir. Prithee hide me.

HORN. Your servant, Pinchwife. – What, he knows us not!

PINCH. *(to his wife aside)* Come along.

MRS. PINCH. *(to* BOOKSELLER*)* Pray, have you any ballads? give me sixpenny worth.

BOOKSELLER. We have no ballads.

MRS. PINCH. Then give me "Covent Garden Drollery,"[11] and a play or two – Oh, here's "Tarugo's Wiles,"[12] and "The Slighted Maiden";[13] I'll have them.

PINCH. *(apart to her)* No; plays are not for your reading. Come along; will you discover yourself?

HORN. Who is that pretty youth with him, Sparkish?

SPARK. I believe his wife's brother, because he's something like her: but I never saw her but once.

HORN. Extremely handsome; I have seen a face like it too. Let us follow 'em.

> *(Exeunt* PINCHWIFE, MRS. PINCHWIFE, ALITHEA, *and*
> LUCY; HORNER *and* DORILANT *following them.)*

HAR. Come, Sparkish, your mistress saw you, and will be angry you go not to her. Besides, I would fain be reconciled to her, which none but you can do, dear friend.

SPARK. Well, that's a better reason, dear friend. I would not go near her now for hers or my own sake; but I can deny you nothing: for though I have known thee a great while, never

---

[11] The subtitle of the work is: "A Collection of all the choice Songs, Poems, Prologues, and Epilogues, sung and spoken at Courts and Theatres. Written by the Refinedst Wits of the Age . . ." (1672). Authorship is uncertain, possibly by Alexander Brome.

[12] a comedy subtitled *The Coffee-House* (1668) by one Thomas St. Serfe, upon which the Earl of Dorset, a friend of Dryden and a poet of some ability, wrote complimentary verses.

[13] *The Slighted Maid*, a comedy by Sir Robert Stapylton (1663), parodied in *The Rehearsal*.

go,[14] if I do not love thee as well as a new acquaintance.

HAR. I am obliged to you indeed, dear friend. I would be well with her, only to be well with thee still; for these ties to wives usually dissolve all ties to friends. I would be contented she should enjoy you a-nights, but I would have you to myself a-days as I have had, dear friend.

SPARK. And thou shalt enjoy me a-days, dear, dear friend, never stir: and I'll be divorced from her, sooner than from thee. Come along.

HAR. *(aside)* So, we are hard put to't, when we make our rival our procurer; but neither she nor her brother would let me come near her now. When all's done, a rival is the best cloak to steal to a mistress under, without suspicion; and when we have once got to her as we desire, we throw him off like other cloaks.

(Exit SPARKISH, HARCOURT following him.)

Re-enter PINCHWIFE and MRS. PINCHWIFE

PINCH. *(to ALITHEA)*[15] Sister, if you will not go, we must leave you. – *(aside)* The fool her gallant and she will muster up all the young saunterers of this place, and they will leave their dear sempstresses to follow us. What a swarm of cuckolds and cuckold-makers are here! – *(aloud)* Come, let's be gone, Mistress Margery.

MRS. PINCH. Don't you believe that; I han't half my bellyful of sights yet.

PINCH. Then walk this way.

MRS. PINCH. Lord, what a power of brave signs are here! stay – the Bull's-Head, the Ram's-Head, and the Stag's-Head,[16] dear —

PINCH. Nay, if every husband's proper sign here were visible, they would be all alike.

---

[14] i.e., may I never go.

[15] Alithea is offstage in the company of Harcourt and Sparkish. Pinchwife calls back to her.

[16] public houses. The irony lies in

Mrs. Pinchwife's innocence that they are all horned animals, and consequently remind her husband of his fear of being cuckolded. His lines indicate that he is painfully aware of the irony.

MRS. PINCH. What d'ye mean by that, bud?

PINCH. 'Tis no matter – no matter, bud.

MRS. PINCH. Pray tell me; nay, I will know.

PINCH. They would all be Bulls, Stags, and Rams-Heads.

(Exeunt PINCHWIFE *and* MRS. PINCHWIFE.*)*

Re-enter SPARKISH, HARCOURT, ALITHEA, *and* LUCY,
at the other side

SPARK. Come, dear madam, for my sake you shall be reconciled to him.

ALITH. For your sake I hate him.

HAR. That's something too cruel, madam, to hate me for his sake.

SPARK. Ay indeed, madam, too, too cruel to me, to hate my friend for my sake.

ALITH. I hate him because he is your enemy; and you ought to hate him too, for making love to me, if you love me.

SPARK. That's a good one! I hate a man for loving you! If he did love you, 'tis but what he can't help; and 'tis your fault, not his, if he admires you. I hate a man for being of my opinion! I'll ne'er do't, by the world.

ALITH. Is it for your honour, or mine, to suffer a man to make love to me, who am to marry you to-morrow?

SPARK. Is it for your honour, or mine, to have me jealous? That he makes love to you, is a sign you are handsome; and that I am not jealous, is a sign you are virtuous. That, I think, is for your honour.

ALITH. But 'tis your honour too I am concerned for.

HAR. But why, dearest madam, will you be more concerned for his honour than he is himself? Let his honour alone, for my sake and his. He! he has no honour —

SPARK. How's that?

HAR. But what my dear friend can guard himself.

SPARK. O ho – that's right again.

HAR. Your care of his honour argues his neglect of it, which is no honour to my dear friend here. Therefore once more, let his honour go which way it will, dear madam.

SPARK. Ay, ay; were it for my honour to marry a woman whose virtue I suspected, and could not trust her in a friend's hands?

ALITH. Are you not afraid to lose me?

HAR. He afraid to lose you, madam! No, no – you may see how the most estimable and most glorious creature in the world is valued by him. Will you not see it?

SPARK. Right, honest Frank, I have that noble value for her that I cannot be jealous of her.

ALITH. You mistake him. He means, you care not for me, nor who has me.

SPARK. Lord, madam, I see you are jealous! Will you wrest a poor man's meaning from his words?

ALITH. You astonish me, sir, with your want of jealousy.

SPARK. And you make me giddy, madam, with your jealousy and fears, and virtue and honour. Gad, I see virtue makes a woman as troublesome as a little reading or learning.

ALITH. Monstrous!

LUCY. (aside) Well, to see what easy husbands these women of quality can meet with! a poor chambermaid can never have such ladylike luck. Besides, he's thrown away upon her. She'll make no use of her fortune, her blessing, none to a gentleman, for a pure cuckold; for it requires good breeding to be a cuckold.[17]

ALITH. I tell you then plainly, he pursues me to marry me.

SPARK. Pshaw!

HAR. Come, madam, you see you strive in vain to make him jealous of me. My dear friend is the kindest creature in the world to me.

SPARK. Poor fellow!

HAR. But his kindness only is not enough for me, without your

[17] Lucy seems to argue that in marrying Sparkish, Alithea will be wasting her endowments upon a man of no breeding, and therefore not worth cuckolding. But were she to marry Harcourt, the gentleman of good breeding, she would be equally matched in the game of love; and if she cuckolded Harcourt, his integrity would remain, in a sense, "pure". If she cuckolded Sparkish, our sympathies would be with her; but if she cuckolded Harcourt, our sympathies would be with him. It is in this sense that Harcourt would be "a pure cuckold".

favour, your good opinion, dear madam: 'tis that must perfect my happiness. Good gentleman, he believes all I say: would you would do so! Jealous of me! I would not wrong him nor you for the world.

SPARK. Look you there. Hear him, hear him, and do not walk away so.

(ALITHEA *walks carelessly to and fro*.)

HAR. I love you, madam, so —

SPARK. How's that? Nay, now you begin to go too far indeed.

HAR. So much, I confess, I say, I love you, that I would not have you miserable, and cast yourself away upon so unworthy and inconsiderable a thing as what you see here.

(*Clapping his hand on his breast, points at* SPARKISH.)

SPARK. No, faith, I believe thou wouldst not: now his meaning is plain: but I knew before thou wouldst not wrong me, nor her.

HAR. No, no, Heavens forbid the glory of her sex should fall so low, as into the embraces of such a contemptible wretch, the least of mankind – my friend here – I injure him!

(*Embracing* SPARKISH.)

ALITH. Very well.

SPARK. No, no, dear friend, I knew it. – Madam, you see he will rather wrong himself than me, in giving himself such names.

ALITH. Do not you understand him yet?

SPARK. Yes: how modestly he speaks of himself, poor fellow!

ALITH. Methinks he speaks impudently of yourself, since – before yourself too; insomuch that I can no longer suffer his scurrilous abusiveness to you, no more than his love to me.

(*Offers to go*.)

SPARK. Nay, nay, madam, pray stay – his love to you! Lord, madam, has he not spoke yet plain enough?

ALITH. Yes, indeed, I should think so.

SPARK. Well then, by the world, a man can't speak civilly to a woman now, but presently she says, he makes love to her. Nay, madam, you shall stay, with your pardon, since you have not yet understood him, till he has made an *éclaircisse-ment*[18] of his love to you, that is, what kind of love it is. Answer to thy catechism, friend; do you love my mistress here?

HAR. Yes, I wish she would not doubt it.

SPARK. But how do you love her?

HAR. With all my soul.

ALITH. I thank him, methinks he speaks plain enough now.

SPARK. *(to* ALITHEA*)* You are out still. – But with what kind of love, Harcourt?

HAR. With the best and truest love in the world.

SPARK. Look you there then, that is with no matrimonial love, I'm sure.

ALITH. How's that? do you say matrimonial love is not best?

SPARK. Gad, I went too far ere I was aware.[19] But speak for thy-self, Harcourt, you said you would not wrong me nor her.

HAR. No, no, madam, e'en take him for Heaven's sake.

SPARK. Look you there, madam.

HAR. Who should in all justice be yours, he that loves you most.
(Claps his hand on his breast.)

ALITH. Look you there, Mr. Sparkish, who's that?

SPARK. Who should it be? – Go on, Harcourt.

HAR. Who loves you more than women titles, or fortune fools.
(Points at SPARKISH.*)*

SPARK. Look you there, he means me still, for he points at me.

ALITH. Ridiculous!

HAR. Who can only match your faith and constancy in love.

SPARK. Ay.

HAR. Who knows, if it be possible, how to value so much beauty and virtue.

SPARK. Ay.

HAR. Whose love can no more be equalled in the world, than that heavenly form of yours.

SPARK. No.

HAR. Who could no more suffer a rival, than your absence, and

---

[18] clarification. Wycherley uses the French term to denote affectation in Sparkish. See also *The Plain Dealer*, IV, ii.

[19] Gad . . . aware: possibly *aside.*

yet could no more suspect your virtue, than his own constancy in his love to you.

SPARK. No.

HAR. Who, in fine, loves you better than his eyes, that first made him love you.

SPARK. Ay – Nay, madam, faith, you shan't go till –

ALITH. Have a care, lest you make me stay too long.

SPARK. But till he has saluted you; that I may be assured you are friends, after his honest advice and declaration. Come, pray, madam, be friends with him.

Re-enter PINCHWIFE *and* MRS. PINCHWIFE

ALITH. You must pardon me, sir, that I am not yet so obedient to you.

PINCH. What, invite your wife to kiss men? Monstrous! are you not ashamed? I will never forgive you.

SPARK. Are you not ashamed, that I should have more confidence in the chastity of your family than you have? You must not teach me; I am a man of honour, sir, though I am frank and free; I am frank, sir –

PINCH. Very frank, sir, to share your wife with your friends.

SPARK. He is an humble, menial friend, such as reconciles the differences of the marriage-bed; you know man and wife do not always agree; I design him for that use, therefore would have him well with my wife.

PINCH. A menial friend! – you will get a great many menial friends, by showing your wife as you do.

SPARK. What then? It may be I have a pleasure in't, as I have to show fine clothes at a play-house, the first day, and count money before poor rogues.

PINCH. He that shows his wife or money, will be in danger of having them borrowed sometimes.

SPARK. I love to be envied, and would not marry a wife that I alone could love; loving alone is as dull as eating alone. Is it not a frank age? and I am a frank person; and to tell you the truth, it may be, I love to have rivals in a wife, they make her seem to a man still but as a kept mistress; and so

good night, for I must to Whitehall. – Madam, I hope you
are now reconciled to my friend; and so I wish you a good
night, madam, and sleep if you can: for to-morrow you
know I must visit you early with a canonical gentleman.
Good night, dear Harcourt. *(Exit.)*

HAR. Madam, I hope you will not refuse my visit to-morrow, if
it should be earlier with a canonical gentleman than Mr.
Sparkish's.

PINCH. This gentlewoman is yet under my care, therefore you
must yet forbear your freedom with her, sir.[20]

(Coming between ALITHEA *and* HARCOURT.*)*

HAR. Must, sir?

PINCH. Yes, sir, she is my sister.

HAR. 'Tis well she is, sir – for I must be her servant, sir. –
Madam —

PINCH. Come away, sister, we had been gone, if it had not been
for you, and so avoided these lewd rake-hells, who seem to
haunt us.

Re-enter HORNER *and* DORILANT

HORN. How now, Pinchwife!

PINCH. Your servant.

HORN. What! I see a little time in the country makes a man turn
wild and unsociable, and only fit to converse with his horses,
dogs, and his herds.

PINCH. I have business, sir, and must mind it; your business is
pleasure, therefore you and I must go different ways.

HORN. Well, you may go on, but this pretty young gentleman —

(Takes hold of MRS. PINCHWIFE.*)*

HAR. The lady —

DOR. And the maid —

HORN. Shall stay with us; for I suppose their business is the same
with ours, pleasure.

PINCH. *(aside)* 'Sdeath, he knows her, she carries it so sillily!

---

20 With these lines Mr. Pinchwife
interrupts the private discourse between Harcourt and Alithea and pre-
vents Alithea from answering Harcourt's question. See Act III, note 22.

yet if he does not, I should be more silly to discover it first.

ALITH. Pray, let us go, sir.

PINCH. Come, come —

HORN. *(to* MRS. PINCHWIFE) Had you not rather stay with us? –
Prithee, Pinchwife, who is this pretty young gentleman?

PINCH. One to whom I'm a guardian. – *(aside)* I wish I could
keep her out of your hands.

HORN. Who is he? I never saw anything so pretty in all my life.

PINCH. Pshaw! do not look upon him so much, he's a poor bashful youth, you'll put him out of countenance. – Come away,
brother.   *(Offers to take her away.)*

HORN. O, your brother!

PINCH. Yes, my wife's brother. – Come, come, she'll stay supper
for us.

HORN. I thought so, for he is very like her I saw you at the play
with, whom I told you I was in love with.

MRS. PINCH. *(aside)* O jeminy![21] is that he that was in love with
me? I am glad on't, I vow, for he's a curious fine gentleman,
and I love him already, too. – *(to* PINCHWIFE) Is this he, bud?

PINCH. *(to his wife)* Come away, come away.

HORN. Why, what haste are you in? why won't you let me talk
with him?

PINCH. Because you'll debauch him; he's yet young and innocent, and I would not have him debauched for anything in
the world. – *(aside)* How she gazes on him! the devil!

HORN. Harcourt, Dorilant, look you here, this is the likeness of
that dowdy he told us of, his wife; did you ever see a love-
lier creature? The rogue has reason to be jealous of his wife,
since she is like him, for she would make all that see her in
love with her.

HAR. And, as I remember now, she is as like him here as can be.

DOR. She is indeed very pretty, if she be like him.

HORN. Very pretty? a very pretty commendation! – she is a glorious creature, beautiful beyond all things I ever beheld.

PINCH. So, so.

[21] another of Mrs. Pinchwife's little
provincialisms.

HAR. More beautiful than a poet's first mistress of imagination.

HORN. Or another man's last mistress of flesh and blood.

MRS. PINCH. Nay, now you jeer, sir; pray don't jeer me.

PINCH. Come, come. – *(aside)* By Heavens, she'll discover herself!

HORN. I speak of your sister, sir.

PINCH. Ay, but saying she was handsome, if like him, made him blush. – *(aside)* I am upon a rack!

HORN. Methinks he is so handsome he should not be a man.

PINCH. *(aside)* O, there 'tis out! he has discovered her! I am not able to suffer any longer. – *(to his wife)* Come, come away, I say.

HORN. Nay, by your leave, sir, he shall not go yet. – *(aside to them)* Harcourt, Dorilant, let us torment this jealous rogue a little.

HAR. DOR. How?

HORN. I'll show you.

PINCH. Come, pray let him go, I cannot stay fooling any longer; I tell you his sister stays supper for us.

HORN. Does she? Come then, we'll all go sup with her and thee.

PINCH. No, now I think on't, having stayed so long for us, I warrant she's gone to bed. – *(aside)* I wish she and I were well out of their hands. – *(to his wife)* Come, I must rise early to-morrow, come.

HORN. Well, then, if she be gone to bed, I wish her and you a good night. But pray, young gentleman, present my humble service to her.

MRS. PINCH. Thank you heartily, sir.

PINCH. *(aside)* 'Sdeath, she will discover herself yet in spite of me. – *(aloud)* He is something more civil to you, for your kindness to his sister, than I am, it seems.

HORN. Tell her, dear sweet little gentleman, for all your brother there, that you have revived the love I had for her at first sight in the playhouse.

MRS. PINCH. But did you love her indeed, and indeed?

PINCH. *(aside)* So, so. – *(aloud)* Away, I say.

HORN. Nay, stay. – Yes, indeed, and indeed, pray do you tell her so, and give her this kiss from me.　　　*(Kisses her.)*

PINCH. *(aside)* O Heavens! what do I suffer? Now 'tis too plain he knows her, and yet —

HORN. And this, and this — *(Kisses her again.)*

MRS. PINCH. What do you kiss me for? I am no woman.

PINCH. *(aside)* So, there, 'tis out. – *(aloud)* Come, I cannot, nor will stay any longer.

HORN. Nay, they shall send your lady a kiss too. Here Harcourt, Dorilant, will you not? *(They kiss her.)*

PINCH. *(aside)* How! do I suffer this? Was I not accusing another just now for this rascally patience, in permitting his wife to be kissed before his face? Ten thousand ulcers gnaw away their lips. – *(aloud)* Come, come.

HORN. Good night, dear little gentleman; madam, good night; farewell, Pinchwife. – *(apart to* HARCOURT *and* DORILANT*)* Did not I tell you I would raise his jealous gall?

(Exeunt HORNER, HARCOURT, *and* DORILANT.*)*

PINCH. So, they are gone at last; stay, let me see first if the coach be at this door. *(Exit.)*

Re-enter HORNER, HARCOURT, *and* DORILANT

HORN. What, not gone yet? Will you be sure to do as I desired you, sweet sir?

MRS. PINCH. Sweet sir, but what will you give me then?

HORN. Anything. Come away into the next walk.

(Exit, haling away MRS. PINCHWIFE.*)*

ALITH. Hold! hold! what d'ye do?

LUCY. Stay, stay, hold —

HAR. Hold, madam, hold, let him present him – he'll come presently; nay, I will never let you go till you answer my question.[22]

LUCY. For God's sake, sir, I must follow 'em.

*(*ALITHEA *and* LUCY, *struggling with* HARCOURT *and* DORILANT.*)*

DOR. *(to* LUCY*)* No, I have something to present you with too, you shan't follow them.

---

[22] his earlier question if he might visit her tomorrow earlier than Sparkish, with a canonical gentleman. Refer to Act III, note 20.

Re-enter PINCHWIFE

PINCH. Where? – how – what's become of? – gone! – whither?

LUCY. He's only gone with the gentleman, who will give him something, an't please your worship.

PINCH. Something! – give him something, with a pox! – where are they?

ALITH. In the next walk only, brother.

PINCH. Only, only! where, where?

(Exit and returns presently, then goes out again.)

HAR. What's the matter with him? why so much concerned? But, dearest madam —

ALITH. Pray let me go, sir; I have said and suffered enough already.

HAR. Then you will not look upon, nor pity, my sufferings?

ALITH. To look upon 'em, when I cannot help 'em, were cruelty, not pity; therefore, I will never see you more.

HAR. Let me then, madam, have my privilege of a banished lover, complaining or railing, and giving you but a farewell reason why, if you cannot condescend to marry me, you should not take that wretch, my rival.

ALITH. He only, not you, since my honour is engaged so far to him, can give me a reason why I should not marry him; but if he be true, and what I think him to me, I must be so to him. Your servant, sir.

HAR. Have women only constancy when 'tis a vice, and are, like Fortune, only true to fools?

DOR. *(to* LUCY, *who struggles to get from him)* Thou sha't not stir, thou robust creature; you see I can deal with you, therefore you should stay the rather, and be kind.

Re-enter PINCHWIFE

PINCH. Gone, gone, not to be found! quite gone! ten thousand plagues go with 'em! Which way went they?

ALITH. But into t'other walk, brother.

LUCY. Their business will be done presently sure, an't please your worship; it can't be long in doing, I'm sure on't.

ALITH. Are they not there?

PINCH. No, you know where they are, you infamous wretch, eternal shame of your family, which you do not dishonour enough yourself, you think, but you must help her to do it too, thou legion of bawds!

ALITH. Good brother —

PINCH. Damned, damned sister!

ALITH. Look you here, she's coming.

Re-enter MRS. PINCHWIFE *running, with her hat full of oranges and dried fruit under her arm,* HORNER *following*

MRS. PINCH. O dear bud, look you here what I have got, see!

PINCH. *(aside, rubbing his forehead)* And what I have got here too, which you can't see.

MRS. PINCH. The fine gentleman has given me better things yet.

PINCH. Has he so? – *(aside)* Out of breath and coloured! – I must hold yet.

HORN. I have only given your little brother an orange, sir.

PINCH. *(to* HORNER*)* Thank you, sir. – *(aside)* You have only squeezed my orange,[23] I suppose, and given it me again; yet I must have a city patience. – *(to his wife)* Come, come away.

MRS. PINCH. Stay, till I have put up my fine things, bud.

Enter SIR JASPAR FIDGET

SIR. JASP. O, Master Horner, come, come, the ladies stay for you; your mistress, my wife, wonders you make not more haste to her.

HORN. I have stayed this half hour for you here, and 'tis your fault I am not now with your wife.

SIR JASP. But, pray, don't let her know so much; the truth on't is, I was advancing a certain project to his majesty about – I'll tell you.

HORN. No, let's go, and hear it at your house. Good night, sweet little gentleman; one kiss more, you'll remember me now,

[23] part of the indecent language of men who frequented the theatre to fondle the orange-wenches.

I hope.   *(Kisses her.)*

DOR. What, Sir Jaspar, will you separate friends? He promised
to sup with us, and if you take him to your house, you'll be
in danger of our company too.

SIR JASP. Alas! gentlemen, my house is not fit for you; there are
none but civil women there, which are not for your turn.
He, you know, can bear with the society of civil women
now, ha! ha! ha! besides, he's one of my family – he's – he!
he! he!

DOR. What is he?

SIR JASP. Faith, my eunuch, since you'll have it; heh! he! he!
                        (Exeunt SIR JASPAR FIDGET *and* HORNER.)

DOR. I rather wish thou wert his or my cuckold. Harcourt, what
a good cuckold is lost there for want of a man to make him
one? Thee and I cannot have Horner's privilege, who can
make use of it.

HAR. Ay, to poor Horner 'tis like coming to an estate at three-
score, when a man can't be the better for't.

PINCH. Come.

MRS. PINCH. Presently, bud.

DOR. Come, let us go too. – *(to* ALITHEA*)* Madam, your servant. –
(to LUCY*)* Good night, strapper.

HAR. Madam, though you will not let me have a good day or
night, I wish you one; but dare not name the other half of
my wish.

ALITH. Good night, sir, for ever.

MRS. PINCH. I don't know where to put this here, dear bud, you
shall eat it; nay, you shall have part of the fine gentleman's
good things, or treat, as you call it, when we come home.

PINCH. Indeed, I deserve it, since I furnished the best part of it.
                        (Strikes away the orange.)

> The gallant treats presents, and gives the ball;
> But 'tis the absent cuckold pays for all.[24]   *(Exeunt.)*

---

[24] The closing couplet echoes Molière,   Le mari dans ces cadeaux
L'Ecole des Femmes, III, ii, 126-7:   Est toujours celui qui paye.

Act IV

SCENE I – PINCHWIFE's *House in the morning*

ALITHEA *dressed in new clothes, and* LUCY

LUCY. Well – madam, now have I dressed you, and set you out
with so many ornaments, and spent upon you ounces of
essence and pulvillio;[1] and all this for no other purpose but
as people adorn and perfume a corpse for a stinking second-
hand grave: such, or as bad, I think Master Sparkish's bed.

ALITH. Hold your peace.

LUCY. Nay, madam, I will ask you the reason why you would
banish poor Master Harcourt for ever from your sight; how
could you be so hard-hearted?

ALITH. 'Twas because I was not hard-hearted.

LUCY. No, no; 'twas stark love and kindness, I warrant.

ALITH. It was so; I would see him no more because I love him.

LUCY. Hey day, a very pretty reason!

ALITH. You do not understand me.

LUCY. I wish you may yourself.

ALITH. I was engaged to marry, you see, another man, whom my
justice will not suffer me to deceive or injure.

LUCY. Can there be a greater cheat or wrong done to a man than
to give him your person without your heart? I should make
a conscience of it.

ALITH. I'll retrieve it for him after I am married a while.

LUCY. The woman that marries to love better, will be as much
mistaken as the wencher that marries to live better. No,
madam, marrying to increase love is like gaming to become
rich; alas! you only lose what little stock you had before.

---

[1] a scented powder.

ALITH. I find by your rhetoric you have been bribed to betray me.

LUCY. Only by his merit, that has bribed your heart, you see, against your word and rigid honour. But what a devil is this honour? 'tis sure a disease in the head, like the megrim or falling-sickness,[2] that always hurries people away to do themselves mischief. Men lose their lives by it; women, what's dearer to 'em, their love, the life of life.

ALITH. Come, pray talk you no more of honour, nor Master Harcourt; I wish the other would come to secure my fidelity to him and his right in me.

LUCY. You will marry him then?

ALITH. Certainly, I have given him already my word, and will my hand too, to make it good, when he comes.

LUCY. Well, I wish I may never stick pin more, if he be not an arrant natural,[3] to t'other fine gentleman.

ALITH. I own he wants the wit of Harcourt, which I will dispense withal for another want he has, which is want of jealousy, which men of wit seldom want.

LUCY. Lord, madam, what should you do with a fool to your husband? You intend to be honest, don't you? then that husbandly virtue, credulity, is thrown away upon you.

ALITH. He only that could suspect my virtue should have cause to do it; 'tis Sparkish's confidence in my truth that obliges me to be so faithful to him.

LUCY. You are not sure his opinion may last.

ALITH. I am satisfied, 'tis impossible for him to be jealous after the proofs I have had of him. Jealousy in a husband – Heaven defend me from it! it begets a thousand plagues to a poor woman, the loss of her honour, her quiet, and her —

LUCY. And her pleasure.

ALITH. What d'ye mean, impertinent?

LUCY. Liberty is a great pleasure, madam.

ALITH. I say, loss of her honour, her quiet, nay, her life some-times; and what's as bad almost, the loss of this town; that

[2] epilepsy.
[3] fool.

is, she is sent into the country, which is the last ill-usage of a husband to a wife, I think.

LUCY. *(aside)* O, does the wind lie there? – *(aloud)* Then of necessity, madam, you think a man must carry his wife into the country, if he be wise. The country is as terrible, I find, to our young English ladies, as a monastery to those abroad; and on my virginity, I think they would rather marry a London jailer, than a high sheriff of a county, since neither can stir from his employment. Formerly women of wit married fools for a great estate, a fine seat, or the like; but now 'tis for a pretty seat only in Lincoln's Inn Fields, St. James's Fields, or the Pall Mall.[4]

Enter SPARKISH, *and* HARCOURT, *dressed like a parson*

SPARK. Madam, your humble servant, a happy day to you, and to us all.

HAR. Amen.

ALITH. Who have we here?

SPARK. My chaplain, faith – O madam, poor Harcourt remembers his humble service to you; and, in obedience to your last commands, refrains coming into your sight.

ALITH. Is that not he?

SPARK. No, fie, no; but to show that he ne'er intended to hinder our match, has sent his brother here to join our hands. When I get me a wife, I must get her a chaplain, according to the custom;[5] this is his brother, and my chaplain.

ALITH. His brother?

LUCY. *(aside)* And your chaplain, to preach in your pulpit then —

ALITH. His brother!

SPARK. Nay, I knew you would not believe it. – I told you, sir, she would take you for your brother Frank.

[4] Lincoln's Inn Fields, St. James's Fields, and Pall Mall were fashionable residential districts in the London of the day. The name Pall Mall derives from a French game *paille-maille* popular in that part of the city.

[5] Private chaplains were *de rigueur* in the households of socially prominent people. In the drama of the time they were generally presented as satiric butts.

ALITH. Believe it!

LUCY. *(aside)* His brother! ha! ha! he! he has a trick left still, it seems.

SPARK. Come, my dearest, pray let us go to church before the canonical hour[6] is past.

ALITH. For shame, you are abused still.

SPARK. By the world, 'tis strange now you are so incredulous.

ALITH. 'Tis strange you are so credulous.

SPARK. Dearest of my life, hear me. I tell you this is Ned Harcourt of Cambridge, by the world; you see he has a sneaking college look. 'Tis true he's something like his brother Frank; and they differ from each other no more than in their age, for they were twins.

LUCY. *(aside)* Ha! ha! he!

ALITH. Your servant, sir; I cannot be so deceived, though you are. But come, let's hear, how do you know what you affirm so confidently?

SPARK. Why, I'll tell you all. Frank Harcourt coming to me this morning to wish me joy, and present his service to you, I asked him if he could help me to a parson. Whereupon he told me, he had a brother in town who was in orders; and he went straight away, and sent him you see there to me.

ALITH. Yes, Frank goes and puts on a black coat, then tells you he is Ned; that's all you have for't.

SPARK. Pshaw! pshaw! I tell you, by the same token, the midwife put her garter about Frank's neck, to know 'em asunder, they were so like.

ALITH. Frank tells you this too?

SPARK. Ay, and Ned there too: nay, they are both in a story.

ALITH. So, so; very foolish.

SPARK. Lord, if you won't believe one, you had best try him by your chambermaid there; for chambermaids must needs know chaplains from other men, they are so used to 'em.

LUCY. Let's see: nay, I'll be sworn he has the canonical smirk,

---

[6] Marriages could be legally performed only during the canonical hours, which at the time were from eight o'clock in the morning until twelve noon. See *The Way of the World*, I.

and the filthy clammy palm of a chaplain.

ALITH. Well, most reverend doctor, pray let us make an end of this fooling.

HAR. With all my soul, divine heavenly creature, when you please.

ALITH. He speaks like a chaplain indeed.

SPARK. Why, was there not soul, divine, heavenly, in what he said?

ALITH. Once more, most impertinent blackcoat, cease your persecution, and let us have a conclusion of this ridiculous love.

HAR. *(aside)* I had forgot, I must suit my style to my coat, or I wear it in vain.

ALITH. I have no more patience left; let us make once an end of this troublesome love, I say.

HAR. So be it, seraphic lady, when your honour shall think it meet and convenient so to do.[7]

SPARK. Gad, I'm sure none but a chaplain could speak so, I think.

ALITH. Let me tell you, sir, this dull trick will not serve your turn; though you delay our marriage, you shall not hinder it.

HAR. Far be it from me, munificent patroness, to delay your marriage; I desire nothing more than to marry you presently, which I might do, if you yourself would; for my noble, good-natured, and thrice generous patron here would not hinder it.

SPARK. No, poor man, not I, faith.

HAR. And now, madam, let me tell you plainly nobody else shall marry you; by Heavens! I'll die first, for I'm sure I should die after it.[8]

LUCY. *(aside)* How his love has made him forget his function, as I have seen it in real parsons!

---

[7] Cf. Book of Common Prayer (Communion Service):
   Priest: Let us give thanks unto our Lord God.
   Answer: It is meet and right so to do.

[8] In the slang of the period, "to die" had the meaning of "to have sexual intercourse". Lucy and Alithea obviously catch the pun.

ALITH. That was spoken like a chaplain too? now you understand him, I hope.

SPARK. Poor man, he takes it heinously to be refused; I can't blame him, 'tis putting an indignity upon him, not to be suffered; but you'll pardon me, madam, it shan't be; he shall marry us; come away, pray, madam.

LUCY. *(aside)* Ha! ha! he! more ado! 'tis late.

ALITH. Invincible stupidity! I tell you, he would marry me as your rival, not as your chaplain.

SPARK. Come, come, madam. *(Pulling her away.)*

LUCY. I pray, madam, do not refuse this reverend divine the honour and satisfaction of marrying you; for I dare say, he has set his heart upon't, good doctor.

ALITH. What can you hope or design by this?

HAR. *(aside)* I could answer her, a reprieve for a day only often revokes a hasty doom. At worst, if she will not take mercy on me, and let me marry her, I have at least the lover's second pleasure, hindering my rival's enjoyment, though but for a time.

SPARK. Come, madam, 'tis e'en twelve o'clock, and my mother charged me never to be married out of the canonical hours. Come, come; Lord, here's such a deal of modesty, I warrant, the first day.

LUCY. Yes, an't please your worship, married women show all their modesty the first day, because married men show all their love the first day. *(Exeunt.)*

SCENE II – *A Bedchamber in* PINCHWIFE'S *House*

PINCHWIFE *and* MRS. PINCHWIFE *discovered*

PINCH. Come, tell me, I say.

MRS. PINCH. Lord! han't I told it an hundred times over?

PINCH. *(aside)* I would try, if in the repetition of the ungrateful tale, I could find her altering it in the least circumstance; for if her story be false, she is so too. – *(aloud)* Come, how was't, baggage?

MRS. PINCH. Lord, what pleasure you take to hear it, sure!

PINCH. No, you take more in telling it, I find; but speak, how was't?

MRS. PINCH. He carried me up into the house next to the Exchange.

PINCH. So, and you two were only in the room!

MRS. PINCH. Yes, for he sent away a youth that was there, for some dried fruit, and China oranges.

PINCH. Did he so? Damn him for it – and for —

MRS. PINCH. But presently came up the gentlewoman of the house.

PINCH. O, 'twas well she did; but what did he do whilst the fruit came?

MRS. PINCH. He kissed me an hundred times, and told me he fancied he kissed my fine sister, meaning me, you know, whom he said he loved with all his soul, and bid me be sure to tell her so, and to desire her to be at her window, by eleven of the clock this morning, and he would walk under it at that time.

PINCH. (aside) And he was as good as his word, very punctual; a pox reward him for't.

MRS. PINCH. Well, and he said if you were not within, he would come up to her, meaning me, you know, bud, still.

PINCH. (aside) So – he knew her certainly; but for this confession, I am obliged to her simplicity.[9] – (aloud) But what, you stood very still when he kissed you?

MRS. PINCH. Yes, I warrant you; would you have had me discovered myself?

PINCH. But you told me he did some beastliness to you, as you called it; what was't?

MRS. PINCH. Why, he put —

PINCH. What?

MRS. PINCH. Why, he put the tip of his tongue between my lips, and so mousled me – and I said, I'd bite it.

[9] An echo of Molière, *L'Ecole des Femmes*, II, v, 19-20:
Cet aveu qu'elle fait avec sincérité,
Me marque pour le moins son ingénuité.

PINCH. An eternal canker seize it, for a dog!

MRS. PINCH. Nay, you need not be so angry with him neither, for to say truth, he has the sweetest breath I ever knew.

PINCH. The devil! you were satisfied with it then, and would do it again?

MRS. PINCH. Not unless he should force me.

PINCH. Force you, changeling! I tell you, no woman can be forced.

MRS. PINCH. Yes, but she may sure, by such a one as he, for he's a proper, goodly, strong man; 'tis hard, let me tell you, to resist him.

PINCH. *(aside)* So, 'tis plain she loves him, yet she has not love enough to make her conceal it from me; but the sight of him will increase her aversion for me and love for him; and that love instruct her how to deceive me and satisfy him, all idiot as she is. Love! 'twas he gave women first their craft, their art of deluding. Out of Nature's hands they came plain, open, silly, and fit for slaves, as she and Heaven intended 'em; but damned Love – well – I must strangle that little monster whilst I can deal with him. – *(aloud)* Go fetch pen, ink, and paper out of the next room.

MRS. PINCH. Yes, bud. *(Exit.)*

PINCH. Why should women have more invention in love than men? It can only be, because they have more desires, more soliciting passions, more lust, and more of the devil.

Re-enter MRS. PINCHWIFE

Come, minx, sit down and write.

MRS. PINCH. Ay, dear bud, but I can't do't very well.

PINCH. I wish you could not at all.

MRS. PINCH. But what should I write for?

PINCH. I'll have you write a letter to your lover.

MRS. PINCH. O Lord, to the fine gentleman a letter!

PINCH. Yes, to the fine gentleman.

MRS. PINCH. Lord, you do but jeer: sure you jest.

PINCH. I am not so merry: come, write as I bid you.

MRS. PINCH. What, do you think I am a fool?

PINCH. *(aside)* She's afraid I would not dictate any love to him,
therefore she's unwilling. – *(aloud)* But you had best begin.

MRS. PINCH. Indeed, and indeed, but I won't, so I won't.

PINCH. Why?

MRS. PINCH. Because he's in town; you may send for him if you
will.

PINCH. Very well, you would have him brought to you; is it come
to this? I say, take the pen and write, or you'll provoke me.

MRS. PINCH. Lord, what d'ye make a fool of me for? Don't I know
that letters are never writ but from the country to London,
and from London into the country? Now he's in town, and
I am in town too; therefore I can't write to him, you know.

PINCH. *(aside)* So, I am glad it is no worse; she is innocent
enough yet. – *(aloud)* Yes, you may, when your husband
bids you, write letters to people that are in town.

MRS. PINCH. O, may I so? then I'm satisfied.

PINCH. Come, begin: – *(dictates)* "Sir" —

MRS. PINCH. Shan't I say, "Dear Sir"? – You know one says always
something more than bare "Sir."

PINCH. Write as I bid you, or I will write whore with this penknife in your face.

MRS. PINCH. Nay, good bud – "Sir"—   *(Writes.)*

PINCH. "Though I suffered last night your nauseous, loathed
kisses and embraces"– Write!

MRS. PINCH. Nay, why should I say so? You know I told you he
had a sweet breath.

PINCH. Write!

MRS. PINCH. Let me but put out "loathed."

PINCH. Write, I say!

MRS. PINCH. Well then.   *(Writes.)*

PINCH. Let's see, what have you writ? – *(Takes the paper and
reads.)* "Though I suffered last night your kisses and embraces" – Thou impudent creature! where is "nauseous"
and "loathed"?

MRS. PINCH. I can't abide to write such filthy words.

PINCH. Once more write as I'd have you, and question it not, or

I will spoil thy writing with this. I will stab out those eyes
that cause my mischief.   *(Holds up the penknife.)*

MRS. PINCH. O Lord! I will.

PINCH. So – so – let's see now. – *(Reads.)* "Though I suffered last
night your nauseous, loathed kisses and embraces"– go on –
"yet I would not have you presume that you shall ever
repeat them"– so —   *(She writes.)*

MRS. PINCH. I have writ it.

PINCH. On, then – "I then concealed myself from your knowledge, to avoid your insolencies."—   *(She writes.)*

MRS. PINCH. So —

PINCH. "The same reason, now I am out of your hands"—
        (She writes.)

MRS. PINCH. So —

PINCH. "Makes me own to you my unfortunate, though innocent
frolic, of being in man's clothes"—   *(She writes.)*

MRS. PINCH. So —

PINCH. "That you may for evermore cease to pursue her, who
hates and detests you"—   *(She writes on.)*

MRS. PINCH. So —   *(Sighs.)*

PINCH. What, do you sigh? – "detests you – as much as she loves
her husband and her honour."

MRS. PINCH. I vow, husband, he'll never believe I should write
such a letter.

PINCH. What, he'd expect a kinder from you? Come, now your
name only.

MRS. PINCH. What, shan't I say "Your most faithful, humble servant till death"?

PINCH. No, tormenting fiend! – *(aside)* Her style, I find, would
be very soft. – *(aloud)* Come, wrap it up now, whilst I go
fetch wax and a candle; and write on the backside, "For
Mr. Horner."   *(Exit.)*

MRS. PINCH. "For Mr. Horner." – So, I am glad he has told me
his name. Dear Mr. Horner! but why should I send thee
such a letter that will vex thee, and make thee angry with
me? – Well, I will not send it. – Ay, but then my husband
will kill me – for I see plainly he won't let me love Mr.

Horner – but what care I for my husband? – I won't, so I won't, send poor Mr. Horner such a letter – But then my husband – but oh, what if I writ at bottom my husband made me write it? – Ay, but then my husband would see't – Can one have no shift? ah, a London woman would have had a hundred presently. Stay – what if I should write a letter, and wrap it up like this, and write upon't too? Ay, but then my husband would see't – I don't know what to do. – But yet yvads[10] I'll try, so I will – for I will not send this letter to poor Mr. Horner, come what will on't.

"Dear, sweet Mr. Horner" – *(Writes and repeats what she writes.)* – so – "my husband would have me send you a base, rude, unmannerly letter; but I won't" – so – "and would have me forbid you loving me; but I won't" – so – "and would have me say to you, I hate you, poor Mr. Horner; but I won't tell a lie for him" – there – "for I'm sure if you and I were in the country at cards together" – so – "I could not help treading on your toe under the table" – so – "or rubbing knees with you, and staring in your face, till you saw me" – very well – "and then looking down, and blushing for an hour together" – so – "but I must make haste before my husband come; and now he has taught me to write letters, you shall have longer ones from me, who am, dear, dear, poor, dear Mr. Horner, your most humble friend, and servant to command till death, – Margery Pinchwife."

Stay, I must give him a hint at bottom[11] – so – now wrap it up just like t'other – so – now write "For Mr. Horner" – But oh now, what shall I do with it? for here comes my husband.

Re-enter PINCHWIFE

PINCH. *(aside)* I have been detained by a sparkish coxcomb, who pretended a visit to me; but I fear 'twas to my wife – *(aloud)* What, have you done?

[10] i' faith (a provincialism).
[11] postscript. See Act IV, note 27.

MRS. PINCH. Ay, ay, bud, just now.

PINCH. Let's see't: what d'ye tremble for? what, you would not have it go?

MRS. PINCH. Here – *(aside)* No, I must not give him that: so I had been served if I had given him this.

(He opens and reads the first letter.)

PINCH. Come, where's the wax and seal?

MRS. PINCH. *(aside)* Lord, what shall I do now? Nay, then I have it – *(aloud)* Pray let me see't. Lord, you will think me so arrant a fool, I cannot seal a letter; I will do't, so I will.

(Snatches the letter from him, changes it for the other, seals it, and delivers it to him.)

PINCH. Nay, I believe you will learn that, and other things too, which I would not have you.

MRS. PINCH. So, han't I done it curiously?[12]– *(aside)* I think I have; there's my letter going to Mr. Horner, since he'll needs have me send letters to folks.

PINCH. 'Tis very well; but I warrant, you would not have it go now?

MRS. PINCH. Yes, indeed, but I would, bud, now.

PINCH. Well, you are a good girl then. Come, let me lock you up in your chamber, till I come back; and be sure you come not within three strides of the window when I am gone, for I have a spy in the street. – *(Exit MRS. PINCHWIFE, PINCHWIFE locks the door.)* At least, 'tis fit she think so. If we do not cheat women, they'll cheat us, and fraud may be justly used with secret enemies, of which a wife is the most dangerous; and he that has a handsome one to keep, and a frontier town, must provide against treachery, rather than open force. Now I have secured all within, I'll deal with the foe without, with false intelligence.

(Holds up the letter. Exit.)

[12] neatly, well.

SCENE III – HORNER'S *Lodging*

HORNER *and* QUACK

QUACK. Well, sir, how fadges[13] the new design? have you not the luck of all your brother projectors, to deceive only yourself at last?

HORN. No, good *domine* doctor, I deceive you, it seems, and others too; for the grave matrons, and old, rigid husbands think me as unfit for love as they are; but their wives, sisters, and daughters know, some of 'em, better things already.

QUACK. Already!

HORN. Already, I say. Last night I was drunk with half-a-dozen of your civil persons, as you call 'em, and people of honour, and so was made free of their society and dressing-rooms for ever hereafter; and am already come to the privileges of sleeping upon their pallets, warming smocks, tying shoes and garters, and the like, doctor, already, already, doctor.

QUACK. You have made good use of your time, sir.

HORN. I tell thee, I am now no more interruption to 'em, when they sing, or talk bawdy, than a little squab[14] French page who speaks no English.

QUACK. But do civil persons and women of honour drink, and sing bawdy songs?

HORN. O, amongst friends, amongst friends. For your bigots in honour are just like those in religion; they fear the eye of the world more than the eye of Heaven; and think there is no virtue but railing at vice, and no sin but giving scandal. They rail at a poor, little, kept player, and keep themselves some young, modest pulpit comedian[15] to be privy to their sins in their closets, not to tell 'em of them in their chapels.

QUACK. Nay, the truth on't is, priests, amongst the women now, have quite got the better of us lay-confessors, physicians.

HORN. And they are rather their patients; but —

Enter LADY FIDGET, *looking about her*

[13] goes, prospers.
[14] dumpy, "squat".

[15] chaplain.

Now we talk of women of honour, here comes one. Step
behind the screen there, and but observe, if I have not particular privileges with the women of reputation already,
doctor, already. *(QUACK retires.)*

LADY FID. Well, Horner, am not I a woman of honour? you see,
I'm as good as my word.

HORN. And you shall see, madam, I'll not be behind-hand with
you in honour; and I'll be as good as my word too, if you
please but to withdraw into the next room.

LADY FID. But first, my dear sir, you must promise to have a care
of my dear honour.

HORN. If we talk a word more of your honour, you'll make me
incapable to wrong it. To talk of honour in the mysteries of
love, is like talking of Heaven or the Deity, in an operation
of witchcraft, just when you are employing the devil: it
makes the charm impotent.

LADY FID. Nay, fy! let us not be smutty. But you talk of mysteries
and bewitching to me; I don't understand you.

HORN. I tell you, madam, the word money in a mistress's mouth,
at such a nick of time, is not a more disheartening sound
to a younger brother, than that of honour to an eager lover
like myself.

LADY FID. But you can't blame a lady of my reputation to be
chary.

HORN. Chary! I have been chary of it already, by the report I
have caused of myself.

LADY FID. Ay, but if you should ever let other women know that
dear secret, it would come out. Nay, you must have a great
care of your conduct; for my acquaintance are so censorious
(oh, 'tis a wicked, censorious world, Mr. Horner!), I say,
are so censorious, and detracting, that perhaps they'll talk
to the prejudice of my honour, though you should not let
them know the dear secret.

HORN. Nay, madam, rather than they shall prejudice your honour, I'll prejudice theirs; and, to serve you, I'll lie with 'em
all, make the secret their own, and then they'll keep it.
I am a Machiavel in love, madam.

LADY FID. Oh, no, sir, not that way.

HORN. Nay, the devil take me, if censorious women are to be silenced any other way.

LADY FID. A secret is better kept, I hope, by a single person than a multitude; therefore pray do not trust anybody else with it, dear, dear Mr. Horner. *(Embracing him.)*

Enter SIR JASPAR FIDGET

SIR JASP. How now!

LADY FID. *(aside)* O my husband! – prevented – and what's almost as bad, found with my arms about another man – that will appear too much – what shall I say? – *(aloud)* Sir Jaspar, come hither: I am trying if Mr. Horner were ticklish, and he's as ticklish as can be. I love to torment the confounded toad; let you and I tickle him.

SIR JASP. No, your ladyship will tickle him better without me, I suppose. But is this your buying china? I thought you had been at the china-house.

HORN. *(aside)* China-house! that's my cue, I must take it.[16]– *(aloud)* A pox! can't you keep your impertinent wives at home? Some men are troubled with the husbands, but I with the wives; but I'd have you to know, since I cannot be your journeyman by night, I will not be your drudge by day, to squire your wife about, and be your man of straw, or scarecrow only to pies[17] and jays, that would be nibbling at your forbidden fruit; I shall be shortly the hackney gentleman-usher[18] of the town.

SIR JASP. *(aside)* Heh! heh! he! poor fellow, he's in the right on't, faith. To squire women about for other folks is as ungrateful an employment, as to tell[19] money for other folks. – *(aloud)* Heh! he! he! be'n't angry, Horner.

LADY FID. No, 'tis I have more reason to be angry, who am left by you, to go abroad indecently alone; or, what is more

---

[16] Horner prepares the audience for the *double entendre* on the word "china" that follows.

[17] magpies.
[18] See Act II, note 23.
[19] count.

indecent, to pin myself upon such ill-bred people of your acquaintance as this is.

SIR JASP. Nay, prithee, what has he done?

LADY FID. Nay, he has done nothing.

SIR JASP. But what d'ye take ill, if he has done nothing?

LADY FID. Ha! ha! ha! faith, I can't but laugh however; why, d'ye think, the unmannerly toad would not come down to me to the coach! I was fain to come up to fetch him, or go without him, which I was resolved not to do; for he knows china very well, and has himself very good, but will not let me see it, lest I should beg some; but I will find it out, and have what I came for yet.

HORN. *(apart to* LADY FIDGET, *as he follows her to the door)* Lock the door, madam. – *(Exit* LADY FIDGET, *and locks the door.)* – *(aloud)* So, she has got into my chamber and locked me out. Oh the impertinency of woman-kind! Well, Sir Jaspar, plain-dealing is a jewel; if ever you suffer your wife to trouble me again here, she shall carry you home a pair of horns; by my lord major she shall; though I cannot furnish you myself, you are sure, yet I'll find a way.

SIR JASP. Ha! ha! he! – *(aside)* At my first coming in, and finding her arms about him, tickling him it seems, I was half jealous, but now I see my folly. – *(aloud)* Heh! he! he! poor Horner.

HORN. Nay, though you laugh now, 'twill be my turn ere long. Oh women, more impertinent, more cunning, and more mischievous than their monkeys, and to me almost as ugly! – Now is she throwing my things about and rifling all I have; but I'll get in to her the back way, and so rifle her for it.

SIR JASP. Ha! ha! ha! poor angry Horner.

HORN. Stay here a little, I'll ferret her out to you presently, I warrant. *(Exit at the other door.)*

> *(*SIR JASPAR *talks through the door to his wife, she answers from within.)*

SIR JASP. Wife! my Lady Fidget! wife! he is coming in to you the back way.

LADY FID. Let him come, and welcome, which way he will.

SIR JASP. He'll catch you, and use you roughly, and be too strong for you.

LADY FID. Don't you trouble yourself, let him if he can.

QUACK. *(aside)* This indeed I could not have believed from him, nor any but my own eyes.

Enter MRS. SQUEAMISH

MRS. SQUEAM. Where's this woman-hater, this toad, this ugly, greasy, dirty sloven?

SIR JASP. *(aside)* So, the women all will have him ugly; methinks he is a comely person, but his wants make his form contemptible to 'em; and 'tis e'en as my wife said yesterday, talking of him, that a proper handsome eunuch was as ridiculous a thing as a gigantic coward.

MRS. SQUEAM. Sir Jaspar, your servant: where is the odious beast?

SIR JASP. He's within in his chamber, with my wife; she's playing the wag with him.

MRS. SQUEAM. Is she so? and he's a clownish beast, he'll give her no quarter, he'll play the wag with her again, let me tell you: come, let's go help her. – What, the door's locked?

SIR JASP. Ay, my wife locked it.

MRS. SQUEAM. Did she so? let us break it open then.

SIR JASP. No, no, he'll do her no hurt.

MRS. SQUEAM. No – *(aside)* But is there no other way to get in to 'em? whither goes this? I will disturb 'em.

(Exit at another door.)

Enter OLD LADY SQUEAMISH

LADY SQUEAM. Where is this harlotry, this impudent baggage, this rambling tomrigg?[20] O Sir Jaspar, I'm glad to see you here; did you not see my vil'd[21] grandchild come in hither just now?

SIR JASP. Yes.

LADY SQUEAM. Ay, but where is she then? where is she? Lord,

[20] tomboy.
[21] probably in the sense of defiled, naughty.

Sir Jaspar, I have e'en rattled myself to pieces in pursuit of her: but can you tell what she makes here? they say below, no woman lodges here.

SIR JASP. No.

LADY SQUEAM. No! what does she here then? say, if it be not a woman's lodging, what makes she here? But are you sure no woman lodges here?

SIR JASP. No, nor no man neither, this is Mr. Horner's lodging.

LADY SQUEAM. Is it so, are you sure?

SIR JASP. Yes, yes.

LADY SQUEAM. So; then there's no hurt in't, I hope. But where is he?

SIR JASP. He's in the next room with my wife.

LADY SQUEAM. Nay, if you trust him with your wife, I may with my Biddy. They say he's a merry, harmless man now, e'en as harmless a man as ever came out of Italy with a good voice,[22] and as pretty, harmless company for a lady, as a snake without his teeth.

SIR JASP. Ay, ay, poor man.

Re-enter MRS. SQUEAMISH

MRS. SQUEAM. I can't find 'em. – Oh, are you here, grandmother? I followed, you must know, my Lady Fidget hither; 'tis the prettiest lodging, and I have been staring on the prettiest pictures —

Re-enter LADY FIDGET *with a piece of china in her hand, and* HORNER *following*

LADY FID. And I have been toiling and moiling for the prettiest piece of china, my dear.

HORN. Nay, she has been too hard for me, do what I could.

MRS. SQUEAM. Oh, lord, I'll have some china too. Good Mr. Horner, don't think to give other people china, and me none; come in with me too.

HORN. Upon my honour, I have none left now.

[22] The reference is to the Italian *castrato* tenor, popular in London musical circles of the time.

MRS. SQUEAM. Nay, nay, I have known you deny your china before now, but you shan't put me off so. Come.

HORN. This lady had the last there.

LADY FID. Yes indeed, madam, to my certain knowledge, he has no more left.

MRS. SQUEAM. O, but it may be he may have some you could not find.

LADY FID. What, d'ye think if he had had any left, I would not have had it too? for we women of quality never think we have china enough.[23]

HORN. Do not take it ill, I cannot make china for you all, but I will have a roll-waggon[24] for you too, another time.

MRS. SQUEAM. Thank you, dear toad.

LADY FID. *(aside to* HORNER*)* What do you mean by that promise?

HORN. *(aside to* LADY FIDGET*)* Alas, she has an innocent, literal understanding.

LADY SQUEAM. Poor Mr. Horner! he has enough to do to please you all, I see.

HORN. Ay, madam, you see how they use me.

LADY SQUEAM. Poor gentleman, I pity you.

HORN. I thank you, madam: I could never find pity, but from such reverend ladies as you are; the young ones will never spare a man.

MRS. SQUEAM. Come, come, beast, and go dine with us; for we shall want a man at ombre after dinner.

HORN. That's all their use of me, madam, you see.

MRS. SQUEAM. Come, sloven, I'll lead you, to be sure of you.

(Pulls him by the cravat.)

LADY SQUEAM. Alas, poor man, how she tugs him! Kiss, kiss her; that's the way to make such nice women quiet.

HORN. No, madam, that remedy is worse than the torment; they know I dare suffer anything rather than do it.

LADY SQUEAM. Prithee kiss her, and I'll give you her picture in little, that you admired so last night; prithee do.

---

[23]For Wycherley's own ironic comment on the "china scene", see the dialogue between Olivia and Eliza in his later play *The Plain Dealer*, II, i.

[24] a toy wagon (probably a china piece). An obscenity is intended.

HORN. Well, nothing but that could bribe me: I love a woman
only in effigy, and good painting as much as I hate them. –
I'll do't, for I could adore the devil well painted.

(*Kisses* MRS. SQUEAMISH.)

MRS. SQUEAM. Foh, you filthy toad! nay, now I've done jesting.

LADY SQUEAM. Ha! ha! ha! I told you so.

MRS. SQUEAM. Foh! a kiss of his —

SIR JASP. Has no more hurt in't than one of my spaniel's.

MRS. SQUEAM. Nor no more good neither.

QUACK. (*aside*) I will now believe anything he tells me.

Enter PINCHWIFE

LADY FID. O lord, here's a man! Sir Jaspar, my mask! my mask!
I would not be seen here for the world.

SIR JASP. What, not when I am with you?

LADY FID. No, no, my honour – let's be gone.

MRS. SQUEAM. Oh grandmother, let us be gone; make haste, make
haste, I know not how he may censure us.

LADY FID. Be found in the lodging of anything like a man! –
Away.

(*Exeunt* SIR JASPAR FIDGET, LADY FIDGET,
OLD LADY SQUEAMISH *and* MRS. SQUEAMISH.)

QUACK. (*aside*) What's here? another cuckold? he looks like one,
and none else sure have any business with him.

HORN. Well, what brings my dear friend hither?

PINCH. Your impertinency.

HORN. My impertinency! – why, you gentlemen that have got
handsome wives, think you have a privilege of saying anything to your friends, and are as brutish as if you were our
creditors.

PINCH. No, sir, I'll ne'er trust you any way.

HORN. But why not, dear Jack? why diffide[25] in me thou know'st
so well?

PINCH. Because I do know you so well.

HORN. Han't I been always thy friend, honest Jack, always ready

[25] distrust.

to serve thee, in love or battle, before thou wert married, and am so still?

PINCH. I believe so; you would be my second now, indeed.

HORN. Well then, dear Jack, why so unkind, so grum, so strange to me? Come, prithee kiss me, dear rogue: gad, I was always, I say, and am still as much thy servant as —

PINCH. As I am yours, sir. What, you would send a kiss to my wife, is that it?

HORN. So, there 'tis – a man can't show his friendship to a married man, but presently he talks of his wife to you. Prithee, let thy wife alone, and let thee and I be all one, as we were wont. What, thou art as shy of my kindness as a Lombard Street alderman of a courtier's civility at Locket's![26]

PINCH. But you are over-kind to me, as kind as if I were your cuckold already; yet I must confess you ought to be kind and civil to me, since I am so kind, so civil to you, as to bring you this: look you there, sir. *(Delivers him a letter.)*

HORN. What is't?

PINCH. Only a love-letter, sir.

HORN. From whom? – how! this is from your wife – *(reads)* – hum – and hum —

PINCH. Even from my wife, sir: am I not wondrous kind and civil to you now too? – *(aside)* But you'll not think her so.

HORN. *(aside)* Ha! is this a trick of his or hers?

PINCH. The gentleman's surprised I find. – What, you expected a kinder letter?

HORN. No faith, not I, how could I?

PINCH. Yes, yes, I'm sure you did. A man so well made as you are, must needs be disappointed, if the women declare not their passion at first sight or opportunity.

HORN. *(aside)* But what should this mean? Stay, the postscript.[27] *(reads aside)* "Be sure you love me, whatsoever my husband says to the contrary, and let him not see this, lest he should

[26] Lombard Street: the financial district of London. Locket's: a famous and fashionable tavern frequently mentioned in the plays of the time. The sense of the lines is that Pinch-wife is as chary of Horner's "kindness" as a financier would be of a courtier's request for a loan.

[27] Refer Act IV, note 11.

come home and pinch me, or kill my squirrel." – *(aside)* It seems he knows not what the letter contains.

PINCH. Come, ne'er wonder at it so much.

HORN. Faith, I can't help it.

PINCH. Now, I think I have deserved your infinite friendship and kindness, and have showed myself sufficiently an obliging kind friend and husband; am I not so, to bring a letter from my wife to her gallant?

HORN. Ay, the devil take me, art thou, the most obliging, kind friend and husband in the world, ha! ha!

PINCH. Well, you may be merry, sir; but in short I must tell you, sir, my honour will suffer no jesting.

HORN. What dost thou mean?

PINCH. Does the letter want a comment? Then, know, sir, though I have been so civil a husband, as to bring you a letter from my wife, to let you kiss and court her to my face, I will not be a cuckold, sir, I will not.

HORN. Thou art mad with jealousy. I never saw thy wife in my life but at the play yesterday, and I know not if it were she or no. I court her, kiss her!

PINCH. I will not be a cuckold, I say; there will be danger in making me a cuckold.

HORN. Why, wert thou not well cured of thy last clap?

PINCH. I wear a sword.

HORN. It should be taken from thee, lest thou shouldst do thyself a mischief with it; thou art mad, man.

PINCH. As mad as I am, and as merry as you are, I must have more reason from you ere we part. I say again, though you kissed and courted last night my wife in man's clothes, as she confesses in her letter —

HORN. *(aside)* Ha!

PINCH. Both she and I say, you must not design it again, for you have mistaken your woman, as you have done your man.

HORN. *(aside)* O – I understand something now – *(aloud)* Was that thy wife! Why wouldst thou not tell me 'twas she? Faith, my freedom with her was your fault, not mine.

PINCH. *(aside)* Faith, so 'twas.

HORN. Fy! I'd never do't to a woman before her husband's face, sure.

PINCH. But I had rather you should do't to my wife before my face, than behind my back; and that you shall never do.

HORN. No – you will hinder me.

PINCH. If it would not hinder you, you see by her letter she would.

HORN. Well, I must e'en acquiesce then, and be contented with what she writes.

PINCH. I'll assure you 'twas voluntarily writ; I had no hand in't, you may believe me.

HORN. I do believe thee, faith.

PINCH. And believe her too, for she's an innocent creature, has no dissembling in her: and so fare you well, sir.

HORN. Pray, however, present my humble service to her, and tell her, I will obey her letter to a tittle, and fulfil her desires, be what they will, or with what difficulty soever I do't; and you shall be no more jealous of me, I warrant her, and you.

PINCH. Well then, fare you well; and play with any man's honour but mine, kiss any man's wife but mine, and welcome.

(Exit.)

HORN. Ha! ha! ha! doctor.

QUACK. It seems, he has not heard the report of you, or does not believe it.

HORN. Ha! ha! – now, doctor, what think you?

QUACK. Pray let's see the letter – *(Reads the letter.)* – hum – "for – dear – love you—"

HORN. I wonder how she could contrive it! What say'st thou to't? 'tis an original.[28]

QUACK. So are your cuckolds too originals: for they are like no other common cuckolds, and I will henceforth believe it not impossible for you to cuckold the Grand Signior[29] amidst his guards of eunuchs, that I say.

HORN. And I say for the letter, 'tis the first love-letter that ever

---

[28] an odd or eccentric person.

[29] "the Great Turk" of Act II, note 20; the sultan of Turkey.

was without flames, darts, fates, destinies,[30] lying and dissembling in't.

Enter SPARKISH *pulling in* PINCHWIFE

SPARK. Come back, you are a pretty brother-in-law, neither go to church nor to dinner with your sister bride!

PINCH. My sister denies her marriage, and you see is gone away from you dissatisfied.

SPARK. Pshaw! upon a foolish scruple, that our parson was not in lawful orders, and did not say all the common-prayer; but 'tis her modesty only, I believe. But let women be never so modest the first day, they'll be sure to come to themselves by night, and I shall have enough of her then. In the meantime, Harry Horner, you must dine with me: I keep my wedding at my aunt's in the Piazza.[31]

HORN. Thy wedding! what stale maid has lived to despair of a husband, or what young one of a gallant?

SPARK. O, your servant, sir – this gentleman's sister then, – no stale maid.

HORN. I'm sorry for't.

PINCH. *(aside)* How comes he so concerned for her?

SPARK. You sorry for't? why, do you know any ill by her?

HORN. No, I know none but by thee; 'tis for her sake, not yours, and another man's sake that might have hoped, I thought —

SPARK. Another man! another man! what is his name?

HORN. Nay, since 'tis past, he shall be nameless. – *(aside)* Poor Harcourt! I am sorry thou hast missed her.

PINCH. *(aside)* He seems to be much troubled at the match.

SPARK. Prithee, tell me – Nay, you shan't go, brother.

PINCH. I must of necessity, but I'll come to you to dinner.

(Exit.)

SPARK. But, Harry, what, have I a rival in my wife already? But with all my heart, for he may be of use to me hereafter; for though my hunger is now my sauce, and I can fall on

[30] the standard clichés of love-letters.
[31] See note on Covent Garden, Act I, note 36.

heartily without, but the time will come when a rival will be as good sauce for a married man to a wife, as an orange to veal.

HORN. O thou damned rogue! thou hast set my teeth on edge with thy orange.

SPARK. Then let's to dinner – there I was with you again. Come.

HORN. But who dines with thee?

SPARK. My friends and relations, my brother Pinchwife, you see, of your acquaintance.

HORN. And his wife?

SPARK. No, gad, he'll ne'er let her come amongst us good fellows; your stingy country coxcomb keeps his wife from his friends, as he does his little firkin of ale, for his own drinking, and a gentleman can't get a smack on't; but his servants, when his back is turned, broach it at their pleasures, and dust it away,[32] ha! ha! ha! – Gad, I am witty, I think, considering I was married to-day, by the world; but come —

HORN. No, I will not dine with you, unless you can fetch her too.

SPARK. Pshaw! what pleasure canst thou have with women now, Harry?

HORN. My eyes are not gone; I love a good prospect yet, and will not dine with you unless she does too; go fetch her therefore, but do not tell her husband 'tis for my sake.

SPARK. Well, I'll go try what I can do; in the meantime, come away to my aunt's lodging, 'tis in the way to Pinchwife's.

HORN. The poor woman has called for aid, and stretched forth her hand, doctor; I cannot but help her over the pale out of the briars.   (*Exeunt.*)

SCENE IV — *A Room in* PINCHWIFE'S *House*

MRS. PINCHWIFE *alone, leaning on her elbow.* – *A table, pen, ink and paper*

MRS. PINCH. Well, 'tis e'en so, I have got the London disease they call love; I am sick of my husband, and for my gallant. I

[32] drink it off quickly.

have heard this distemper called a fever, but methinks 'tis
liker an ague; for when I think of my husband, I tremble,
and am in a cold sweat, and have inclinations to vomit;
but when I think of my gallant, dear Mr. Horner, my hot
fit comes, and I am all in a fever indeed; and, as in other
fevers, my own chamber is tedious to me, and I would be
fain removed to his, and then methinks I should be well.
Ah, poor Mr. Horner! Well, I cannot, will not stay here;
therefore I'll make an end of my letter to him, which shall
be a finer letter than my last, because I have studied it like
anything. Oh sick! sick! *(Takes a pen and writes.)*

Enter PINCHWIFE, *who seeing her writing, steals softly behind her and looking over her shoulder, snatches the paper
from her.*

PINCH. What, writing more letters?
MRS. PINCH. O Lord, bud, why d'ye fright me so?
(She offers to run out; he stops her, and reads.)
PINCH. How's this? nay, you shall not stir, madam: – "Dear,
dear, dear Mr. Horner" – very well – I have taught you to
write letters to good purpose – but let's see't. "First, I am
to beg your pardon for my boldness in writing to you, which
I'd have you to know I would not have done, had not you
said first you loved me so extremely, which if you do, you
will never suffer me to lie in the arms of another man whom
I loathe, nauseate, and detest." – Now you can write these
filthy words. But what follows? – "Therefore, I hope you
will speedily find some way to free me from this unfortunate
match, which was never, I assure you, of my choice, but I'm
afraid 'tis already too far gone; however, if you love me, as
I do you, you will try what you can do; but you must help
me away before to-morrow, or else, alas! I shall be for ever
out of your reach, for I can defer no longer our — *(The letter concludes.)* – our —" what is to follow "our"? – speak,
what – our journey into the country, I suppose – Oh woman,
damned woman! and Love, damned Love, their old temp-
ter! for this is one of his miracles; in a moment he can make

those blind that could see, and those see that were blind,
those dumb that could speak, and those prattle who were
dumb before;[33] nay, what is more than all, make these
dough-baked, senseless, indocile animals, women, too hard
for us their politic lords and rulers, in a moment. But make
an end of your letter, and then I'll make an end of you
thus, and all my plagues together.   *(Draws his sword.)*

MRS. PINCH. O Lord, O Lord, you are such a passionate man,
bud!

Enter SPARKISH

SPARK. How now, what's here to do?

PINCH. This fool here now!

SPARK. What! drawn upon your wife? You should never do that,
but at night in the dark, when you can't hurt her. This is
my sister-in-law, is it not? *(pulls aside her handkerchief)* ay,
faith, e'en our country Margery; one may know her. Come,
she and you must go dine with me; dinner's ready, come.
But where's my wife? is she not come home yet? where is she?

PINCH. Making you a cuckold; 'tis that they all do, as soon as
they can.

SPARK. What, the wedding-day? no, a wife that designs to make
a cully of her husband will be sure to let him win the first
stake of love, by the world. But come, they stay dinner for
us: come, I'll lead down our Margery.

MRS.[34] PINCH. No – sir, go, we'll follow you.

SPARK. I will not wag without you.

PINCH. *(aside)* This coxcomb is a sensible torment to me amidst
the greatest in the world.

SPARK. Come, come, Madam Margery.

PINCH. No; I'll lead her my way: what, would you treat your

---

[33] Cf. Isaiah, 35, verse 5: "Then the eyes of the blind shall be opened, and the ears of the deaf shall be unstopped." The preceding verse (4) is especially apposite to the general context: "Say to them that are of a fearful heart, Be strong, fear not: behold, your God will come with vengeance, even God with a recompence; he will come and save you. [34] Some editions have, without textual authority, attributed this line to Mr. Pinchwife.

friends with mine, for want of your own wife? – *(Leads her to the other door, and locks her in and returns.) (aside)* I am contented my rage should take breath —

SPARK. I told Horner this.

PINCH. Come now.

SPARK. Lord, how shy you are of your wife! but let me tell you, brother, we men of wit have amongst us a saying, that cuckolding, like the small-pox, comes with a fear; and you may keep your wife as much as you will out of danger of infection, but if her constitution incline her to't, she'll have it sooner or later, by the world, say they.

PINCH. *(aside)* What a thing is a cuckold, that every fool can make him ridiculous! – *(aloud)* Well, sir – but let me advise you, now you are come to be concerned, because you suspect the danger, not to neglect the means to prevent it, especially when the greatest share of the malady will light upon your own head, for

> Hows'e'er the kind wife's belly comes to swell,
> The husband breeds for her, and first is ill.

(Exeunt.)

Act V

Scene I – PINCHWIFE's *House*

Enter PINCHWIFE *and* MRS. PINCHWIFE. *A table and candle.*

PINCH. Come, take the pen and make an end of the letter, just as you intended; if you are false in a tittle, I shall soon perceive it, and punish you with this as you deserve. – *(Lays his hand on his sword.)* Write what was to follow – let's see – "You must make haste, and help me away before to-morrow, or else I shall be for ever out of your reach, for I can defer no longer our" – What follows "our"?

MRS. PINCH. Must all out, then, bud? – *(*MRS. PINCHWIFE *takes the pen and writes.)* Look you there, then.

PINCH. Let's see – "For I can defer no longer our – wedding – your slighted Alithea." – What's the meaning of this? my sister's name to't? speak, unriddle.

MRS. PINCH. Yes, indeed, bud.

PINCH. But why her name to't? speak – speak, I say.

MRS. PINCH. Ay, but you'll tell her then again. If you would not tell her again —

PINCH. I will not: – I am stunned, my head turns round. – Speak.

MRS. PINCH. Won't you tell her, indeed, and indeed?

PINCH. No; speak, I say.

MRS. PINCH. She'll be angry with me; but I had rather she should be angry with me than you, bud; and, to tell you the truth, 'twas she made me write the letter, and taught me what I should write.

PINCH. Ha! *(aside)* I thought the style was somewhat better than her own. – *(aloud)* But how could she come to you to teach you, since I had locked you up alone?

MRS. PINCH. O, through the key-hole, bud.

PINCH. But why should she make you write a letter for her to him, since she can write herself?

MRS. PINCH. Why, she said because – for I was unwilling to do it —

PINCH. Because what – because?

MRS. PINCH. Because, lest Mr. Horner should be cruel, and refuse her; or be vain afterwards, and show the letter, she might disown it, the hand not being hers.

PINCH. *(aside)* How's this? Ha! – then I think I shall come to myself again. – This changeling could not invent this lie: but if she could, why should she? she might think I should soon discover it. – Stay – now I think on't too, Horner said he was sorry she had married Sparkish; and her disowning her marriage to me makes me think she has evaded it for Horner's sake: yet why should she take this course? But men in love are fools; women may well be so – *(aloud)* But hark you, madam, your sister went out in the morning, and I have not seen her within since.

MRS. PINCH. Alack-a-day, she has been crying all day above, it seems, in a corner.

PINCH. Where is she? let me speak with her.

MRS. PINCH. *(aside)* O Lord, then he'll discover all![1] – *(aloud)* Pray hold, bud; what, d'ye mean to discover me? she'll know I have told you then. Pray, bud, let me talk with her first.

PINCH. I must speak with her, to know whether Horner ever made her any promise, and whether she be married to Sparkish or no.

MRS. PINCH. Pray, dear bud, don't, till I have spoken with her, and told her that I have told you all; for she'll kill me else.

PINCH. Go then, and bid her come out to me.

MRS. PINCH. Yes, yes, bud.

PINCH. Let me see — *(Pausing.)*

MRS. PINCH. *(aside)* I'll go, but she is not within to come to him: I have just got time to know of Lucy her maid, who first

1 Some editions read "she'll" for "he'll". But Mrs. Pinchwife fears that her husband will "discover" (i.e., reveal) the ruse to Alithea.

set me on work, what lie I shall tell next; for I am e'en at my wits' end.   *(Exit.)*

PINCH. Well, I resolve it, Horner shall have her: I'd rather give him my sister than lend him my wife; and such an alliance will prevent his pretensions to my wife, sure. I'll make him of kin to her, and then he won't care for her.

Re-enter MRS. PINCHWIFE

MRS. PINCH. O Lord, bud! I told you what anger you would make me with my sister.

PINCH. Won't she come hither?

MRS. PINCH. No, no. Alack-a-day, she's ashamed to look you in the face: and she says, if you go in to her, she'll run away downstairs, and shamefully go herself to Mr. Horner, who has promised her marriage, she says; and she will have no other, so she won't.

PINCH. Did he so? – promise her marriage! – then she shall have no other. Go tell her so; and if she will come and discourse with me a little concerning the means, I will about it immediately. Go. – *(Exit* MRS. PINCHWIFE.*)* His estate is equal to Sparkish's, and his extraction as much better than his, as his parts are; but my chief reason is, I'd rather be of kin to him by the name of brother-in-law than that of cuckold.

Re-enter MRS. PINCHWIFE

Well, what says she now?

MRS. PINCH. Why, she says, she would only have you lead her to Horner's lodging; with whom she first will discourse the matter before she talk with you, which yet she cannot do; for alack, poor creature, she says she can't so much as look you in the face, therefore, she'll come to you in a mask. And you must excuse her, if she make you no answer to any question of yours, till you have brought her to Mr. Horner; and if you will not chide her, nor question her, she'll come out to you immediately.

PINCH. Let her come: I will not speak a word to her, nor require a word from her.

MRS. PINCH. Oh, I forgot: besides she says, she cannot look you in the face, though through a mask; therefore would desire you to put out the candle.

PINCH. I agree to all. Let her make haste. – *(Puts out the candle.)* There, 'tis out. – *(Exit* MRS. PINCHWIFE.*)* My case is something better: I'd rather fight with Horner for not lying with my sister, than for lying with my wife; and of the two, I had rather find my sister too forward than my wife. I expected no other from her free education, as she calls it, and her passion for the town. Well, wife and sister are names which make us expect love and duty, pleasure and comfort; but we find 'em plagues and torments, and are equally, though differently, troublesome to their keeper; for we have as much ado to get people to lie with our sisters as to keep 'em from lying with our wives.

Re-enter MRS. PINCHWIFE *masked, and in hoods and scarves, and a night-gown and petticoat of* ALITHEA'S, *in the dark*

What, are you come, sister? let us go then. – But first, let me lock up my wife. Mrs. Margery, where are you?

MRS. PINCH. Here, bud.

PINCH. Come hither, that I may lock you up: get you in. – *(Locks the door.)* Come, sister, where are you now?

> *(*MRS. PINCHWIFE *gives him her hand; but when he lets her go, she steals softly on to the other side of him, and is led away by him for his sister,* ALITHEA.*)*

SCENE II – HORNER'S *Lodging*

HORNER *and* QUACK

QUACK. What, all alone? not so much as one of your cuckolds here, nor one of their wives! They use to take their turns with you, as if they were to watch you.

HORN. Yes, it often happens that a cuckold is but his wife's spy, and is more upon family duty when he is with her gallant abroad, hindering his pleasure, than when he is at home with her playing the gallant. But the hardest duty a married woman imposes upon a lover is keeping her husband company always.

QUACK. And his fondness wearies you almost as soon as hers.

HORN. A pox! keeping a cuckold company, after you have had his wife, is as tiresome as the company of a country squire to a witty fellow of the town, when he has got all his money.

QUACK. And as at first a man makes a friend of the husband to get the wife, so at last you are fain to fall out with the wife to be rid of the husband.

HORN. Ay, most cuckold-makers are true courtiers; when once a poor man has cracked his credit for 'em, they can't abide to come near him.

QUACK. But at first, to draw him in, are so sweet, so kind, so dear! just as you are to Pinchwife. But what becomes of that intrigue with his wife?

HORN. A pox! he's as surly as an alderman that has been bit; and since he's so coy, his wife's kindness is in vain, for she's a silly innocent.

QUACK. Did she not send you a letter by him?

HORN. Yes; but that's a riddle I have not yet solved. Allow the poor creature to be willing, she is silly too, and he keeps her up so close —

QUACK. Yes, so close, that he makes her but the more willing, and adds but revenge to her love; which two, when met, seldom fail of satisfying each other one way or other.

HORN. What! here's the man we are talking of, I think.

Enter PINCHWIFE, *leading in his wife masked, muffled, and in her sister's gown*

Pshaw!

QUACK. Bringing his wife to you is the next thing to bringing a love-letter from her.

HORN. What means this?

PINCH. The last time, you know, sir, I brought you a love-letter;

now, you see, a mistress; I think you'll say I am a civil man to you.

HORN. Ay, the devil take me, will I say thou art the civillest man I ever met with; and I have known some. I fancy I understand thee now better than I did the letter. But, hark thee, in thy ear —

PINCH. What?

HORN. Nothing but the usual question, man: is she sound, on thy word?

PINCH. What, you take her for a wench, and me for a pimp?

HORN. Pshaw! wench and pimp, paw[2] words; I know thou art an honest fellow, and hast a great acquaintance among the ladies, and perhaps hast made love for me, rather than let me make love to thy wife.

PINCH. Come, sir, in short, I am for no fooling.

HORN. Nor I neither: therefore prithee, let's see her face presently. Make her show, man: art thou sure I don't know her?

PINCH. I am sure you do know her.

HORN. A pox! why dost thou bring her to me then?

PINCH. Because she's a relation of mine —

HORN. Is she, faith, man? then thou art still more civil and obliging, dear rogue.

PINCH. Who desired me to bring her to you.

HORN. Then she is obliging, dear rogue.

PINCH. You'll make her welcome for my sake, I hope.

HORN. I hope she is handsome enough to make herself welcome. Prithee let her unmask.

PINCH. Do you speak to her; she would never be ruled by me.

HORN. Madam — (MRS. PINCHWIFE whispers to HORNER.) She says she must speak with me in private. Withdraw, prithee.

PINCH. (aside) She's unwilling, it seems, I should know all her undecent conduct in this business. – (aloud) Well then, I'll leave you together, and hope when I am gone, you'll agree; if not, you and I shan't agree, sir.

---

[2] obscene, improper.

HORN. *(aside)* What means the fool? – *(aloud)* If she and I agree
'tis no matter what you and I do.

> *(Whispers to* MRS. PINCHWIFE, *who makes
> signs with her hand for him to be gone.)*

PINCH. In the meantime I'll fetch a parson, and find out Sparkish, and disabuse him. You would have me fetch a parson,
would you not? Well then – now I think I am rid of her,
and shall have no more trouble with her – our sisters and
daughters, like usurers' money, are safest when put out;
but our wives, like their writings, never safe but in our
closets under lock and key.   *(Exit.)*

Enter BOY

BOY. Sir Jaspar Fidget, sir, is coming up.   *(Exit.)*

HORN. *(aside to* QUACK) Here's the trouble of a cuckold now we
are talking of. A pox on him! has he not enough to do to
hinder his wife's sport, but he must other women's too? –
Step in here, madam.   *(Exit* MRS. PINCHWIFE.)

Enter SIR JASPAR FIDGET

SIR JASP. My best and dearest friend.

HORN. *(aside to* QUACK) The old style, doctor. – *(aloud)* Well, be
short, for I am busy. What would your impertinent wife
have now?

SIR JASP. Well guessed, i'faith; for I do come from her.

HORN. To invite me to supper! Tell her, I can't come: go.

SIR JASP. Nay, now you are out, faith; for my lady, and the whole
knot of the virtuous gang, as they call themselves, are resolved upon a frolic of coming to you to-night in masquerade, and are all dressed already.

HORN. I shan't be at home.

SIR JASP. *(aside)* Lord, how churlish he is to women! – *(aloud)*
Nay, prithee don't disappoint 'em; they'll think 'tis my
fault: prithee don't. I'll send in the banquet and the fiddles.
But make no noise on't; for the poor virtuous rogues would
not have it known, for the world, that they go a-masquerad-
ing; and they would come to no man's ball but yours.

HORN. Well, well – get you gone; and tell 'em, if they come,
'twill be at the peril of their honour and yours.

SIR JASP. Heh! he! he! – we'll trust you for that: farewell.

(Exit.)

HORN. Doctor, anon you too shall be my guest,
But now I'm going to a private feast.

(Exeunt severally.)

SCENE III – *The Piazza of Covent Garden*

SPARKISH *with the letter*[3] *in his hand,* PINCHWIFE *following*

SPARK. But who would have thought a woman could have been
false to me? By the world, I could not have thought it.

PINCH. You were for giving and taking liberty: she has taken it
only, sir, now you find in that letter. You are a frank person, and so is she, you see there.

SPARK. Nay, if this be her hand – for I never saw it.

PINCH. 'Tis no matter whether that be her hand or no; I am
sure this hand, at her desire, led her to Mr. Horner, with
whom I left her just now, to go fetch a parson to 'em at
their desire too, to deprive you of her for ever; for it seems
yours was but a mock marriage.

SPARK. Indeed, she would needs have it that 'twas Harcourt
himself, in a parson's habit, that married us; but I'm sure
he told me 'twas his brother Ned.

PINCH. O, there 'tis out; and you were deceived, not she: for
you are such a frank person. But I must be gone. – You'll
find her at Mr. Horner's. Go, and believe your eyes. *(Exit.)*

SPARK. Nay, I'll to her, and call her as many crocodiles, sirens,
harpies, and other heathenish names, as a poet would do a
mistress who had refused to hear his suit, nay more, his
verses on her. – But stay, is not that she following a torch
at t'other end of the Piazza? and from Horner's certainly –
'tis so.

Enter ALITHEA *following a torch, and* LUCY *behind*

[3] i.e., Margery's letter to Horner,   Act IV, scene iv.
signed with Alithea's name. Refer

You are well met, madam, though you don't think so. What, you have made a short visit to Mr. Horner, but I suppose you'll return to him presently, by that time the parson can be with him.

ALITH. Mr. Horner and the parson, sir!

SPARK. Come, madam, no more dissembling, no more jilting; for I am no more a frank person.

ALITH. How's this?

LUCY. *(aside)* So, 'twill work, I see.

SPARK. Could you find out no easy country fool to abuse? none but me, a gentleman of wit and pleasure about the town? But it was your pride to be too hard for a man of parts, unworthy false woman! false as a friend that lends a man money to lose; false as dice, who undo those that trust all they have to 'em.

LUCY. *(aside)* He has been a great bubble, by his similes,[4] as they say.

ALITH. You have been too merry, sir, at your wedding-dinner, sure.

SPARK. What, d'ye mock me too?

ALITH. Or you have been deluded.

SPARK. By you.

ALITH. Let me understand you.

SPARK. Have you the confidence (I should call it something else, since you know your guilt) to stand my just reproaches? you did not write an impudent letter to Mr. Horner? who I find now has clubbed with you in deluding me with his aversion for women, that I might not, forsooth, suspect him for my rival.

LUCY. *(aside to ALITHEA)* D'ye think the gentleman can be jealous now, madam?

ALITH. I write a letter to Mr. Horner!

SPARK. Nay, madam, do not deny it. Your brother showed it me just now; and told me likewise, he left you at Horner's lodging to fetch a parson to marry you to him: and I wish

[4] i.e., "to judge by his similes, he has been often duped, cheated."

you joy, madam, joy, joy; and to him too, much joy; and to myself more joy, for not marrying you.

ALITH. *(aside)* So, I find my brother would break off the match; and I can consent to't, since I see this gentleman can be made jealous. – *(aloud)* O Lucy, by his rude usage and jealousy, he makes me almost afraid I am married to him. Art thou sure 'twas Harcourt himself, and no parson, that married us?

SPARK. No, madam, I thank you. I suppose, that was a contrivance too of Mr. Horner's and yours, to make Harcourt play the parson; but I would as little as you have him one now, no, not for the world. For, shall I tell you another truth? I never had any passion for you till now, for now I hate you. 'Tis true, I might have married your portion, as other men of parts of the town do sometimes: and so, your servant. And to show my unconcernedness, I'll come to your wedding, and resign you with as much joy as I would a stale wench to a new cully; nay, with as much joy as I would after the first night, if I had been married to you. There's for you; and so your servant, servant. *(Exit.)*

ALITH. How was I deceived in a man!

LUCY. You'll believe then a fool may be made jealous now? for that easiness in him that suffers him to be led by a wife, will likewise permit him to be persuaded against her by others.

ALITH. But marry Mr. Horner! my brother does not intend it, sure: if I thought he did, I would take thy advice, and Mr. Harcourt for my husband. And now I wish, that if there be any overwise woman of the town, who, like me, would marry a fool for fortune, liberty, or title, first, that her husband may love play, and be a cully to all the town but her, and suffer none but Fortune to be mistress of his purse; then, if for liberty, that he may send her into the country, under the conduct of some housewifely mother-in-law; and if for title, may the world give 'em none but that of cuckold.

LUCY. And for her greater curse, madam, may he not deserve it.

ALITH. Away, impertinent! Is not this my old Lady Lanterlu's?[5]

---

[5] a reference to the fashionable card game called loo.

LUCY. Yes, madam. – *(aside)* And here I hope we shall find Mr. Harcourt. *(Exeunt.)*

SCENE IV – HORNER's *Lodging. A table, banquet, and bottles*

HORNER, LADY FIDGET, MRS. DAINTY FIDGET, *and* MRS. SQUEAMISH

HORN. *(aside)* A pox! they are come too soon – before I have sent back my new – mistress. All I have now to do is to lock her in, that they may not see her.

LADY FID. That we may be sure of our welcome, we have brought our entertainment with us, and are resolved to treat thee, dear toad.

MRS. DAIN. And that we may be merry to purpose, have left Sir Jaspar and my old Lady Squeamish quarrelling at home at backgammon.

MRS. SQUEAM. Therefore let us make use of our time, lest they should chance to interrupt us.

LADY FID. Let us sit then.

HORN. First, that you may be private, let me lock this door and that, and I'll wait upon you presently.

LADY FID. No, sir, shut 'em only, and your lips for ever; for we must trust you as much as our women.

HORN. You know all vanity's killed in me; I have no occasion for talking.

LADY FID. Now, ladies, supposing we had drank each of us our two bottles, let us speak the truth of our hearts.

MRS. DAIN. *and* MRS. SQUEAM. Agreed.

LADY FID. By this brimmer, for truth is nowhere else to be found – *(aside to* HORNER*)* not in thy heart, false man!

HORN. *(aside to* LADY FIDGET*)* You have found me a true man, I'm sure.

LADY FID. *(aside to* HORNER*)* Not every way. – *(aloud)* But let us sit and be merry. *(Sings.)*

I

Why should our damn'd tyrants oblige us to live
On the pittance of pleasure which they only give?
    We must not rejoice
    With wine and with noise:
In vain we must wake in a dull bed alone,
Whilst to our warm rival the bottle they're gone.
    Then lay aside charms,
    And take up these arms.[6]

II

'Tis wine only gives 'em their courage and wit;
Because we live sober, to men we submit.
    If for beauties you'd pass,
    Take a lick of the glass,
'Twill mend your complexions, and when they are
    gone,
The best red we have is the red of the grape:
    Then, sisters, lay't on,
    And damn a good shape.

MRS. DAIN. Dear brimmer! Well, in token of our openness and plain-dealing, let us throw our masks over our heads.

HORN. *(aside)* So, 'twill come to the glasses anon.

MRS. SQUEAM. Lovely brimmer! let me enjoy him first.

LADY FID. No, I never part with a gallant till I've tried him. Dear brimmer! that makest our husbands short-sighted.

MRS. DAIN. And our bashful gallants bold.

MRS. SQUEAM. And, for want of a gallant, the butler lovely in our eyes. – Drink, eunuch.

LADY FID. Drink, thou representative of a husband. Damn a husband!

MRS. DAIN. And, as it were a husband, an old keeper.

MRS. SQUEAM. And an old grandmother.

HORN. And an English bawd, and a French chirurgeon.

---

[6] glasses.

LADY FID. Ay, we have all reason to curse 'em.

HORN. For my sake, ladies?

LADY FID. No, for our own; for the first spoils all young gallants' industry.

MRS. DAIN. And the other's art makes 'em bold only with common women.

MRS. SQUEAM. And rather run the hazard of the vile distemper amongst them, than of a denial amongst us.

MRS. DAIN. The filthy toads choose mistresses now as they do stuffs, for having been fancied and worn by others.

MRS. SQUEAM. For being common and cheap.

LADY FID. Whilst women of quality, like the richest stuffs, lie untumbled, and unasked for.

HORN. Ay, neat, and cheap, and new, often they think best.

MRS. DAIN. No, sir, the beasts will be known by a mistress longer than by a suit.

MRS. SQUEAM. And 'tis not for cheapness neither.

LADY FID. No; for the vain fops will take up druggets and embroider 'em. But I wonder at the depraved appetites of witty men; they use to be out of the common road, and hate imitation. Pray tell me, beast, when you were a man, why you rather chose to club with a multitude in a common house for an entertainment, than to be the only guest at a good table.

HORN. Why, faith, ceremony and expectation are unsufferable to those that are sharp bent. People always eat with the best stomach at an ordinary,[7] where every man is snatching for the best bit.

LADY FID. Though he get a cut over the fingers. – But I have heard, people eat most heartily of another man's meat, that is, what they do not pay for.

HORN. When they are sure of their welcome and freedom; for ceremony in love and eating is as ridiculous as in fighting: falling on briskly is all should be done in those occasions.

LADY FID. Well, then, let me tell you, sir, there is nowhere more

7 an eating-house with a *table d'hôte* menu.

freedom than in our houses; and we take freedom from a young person as a sign of good breeding; and a person may be as free as he pleases with us, as frolic, as gamesome, as wild as he will.

HORN. Han't I heard you all declaim against wild men?

LADY FID. Yes; but for all that, we think wildness in a man as desirable a quality as in a duck or rabbit: a tame man! foh!

HORN. I know not, but your reputations frightened me as much as your faces invited me.

LADY FID. Our reputation! Lord, why should you not think that we women make use of our reputation, as you men of yours, only to deceive the world with less suspicion? Our virtue is like the state-man's religion, the Quaker's word, the game-ster's oath, and the great man's honour; but to cheat those that trust us.

MRS. SQUEAM. And that demureness, coyness, and modesty, that you see in our faces in the boxes at plays, is as much a sign of a kind woman, as a vizard-mask in the pit.

MRS. DAIN. For, I assure you, women are least masked when they have the velvet vizard[8] on.

LADY FID. You would have found us modest women in our de-nials only.

MRS. SQUEAM. Our bashfulness is only the reflection of the men's.

MRS. DAIN. We blush, when they are shamefaced.

HORN. I beg your pardon, ladies, I was deceived in you devil-ishly. But why that mighty pretence to honour?

LADY FID. We have told you; but sometimes 'twas for the same reason you men pretend business often, to avoid ill com-pany, to enjoy the better and more privately those you love.

HORN. But why would you ne'er give a friend a wink then?

LADY FID. Faith, your reputation frightened us, as much as ours did you, you were so notoriously lewd.

HORN. And you so seemingly honest.

LADY FID. Was that all that deterred you?

HORN. And so expensive – you allow freedom, you say.

LADY FID. Ay, ay.

[8] the mark of the whore.

HORN. That I was afraid of losing my little money, as well as my little time, both which my other pleasures required.

LADY FID. Money! foh! you talk like a little fellow now: do such as we expect money?

HORN. I beg your pardon, madam; I must confess, I have heard that great ladies, like great merchants, set but the higher prices upon what they have, because they are not in necessity of taking the first offer.

MRS. DAIN. Such as we make sale of our hearts?

MRS. SQUEAM. We bribed for our love? foh!

HORN. With your pardon, ladies, I know, like great men in offices, you seem to exact flattery and attendance only from your followers; but you have receivers about you, and such fees to pay, a man is afraid to pass your grants.[9] Besides, we must let you win at cards, or we lose your hearts; and if you make an assignation, 'tis at a goldsmith's, jeweller's, or china-house;[10] where for your honour you deposit to him, he must pawn his to the punctual cit, and so paying for what you take up, pays for what he takes up.

MRS. DAIN. Would you not have us assured of our gallants' love?

MRS. SQUEAM. For love is better known by liberality than by jealousy.

LADY FID. For one may be dissembled, the other not. – (aside) But my jealousy can be no longer dissembled, and they are telling ripe. – (aloud) Come, here's to our gallants in waiting, whom we must name, and I'll begin. This is my false rogue.   (Claps him on the back.)

MRS. SQUEAM. How!

HORN. (aside) So, all will out now.

MRS. SQUEAM. (aside to HORNER) Did you not tell me, 'twas for my sake only you reported yourself no man?

MRS. DAIN. (aside to HORNER) Oh, wretch! did you not swear to me, 'twas for my love and honour you passed for that thing you do?

HORN. So, so.

---

9 accept the favours you offer.
10 a house where fine china was displayed; a favourite place of assignation.

LADY FID. Come, speak, ladies: this is my false villain.

MRS. SQUEAM. And mine too.

MRS. DAIN. And mine.

HORN. Well, then, you are all three my false rogues too, and there's an end on't.

LADY FID. Well then, there's no remedy; sister sharers, let us not fall out, but have a care of our honour. Though we get no presents, no jewels of him, we are savers of our honour, the jewel of most value and use, which shines yet to the world unsuspected, though it be counterfeit.

HORN. Nay, and is e'en as good as if it were true, provided the world think so; for honour, like beauty now, only depends on the opinion of others.

LADY FID. Well, Harry Common, I hope you can be true to three. Swear; but 'tis to no purpose to require your oath, for you are as often forsworn as you swear to new women.

HORN. Come, faith, madam, let us e'en pardon one another; for all the difference I find betwixt we men and you women, we forswear ourselves at the beginning of an amour, you, as long as it lasts.

Enter SIR JASPAR FIDGET, *and* OLD LADY SQUEAMISH

SIR JASP. Oh, my Lady Fidget, was this your cunning, to come to Mr. Horner without me? but you have been nowhere else, I hope.

LADY FID. No, Sir Jaspar.

LADY SQUEAM. And you came straight hither, Biddy?

MRS. SQUEAM. Yes, indeed, lady grandmother.

SIR JASP. 'Tis well, 'tis well; I knew when once they were thoroughly acquainted with poor Horner, they'd ne'er be from him: you may let her masquerade it with my wife and Horner, and I warrant her reputation safe.

Enter BOY

BOY. O, sir, here's the gentleman come, whom you bid me not suffer to come up, without giving you notice, with a lady too, and other gentlemen.

HORN. Do you all go in there, whilst I send 'em away; and, boy, do you desire 'em to stay below till I come, which shall be immediately.

(Exeunt SIR JASPAR FIDGET, LADY FIDGET, LADY SQUEAMISH, MRS. SQUEAMISH, *and* MRS. DAINTY FIDGET.)

BOY. Yes, sir. *(Exit.)*

(Exit HORNER *at the other door, and returns with* MRS. PINCHWIFE.)

HORN. You would not take my advice, to be gone home before your husband came back, he'll now discover all; yet pray, my dearest, be persuaded to go home, and leave the rest to my management; I'll let you down the back way.

MRS. PINCH. I don't know the way home, so I don't.

HORN. My man shall wait upon you.

MRS. PINCH. No, don't you believe that I'll go at all; what, are you weary of me already?

HORN. No, my life, 'tis that I may love you long, 'tis to secure my love, and your reputation with your husband; he'll never receive you again else.

MRS. PINCH. What care I? d'ye think to frighten me with that? I don't intend to go to him again; you shall be my husband now.

HORN. I cannot be your husband, dearest, since you are married to him.

MRS. PINCH. O, would you make me believe that? Don't I see every day at London here, women leave their first husbands, and go and live with other men as their wives? pish, pshaw! you'd make me angry, but that I love you so mainly.

HORN. So, they are coming up – In again, in, I hear 'em. – *(Exit* MRS. PINCHWIFE.)* Well, a silly mistress is like a weak place, soon got, soon lost, a man has scarce time for plunder; she betrays her husband first to her gallant, and then her gallant to her husband.

Enter PINCHWIFE, ALITHEA, HARCOURT, SPARKISH, LUCY, *and a parson*

PINCH. Come, madam, 'tis not the sudden change of your dress, the confidence of your asseverations, and your false witness there, shall persuade me I did not bring you hither just now; here's my witness, who cannot deny it, since you must be confronted. – Mr. Horner, did not I bring this lady to you just now?

HORN. *(aside)* Now must I wrong one woman for another's sake, – but that's no new thing with me, for in these cases I am still on the criminal's side against the innocent.

ALITH. Pray speak, sir.

HORN. *(aside)* It must be so. I must be impudent, and try my luck; impudence uses to be too hard for truth.

PINCH. What, you are studying an evasion or excuse for her! Speak, sir.

HORN. No, faith, I am something backward only to speak in women's affairs or disputes.

PINCH. She bids you speak.

ALITH. Ah, pray, sir, do, pray satisfy him.

HORN. Then truly, you did bring that lady to me just now.

PINCH. O ho!

ALITH. How, sir?

HAR. How, Horner?

ALITH. What mean you, sir? I always took you for a man of honour.

HORN. *(aside)* Ay, so much a man of honour, that I must save my mistress, I thank you, come what will on't.

SPARK. So, if I had had her, she'd have made me believe the moon had been made of a Christmas pie.

LUCY. *(aside)* Now could I speak, if I durst, and solve the riddle, who am the author of it.

ALITH. O unfortunate woman! *(to HARCOURT)* A combination against my honour! which most concerns me now, because you share in my disgrace, sir, and it is your censure, which I must now suffer, that troubles me, not theirs.

HAR. Madam, then have no trouble, you shall now see 'tis possible for me to love too, without being jealous; I will not only believe your innocence myself, but make all the world believe it. – *(aside to HORNER)* Horner, I must now be concerned for this lady's honour.

HORN. And I must be concerned for a lady's honour too.

HAR. This lady has her honour, and I will protect it.

HORN. My lady has not her honour but has given it me to keep, and I will preserve it.

HAR. I understand you not.

HORN. I would not have you.

MRS. PINCH. *(peeping in behind)* What's the matter with 'em all?

PINCH. Come, come, Mr. Horner, no more disputing; here's the parson, I brought him not in vain.

HAR. No, sir, I'll employ him, if this lady please.

PINCH. How! what d'ye mean?

SPARK. Ay, what does he mean?

HORN. Why, I have resigned your sister to him, he has my consent.

PINCH. But he has not mine, sir; a woman's injured honour, no more than a man's, can be repaired or satisfied by any but him that first wronged it; and you shall marry her presently, or — *(Lays his hand on his sword.)*

Re-enter MRS. PINCHWIFE

MRS. PINCH. O Lord, they'll kill poor Mr. Horner! besides, he shan't marry her whilst I stand by, and look on; I'll not lose my second husband so.

PINCH. What do I see?

ALITH. My sister in my clothes!

SPARK. Ha!

MRS. PINCH. *(to* PINCHWIFE*)* Nay, pray now don't quarrel about finding work for the parson, he shall marry me to Mr. Horner; for now, I believe, you have enough of me.

HORN. *(aside)* Damned, damned loving changeling!

MRS. PINCH. Pray, sister, pardon me for telling so many lies of you.

HORN. I suppose the riddle is plain now.

LUCY. No, that must be my work. – Good sir, hear me.

> *(Kneels to* PINCHWIFE, *who stands doggedly with his hat over his eyes.)*

PINCH. I will never hear woman again, but make 'em all silent,
 thus —   *(Offers to draw upon his wife.)*

HORN. No, that must not be.

PINCH. You then shall go first, 'tis all one to me.
 (Offers to draw on HORNER, *but is stopped by* HARCOURT.*)*

HAR. Hold!

Re-enter SIR JASPAR FIDGET, LADY FIDGET, LADY SQUEAMISH,
MRS. DAINTY FIDGET, *and* MRS. SQUEAMISH

SIR JASP. What's the matter? what's the matter? pray, what's the
matter, sir? I beseech you communicate, sir.

PINCH. Why, my wife has communicated, sir, as your wife may
have done too, sir, if she knows him, sir.

SIR JASP. Pshaw, with him! ha! ha! he!

PINCH. D'ye mock me, sir? a cuckold is a kind of a wild beast;
have a care, sir.

SIR JASP. No, sure, you mock me, sir. He cuckold you! it can't
be, ha! ha! he! why, I'll tell you, sir — *(Offers to whisper.)*

PINCH. I tell you again, he has whored my wife, and yours too,
if he knows her, and all the women he comes near; 'tis not
his dissembling, his hypocrisy, can wheedle me.

SIR JASP. How! does he dissemble? is he a hypocrite? Nay, then —
how – wife – sister, is he a hypocrite?

LADY SQUEAM. A hypocrite! a dissembler! Speak, young harlotry,
speak, how?

SIR JASP. Nay, then – O my head too![11] – O thou libidinous lady!

LADY SQUEAM. O thou harloting harlotry! hast thou done't then?

SIR JASP. Speak, good Horner, art thou a dissembler, a rogue?
hast thou —

HORN. So!

LUCY. *(apart to* HORNER) I'll fetch you off, and her too, if she will
but hold her tongue.

HORN. *(apart to* LUCY) Canst thou? I'll give thee —

LUCY. *(to* PINCHWIFE) Pray have but patience to hear me, sir,

[11] He is suddenly aware that cuckold's
horns are on his forehead too.

who am the unfortunate cause of all this confusion. Your wife is innocent, I only culpable; for I put her upon telling you all these lies concerning my mistress, in order to the breaking off the match between Mr. Sparkish and her, to make way for Mr. Harcourt.

SPARK. Did you so, eternal rotten tooth? Then, it seems, my mistress was not false to me, I was only deceived by you. Brother, that should have been, now man of conduct, who is a frank person now, to bring your wife to her lover, ha?

LUCY. I assure you, sir, she came not to Mr. Horner out of love, for she loves him no more —

MRS. PINCH. Hold, I told lies for you, but you shall tell none for me, for I do love Mr. Horner with all my soul, and nobody shall say me nay; pray, don't you go to make poor Mr. Horner believe to the contrary; 'tis spitefully done of you, I'm sure.

HORN. *(aside to* MRS. PINCHWIFE*)* Peace, dear idiot.

MRS. PINCH. Nay, I will not peace.

PINCH. Not till I make you.

Enter DORILANT *and* QUACK

DOR. Horner, your servant; I am the doctor's guest, he must excuse our intrusion.

QUACK. But what's the matter, gentlemen? for Heaven's sake, what's the matter?

HORN. Oh, 'tis well you are come. 'Tis a censorious world we live in; you may have brought me a reprieve, or else I had died for a crime I never committed, and these innocent ladies had suffered with me; therefore, pray satisfy these worthy, honourable, jealous gentleman – that —   *(Whispers.)*

QUACK. O, I understand you, is that all? – Sir Jaspar, by Heavens, and upon the word of a physician, sir —

(Whispers to SIR JASPAR.*)*

SIR JASP. Nay, I do believe you truly. – Pardon me, my virtuous lady, and dear of honour.

LADY SQUEAM. What, then all's right again?

SIR JASP. Ay, ay, and now let us satisfy him too.

(They whisper with PINCHWIFE.*)*

PINCH. An eunuch! Pray, no fooling with me.

QUACK. I'll bring half the chirurgeons in town to swear it.

PINCH. They! – they'll swear a man that bled to death through his wounds, died of an apoplexy.

QUACK. Pray, hear me, sir – why, all the town has heard the report of him.

PINCH. But does all the town believe it?

QUACK. Pray, inquire a little, and first of all these.

PINCH. I'm sure when I left the town, he was the lewdest fellow in't.

QUACK. I tell you, sir, he has been in France since; pray, ask but these ladies and gentlemen, your friend Mr. Dorilant. Gentlemen and ladies, han't you all heard the late sad report of poor Mr. Horner?

ALL THE LADIES. Ay, ay, ay.

DOR. Why, thou jealous fool, dost thou doubt it? he's an arrant French capon.

MRS. PINCH. 'Tis false, sir, you shall not disparage poor Mr. Horner, for to my certain knowledge —

LUCY. O, hold!

MRS. SQUEAM. *(aside to LUCY)* Stop her mouth!

LADY FID. *(to PINCHWIFE)* Upon my honour, sir, 'tis as true —

MRS. DAIN. D'ye think we would have been seen in his company?

MRS. SQUEAM. Trust our unspotted reputations with him?

LADY FID. *(aside to HORNER)* This you get, and we too, by trusting your secret to a fool.

HORN. Peace, madam. – *(aside to QUACK)* Well, doctor, is not this a good design, that carries a man on unsuspected, and brings him off safe?

PINCH. *(aside)* Well, if this were true – but my wife —

(DORILANT whispers with MRS. PINCHWIFE.)

ALITH. Come, brother, your wife is yet innocent, you see; but have a care of too strong an imagination, lest, like an overconcerned timorous gamester, by fancying an unlucky cast, it should come. Women and fortune are truest still to those that trust 'em.

LUCY. And any wild thing grows but the more fierce and hungry for being kept up, and more dangerous to the keeper.

ALITH. There's doctrine for all husbands, Mr. Harcourt.

HAR. I edify, madam, so much, that I am impatient till I am one.

DOR. And I edify so much by example, I will never be one.

SPARK. And because I will not disparage my parts, I'll ne'er be one.

HORN. And I, alas! can't be one.

PINCH. But I must be one – against my will to a country wife, with a country murrain[12] to me!

MRS. PINCH. *(aside)* And I must be a country wife still too, I find; for I can't, like a city one, be rid of my musty husband, and do what I list.

HORN. Now, sir, I must pronounce your wife innocent, though I blush whilst I do it; and I am the only man by her now exposed to shame, which I will straight drown in wine, as you shall your suspicion; and the ladies' troubles we'll divert with a ballet. – Doctor, where are your maskers?

LUCY. Indeed, she's innocent, sir, I am her witness; and her end of coming out was but to see her sister's wedding; and what she has said to your face of her love to Mr. Horner, was but the usual innocent revenge on a husband's jealousy – was it not, madam, speak?

MRS. PINCH. *(aside to* LUCY *and* HORNER*)* Since you'll have me tell more lies – *(aloud)* Yes, indeed, bud.

PINCH. For my own sake fain I would all believe;
Cuckolds, like lovers, should themselves deceive.
But — *(Sighs.)*
His honour is least safe (too late I find)
Who trusts it with a foolish wife or friend.

A Dance of Cuckolds

HORN. Vain fops but court and dress, and keep a pother,
To pass for women's men with one another;
But he who aims by women to be prized,
First by the men, you see, must be despised.

(Exeunt.)

---

[12] "plague" (usually referring to cattle), used in oaths and curses.

Epilogue

SPOKEN BY MRS. KNEP [LADY FIDGET]

Now you the vigorous, who daily here
O'er vizard-mask in public domineer,
And what you'd do to her, if in place where;
Nay, have the confidence to cry, "Come out!"
Yet when she says, "Lead on!" you are not stout;   5
But to your well-dress'd brother straight turn round,
And cry, "Pox on her, Ned, she can't be sound!"
Then slink away, a fresh one to engage,
With so much seeming heat and loving rage,
You'd frighten list'ning actress on the stage;   10
Till she at last has seen you huffing come,
And talk of keeping in the tiring-room,
Yet cannot be provok'd to lead her home.
Next, you Falstaffs of fifty, who beset
Your buckram maidenheads, which your friends get;   15
And whilst to them you of achievements boast,
They share the booty, and laugh at your cost.
In fine, you essenc'd boys, both old and young,
Who would be thought so eager, brisk, and strong,
Yet do the ladies, not their husbands wrong;   20
Whose purses for your manhood make excuse,
And keep your Flanders mares for show, not use;
Encourag'd by our woman's man to-day,
A Horner's part may vainly think to play;
And may intrigues so bashfully disown,   25
That they may doubted be by few or none;
May kiss the cards at picquet, ombre, loo,

And so be thought[1] to kiss the lady too;
But, gallants, have a care, faith, what you do.
The world, which to no man his due will give,   30
You by experience know you can deceive,
And men may still believe you vigorous,
But then we women – there's no coz'ning us.

---

[1] Many editions read "taught", but
only "thought" (the reading of the
first quarto) carries the sense of the
epilogue.

The Way of the World

WILLIAM CONGREVE

Audire est operae pretium, procedere recte
Qui moechis non vultis. — Hor. Sat. 2, liber I.[1]

— Metuat doti deprensa. — *Ibid.*[2]

[1] Horace, *Satires*, Book I, Satire 2, lines 37-8. "Ye that do not wish well to the proceedings of adulterers, it is worth your while to hear how they are hampered on all sides." (Trans. Christopher Smart).

[2] *Ibid.*, line 131. The context of the lines in which the epigraph appears is: "Nor am I apprehensive, while I am in her company, . . . lest the maid . . . should be in apprehension for her limbs, *the detected wife for her portion* [dowry], I for myself." (Trans. Smart).

William Congreve

BIOGRAPHICAL DATA

1670 Born at Bardsey, near Leeds, Yorkshire. His father's military appointments took the family to Ireland shortly after this date.

1682 Entered Kilkenny School in Ireland. Swift was a fellow student, his senior by about two years.

1686 Entered Trinity College, Dublin. His tutor was St. George Ashe, formerly the tutor of Swift.

1691 London, where he was admitted as a student of law at the Middle Temple.

1692 Published Incognita, *a short novel, under the name of Cleophil. Wrote some occasional verse, and contributed his translation of Juvenal's eleventh satire to Dryden's* Juvenal.

1693 Published The Old Bachelor, *the first of his comedies.*
The beginning of a long and intimate relationship with the celebrated actress Mrs. Anne Bracegirdle.

1694 Published The Double-Dealer, *a comedy; produced earlier, in 1693. Wrote* The Mourning Muse of Alexis, *an elegy upon the death of Queen Mary, wife of William III.*
Obtained a minor governmental post.

1695 Published Love for Love, *a comedy. Wrote* A Pindaric Ode to the King *and his famous essay* Concerning Humour in Comedy.
Appointed Commissioner for licensing Hackney Coaches.

1697 Published The Mourning Bride, *his only tragedy, and some verse.*

1698 July — published his prose Amendments of Mr. Collier's False and Imperfect Citations *in answer to Jeremy Collier's* A Short View of the Immorality and Profaneness of the English Stage *of the previous April.*

1700 Published The Way of the World.

1701 Published The Judgment of Paris, *a masque, and* An Ode for St. Cecilia's Day.

1704 *Collaborated with Vanbrugh and Walsh in the writing of a farce entitled* Squire Trelooby, *an adaptation of Molière's* Monsieur de Pourceaugnac.

1705 The Tears of Amaryllis, *a poem.*
Given a post in the Customs as Commissioner of Wine Licences.

1706 A Pindaric Ode on the Victorious Progress of Her Majesty's Arms *together with a prose* Discourse on the Pindaric Ode.

1710 *Publication of the first collected edition of his* Works, *including* Semele, *an opera, published by Jacob Tonson.*

1714 Appointed Secretary to the Island of Jamaica.

1720 Pope's dedication of his translation of Homer's *Iliad* to Congreve.

1722 Steele's dedication of his edition of Addison's play *The Drummer* to Congreve.

1726 Visited by Voltaire.

1729 January 19, died. In his will he bequeathed a legacy of two hundred pounds to Mrs. Bracegirdle, but most of his property was left to Henrietta, Duchess of Marlborough, daughter of the great duke, with the proviso that upon her death it revert to Lady Mary Godolphin, the Duchess's (and possibly Congreve's) daughter. Buried in the south transept of Westminster Abbey.

Commendatory Verses

To MR. CONGREVE, occasioned by his Comedy called "The Way of the World."

When pleasure's falling to the low delight,
In the vain joys of the uncertain sight;
No sense of wit when rude spectators know,
But in distorted gesture, farce and show;
How could, great author, your aspiring mind   5
Dare to write only to the few refin'd?
Yet though that nice ambition you pursue,
'Tis not in Congreve's power to please but few.
Implicitly devoted to his fame,
Well-dress'd barbarians know his awful name;   10
Though senseless they're of mirth, but when they laugh,
As they feel wine, but when, till drunk, they quaff.[1]
On you from fate a lavish portion fell
In ev'ry way of writing to excel.
Your muse applause to Arabella[2] brings,   15
In notes as sweet as Arabella sings.
Whene'er you draw an undissembled woe,
With sweet distress your rural numbers[3] flow;
Pastora's[4] the complaint of ev'ry swain,
Pastora still the echo of the plain!   20
Or if your muse describe, with warming force,
The wounded Frenchman falling from his horse;
And her own William[5] glorious in the strife,

---

[1] The sense of the couplet is: "As they feel the effects of wine only when they have drunk to excess, so they are insensible to mirth except when they laugh."

[2] the Arabella of Congreve's ode *On Mrs. Arabella Hunt, Singing.*

[3] verbal cadences.

[4] In his poem *The Mourning Muse of Alexis,* Congreve laments the death in 1694 of Queen Mary, who appears in the poem in the guise of Pastora.

[5] Mary's husband, King William III, whose military victory at Namur Congreve celebrated in an ode.

Bestowing on the prostrate foe his life:
You the great act as gen'rously rehearse,   **25**
And all the English fury's in your verse.
By your selected scenes and handsome choice,
Ennobled Comedy exalts her voice,[6]
You check unjust esteem and fond desire,
And teach to scorn what else we should admire;   **30**
The just impression taught by you we bear,
The player acts the world, the world the player,
Whom still that world unjustly disesteems,
Though he alone professes what he seems.
But when your muse assumes her tragic part,   **35**
She conquers and she reigns in ev'ry heart;
To mourn with her men cheat their private woe,
And gen'rous pity's all the grief they know.
The widow, who, impatient of delay,
From the town-joys must mask it to the play,   **40**
Joins with your Mourning Bride's[7] resistless moan,
And weeps a loss she slighted, when her own;
You give us torment, and you give us ease,
And vary our afflictions as you please;
Is not a heart so kind as yours in pain,   **45**
To load your friends with cares you only feign;
Your friends in grief, compos'd yourself, to leave?
But 'tis the only way you'll e'er deceive.
Then still, great sir, your moving pow'r employ,
To lull our sorrow, and correct our joy.   **50**

                             R. STEELE[8]

[6] Cf. Horace, *Ars Poetica*, line 93: "vocem Comoedia tollit."

[7] Congreve's one tragedy, *The Mourning Bride* (1697).

[8] Sir Richard Steele (1672-1729), the editor of *The Tatler*, and collaborator with Joseph Addison in *The Spectator*.

Worth between 1689 - 1705 (handwritten)

To the Right Honourable

RALPH, EARL OF MONTAGUE,[1] &c.

MY LORD,

Whether the world will arraign me of vanity or not, that I have presumed to dedicate this comedy to your Lordship, I am yet in doubt, though it may be it is some degree of vanity even to doubt of it. One who has at any time had the honour of your Lordship's conversation, cannot be supposed to think very meanly of that which he would prefer[2] to your perusal; yet it were to incur the imputation of too much sufficiency, to pretend to such a merit as might abide the test of your Lordship's censure.

Whatever value may be wanting to this play while yet it is mine, will be sufficiently made up to it when it is once become your Lordship's; and it is my security that I cannot have overrated it more by my dedication than your Lordship will dignify it by your patronage.

That it succeeded on the stage was almost beyond my expectation; for but little of it was prepared for that general taste which seems now to be predominant in the palates of our audience.

Those characters which are meant to be ridiculed in most of our comedies, are of fools so gross that, in my humble opinion, they should rather disturb than divert the well-natured and reflecting part of an audience; they are rather objects of charity than contempt; and instead of moving our mirth, they ought very often to excite our compassion.

This reflection moved me to design some characters which should appear ridiculous, not so much through a natural folly (which is incorrigible, and therefore not proper for the stage)

---

[1] a Restoration courtier, created earl in 1689 and duke in 1705. [2] offer.

as through an affected wit; a wit which, at the same time that it
is affected, is also false. As there is some difficulty in the formation of a character of this nature, so there is some hazard which
attends the progress of its success upon the stage; for many
come to a play so overcharged with criticism that they very often
let fly their censure, when through their rashness they have mistaken their aim. This I had occasion lately to observe; for this
play had been acted two or three days, before some of these
hasty judges could find the leisure to distinguish betwixt the
character of a Witwoud[3] and a Truewit.[4]

I must beg your Lordship's pardon for this digression from
the true course of this epistle; but that it may not seem altogether
impertinent, I beg that I may plead the occasion of it, in part
of that excuse of which I stand in need, for recommending this
comedy to your protection. It is only by the countenance of your
Lordship, and the *few* so qualified, that such who write with
care and pains can hope to be distinguished; for the prostituted
name of *poet* promiscuously levels all that bear it.

Terence,[5] the most correct writer in the world, had a Scipio
and a Lælius,[6] if not to assist him, at least to support him in his
reputation; and notwithstanding his extraordinary merit, it may
be their countenance was not more than necessary.

The purity of his style, the delicacy of his turns, and the justness of his characters were all of them beauties which the greater
part of his audience were incapable of tasting; some of the
coarsest strokes of Plautus,[7] so severely censured by Horace,[8]
were more likely to affect the multitude, such who come with
expectation to laugh at the last act of a play and are better
entertained with two or three unseasonable jests than with the
artful solution of the *fable*.[9]

As Terence excelled in his performances, so had he great

---

[3] a generic term for a false pretender
to wit: the Witwoud of Congreve's
play.

[4] a character in Jonson's *Epicoene: or,
The Silent Woman* (1609).

[5] the Roman comic dramatist (190?-
159? B.C.).

[6] friends and patrons of Terence.

[7] Roman comic dramatist (254?-184
B.C.).

[8] In his *Ars Poetica* Horace censures
the reader who admires Plautus's
scurrilous passages.

[9] plot.

advantages to encourage his undertakings, for he built most on the foundations of Menander;[10] his plots were generally modelled, and his characters ready drawn to his hand. He copied Menander, and Menander had no less light in the formation of his characters from the observations of Theophrastus,[11] of whom he was a disciple; and Theophrastus, it is known, was not only the disciple, but the immediate successor of Aristotle, the first and greatest judge of poetry.[12] These were great models to design by; and the further advantage which Terence possessed, towards giving his plays the due ornaments of purity of style and justness of manners, was not less considerable from the freedom of conversation which was permitted him with Lælius and Scipio, two of the greatest and most polite men of his age. And indeed the privilege of such a conversation is the only certain means of attaining to the perfection of dialogue.

If it has happened in any part of this comedy that I have gained a turn of style or expression more correct, or at least more corrigible, than in those which I have formerly written, I must, with equal pride and gratitude, ascribe it to the honour of your Lordship's admitting me into your conversation, and that of a society where everybody else was so well worthy of you, in your retirement last summer from the town; for it was immediately after, that this comedy was written. If I have failed in my performance, it is only to be regretted, where there were so many not inferior either to a Scipio or a Lælius, that there should be one wanting equal in capacity to a Terence.

If I am not mistaken, poetry is almost the only art which has not yet laid claim to your Lordship's patronage. Architecture and painting, to the great honour of our country, have flourished under your influence and protection. In the meantime, poetry, the eldest sister of all arts, and parent of most, seems to have resigned her birthright, by having neglected to pay her duty to your Lordship, and by permitting others of a later

[10] Greek comic dramatist (342?-291 B.C.).
[11] Greek author (372?-287 B.C.) famous in seventeenth-century England

for his *Characters*.
[12] The reference is to Aristotle's *Poetics*.

extraction to prepossess that place in your esteem to which none can pretend a better title. Poetry, in its nature, is sacred to the good and great; the relation between them is reciprocal, and they are ever propitious to it. It is the privilege of poetry to address to them, and it is their prerogative alone to give it protection.

This received maxim is a general apology for all writers who consecrate their labours to great men; but I could wish at this time that this address were exempted from the common pretence of all dedications; and that, as I can distinguish your Lordship even among the most deserving, so this offering might become remarkable by some particular instance of respect, which should assure your Lordship that I am, with all due sense of your extreme worthiness and humanity,

MY LORD,

Your Lordship's most obedient and
most obliged humble Servant

WILL. CONGREVE

Restoration

Charles II — 1660 — 1685

James II — 1685 — 1688

Succeeded by Wm

Precarious State of Poets

Prologue

SPOKEN BY MR. BETTERTON [MR. FAINALL]

Of those few fools who with ill stars are curst,
Sure scribbling fools, call'd poets, fare the worst;
For they're a sort of fools which Fortune makes,
And after she has made 'em fools, forsakes.
With Nature's oafs 'tis quite a different case,   5
For Fortune favours all her idiot-race;
In her own nest[1] the cuckoo-eggs we find,
O'er which she broods to hatch the changeling-kind.[2]
No portion for her own she has to spare,
So much she dotes on her adopted care.   10
   Poets are bubbles,[3] by the town drawn in,
Suffer'd at first some trifling stakes to win;
But what unequal hazards do they run!
Each time they write, they venture all they've won;
The squire that's buttered[4] still, is sure to be undone.   15
This author, heretofore, has found your favour, *audience*
But pleads no merit from his past behaviour.
To build on that might prove a vain presumption,
Should grants to poets made admit resumption;
And in Parnassus[5] he must lose his seat,   20
If that be found a forfeited estate.
   He owns, with toil he wrought the following scenes,
But, if they're naught, ne'er spare him for his pains;
Damn him the more; have no commiseration
For dullness on mature deliberation.   25

---

[1] Fortune's.
[2] The cuckoo lays its eggs in the nests of other birds to whom they are left to be hatched. The implication is that Fortune is favourable to fools.
[3] dupes.
[4] fulsomely flattered.
[5] the Greek mountain sacred to Apollo and the Muses.

He swears he'll not resent one hiss'd-off scene,
Nor, like those peevish wits, his play maintain,
Who, to assert their sense, your taste arraign.
Some plot we think he has, and some new thought;
Some humour too, no farce; but that's a fault.   30
Satire, he thinks, you ought not to expect;
For so reform'd a town who dares correct?
To please, this time, has been his sole pretence;
He'll not instruct, lest it should give offence.
Should he by chance a knave or fool expose,   35
That hurts none here, sure here are none of those.
In short, our play shall (with your leave to show it)
Give you one instance of a passive poet,
Who to your judgments yields all resignation;
So save or damn, after your own discretion.   40

Dramatis Personae

Men

FAINALL, *in love with* MRS. MARWOOD
MIRABELL, *in love with* MRS. MILLAMANT
WITWOUD, } *followers of* MRS. MILLAMANT
PETULANT, }
SIR WILFULL WITWOUD, *half brother to* WITWOUD, *and*
   nephew to LADY WISHFORT
WAITWELL, *servant to* MIRABELL

Women

LADY WISHFORT, *enemy to* MIRABELL, *for having falsely*
   pretended love to her
MRS. MILLAMANT, *a fine lady, niece to* LADY WISHFORT,
   and loves MIRABELL
MRS. MARWOOD, *friend to* MR. FAINALL, *and likes* MIRABELL
MRS. FAINALL, *daughter to* LADY WISHFORT, *and wife to* FAINALL,
   formerly friend to MIRABELL
FOIBLE, *woman to* LADY WISHFORT
MINCING, *woman to* MRS. MILLAMANT
BETTY, *waiting-maid at a chocolate-house*
PEG, *maid to* LADY WISHFORT

Dancers, Footmen, and Attendants

SCENE: *London*

The time equal to that of the presentation

THE WAY OF THE WORLD

Act I

A Chocolate-House

MIRABELL *and* FAINALL, *rising from cards;* BETTY *waiting*

MIR. You are a fortunate man, Mr. Fainall.

FAIN. Have we done?

MIR. What you please. I'll play on to entertain you.

FAIN. No, I'll give you your revenge another time, when you are not so indifferent; you are thinking of something else now, and play too negligently. The coldness of a losing gamester lessens the pleasure of the winner. I'd no more play with a man that slighted his ill fortune than I'd make love to a woman who undervalued the loss of her reputation.

MIR. You have a taste extremely delicate and are for refining on your pleasures.

FAIN. Prithee, why so reserved? Something has put you out of humour.

MIR. Not at all. I happen to be grave to-day, and you are gay; that's all.

FAIN. Confess, Millamant and you quarrelled last night, after I left you; my fair cousin has some humours[1] that would tempt the patience of a Stoic.[2] What, some coxcomb came in, and was well received by her, while you were by.

MIR. Witwoud and Petulant, and what was worse, her aunt, your wife's mother, my evil genius; or to sum up all in her own name, my old Lady Wishfort came in.

FAIN. Oh, there it is then! She has a lasting passion for you, and with reason. What, then my wife was there?

---

[1] moods.

[2] one who subscribes to the Stoic school of philosophy, which teaches freedom from passion, and indifference to pleasure and pain.

MIR. Yes, and Mrs. Marwood, and three or four more, whom I never saw before. Seeing me, they all put on their grave faces, whispered one another; then complained aloud of the vapours,[3] and after fell into a profound silence.

FAIN. They had a mind to be rid of you.

MIR. For which reason I resolved not to stir. At last the good old lady broke through her painful taciturnity with an invective against long visits. I would not have understood her, but Millamant joining in the argument, I rose, and, with a constrained smile, told her, I thought nothing was so easy as to know when a visit began to be troublesome. She reddened, and I withdrew, without expecting[4] her reply.

FAIN. You were to blame to resent what she spoke only in compliance with her aunt.

MIR. She is more mistress of herself than to be under the necessity of such a resignation.

FAIN. What? though half her fortune depends upon her marrying with my lady's approbation?

MIR. I was then in such a humour that I should have been better pleased if she had been less discreet.

FAIN. Now I remember, I wonder not they were weary of you. Last night was one of their cabal-nights; they have 'em three times a week, and meet by turns at one another's apartments, where they come together like the coroner's inquest, to sit upon the murdered reputations of the week. You and I are excluded; and it was once proposed that all the male sex should be excepted. But somebody moved that, to avoid scandal, there might be one man of the community; upon which motion Witwoud and Petulant were enrolled members.[5]

MIR. And who may have been the foundress of this sect? My Lady Wishfort, I warrant, who publishes her detestation of mankind, and full of the vigour of fifty-five, declares for a

---

[3] boredom.
[4] awaiting.

[5] The implication is that Witwoud and Petulant are but half-men.

friend[6] and ratafia,[7] and let posterity shift for itself, she'll breed no more.

FAIN. The discovery of your sham addresses to her, to conceal your love to her niece, has provoked this separation; had you dissembled better, things might have continued in the state of nature.

MIR. I did as much as man could, with any reasonable conscience; I proceeded to the very last act of flattery with her, and was guilty of a song in her commendation. Nay, I got a friend to put her into a lampoon, and compliment her with the imputation of an affair with a young fellow, which I carried so far that I told her the malicious town took notice that she was grown fat of a sudden; and when she lay in of a dropsy,[8] persuaded her she was reported to be in labour. The devil's in't, if an old woman is to be flattered further, unless a man should endeavour downright personally to debauch her; and that my virtue forbade me. But for the discovery of this amour I am indebted to your friend, or your wife's friend, Mrs. Marwood.

FAIN. What should provoke her to be your enemy, unless she has made you advances which you have slighted? Women do not easily forgive omissions of that nature.

MIR. She was always civil to me till of late. I confess I am not one of those coxcombs who are apt to interpret a woman's good manners to her prejudice, and think that she who does not refuse 'em everything can refuse 'em nothing.

FAIN. You are a gallant man, Mirabell; and though you may have cruelty enough not to satisfy a lady's longing, you have too much generosity not to be tender of her honour. Yet you speak with an indifference which seems to be affected, and confesses you are conscious of a negligence.

MIR. You pursue the argument with a distrust that seems to be unaffected, and confesses you are conscious of a concern

---

[6] lover. When applied to a lady, the word carries the meaning of "mistress".

[7] a cordial flavoured with fruit kernels.

[8] an excessive accumulation of fluid in the body.

Foible/Waitwell, just married

for which the lady is more indebted to you than is your wife.

FAIN. Fie, fie, friend! If you grow censorious, I must leave you. I'll look upon the gamesters in the next room.

MIR. Who are they?

FAIN. Petulant and Witwoud. *(to BETTY)* Bring me some chocolate. *(Exit.)*

MIR. Betty, what says your clock?

BET. Turned of the last canonical hour,[9] sir. *(Exit.)*

MIR. How pertinently the jade answers me! *(looking on his watch)* Ha? almost one o'clock! O, y'are come!

Enter a FOOTMAN

Well, is the grand affair over? You have been something tedious.

FOOT. Sir, there's such coupling at Pancras[10] that they stand behind one another, as 'twere in a country dance. Ours was the last couple to lead up, and no hopes appearing of dispatch, besides the parson growing hoarse, we were afraid his lungs would have failed before it came to our turn; so we drove round to Duke's place,[11] and there they were riveted in a trice.

MIR. So, so, you are sure they are married.

FOOT. Married and bedded, sir; I am witness.

MIR. Have you the certificate?

FOOT. Here it is, sir.

MIR. Has the tailor brought Waitwell's clothes home, and the new liveries?

FOOT. Yes, sir.

MIR. That's well. Do you go home again, d'ye hear, and adjourn the consummation till farther order; bid Waitwell shake his ears, and Dame Partlet[12] rustle up her feathers, and meet

---

[9] It was only during the canonical hours (eight in the morning to twelve noon) that marriages could be legally performed. See *The Country Wife,* IV, i.

[10] St. Pancras Church, where marriages were performed without licence and outside the canonical hours.

[11] St. James's Church, Aldgate. See note above.

[12] Refers to Foible, who has just been married to Waitwell. "Partlet" derives from Pertelote, the hen in Chaucer's *Nun's Priest's Tale.*

M's "matter of some mirth"

M's feeling for Millmant

me at one o'clock by Rosamond's Pond,[18] that I may see her before she returns to her lady; and as you tender your ears, be secret.

(Exit FOOTMAN.*)*

Re-enter FAINALL *and* BETTY

FAIN. Joy of your success, Mirabell; you look pleased.

MIR. Aye, I have been engaged in a matter of some sort of mirth, which is not yet ripe for discovery. I am glad this is not a cabal-night. I wonder, Fainall, that you who are married, and of consequence should be discreet, will suffer your wife to be of such a party.

FAIN. Faith, I am not jealous. Besides, most who are engaged are women and relations; and for the men, they are of a kind too contemptible to give scandal.

MIR. I am of another opinion. The greater the coxcomb, always the more the scandal; for a woman who is not a fool can have but one reason for associating with a man who is one.

FAIN. Are you jealous as often as you see Witwoud entertained by Millamant?

MIR. Of her understanding I am, if not of her person.

FAIN. You do her wrong; for, to give her her due, she has wit.

MIR. She has beauty enough to make any man think so, and complaisance enough not to contradict him who shall tell her so.

FAIN. For a passionate lover, methinks you are a man somewhat too discerning in the failings of your mistress.

MIR. And for a discerning man, somewhat too passionate a lover; for I like her with all her faults, nay, like her for her faults. Her follies are so natural, or so artful, that they become her; and those affectations which in another woman would be odious, serve but to make her more agreeable. I'll tell thee, Fainall, she once used me with that insolence, that in revenge I took her to pieces, sifted[14] her, and separated her failings; I studied 'em, and got 'em by rote.[15] The catalogue

[18] a lake in St. James's Park.
[14] examined closely.
[15] in a mechanical way.

was so large that I was not without hopes one day or other to hate her heartily: to which end I so used[16] myself to think of 'em that at length, contrary to my design and expectation, they gave me every hour less and less disturbance; till in a few days it became habitual to me to remember 'em without being displeased. They are now grown as familiar to me as my own frailties; and in all probability, in a little time longer I shall like 'em as well.

FAIN. Marry her, marry her! Be half as well acquainted with her charms as you are with her defects, and my life on't, you are your own man again.

MIR. Say you so?

FAIN. Aye, aye, I have experience; I have a wife, and so forth.

Enter a MESSENGER

MES. Is one Squire Witwoud here?

BET. Yes; what's your business?

MES. I have a letter for him, from his brother Sir Wilfull, which I am charged to deliver into his own hands.

BET. He's in the next room, friend; that way.

(Exit MESSENGER.*)*

MIR. What, is the chief of that noble family in town, Sir Wilfull Witwoud?

FAIN. He is expected to-day. Do you know him?

MIR. I have seen him. He promises to be an extraordinary[17] person; I think you have the honour to be related to him.

FAIN. Yes, he is half brother to this Witwoud by a former wife, who was sister to my Lady Wishfort, my wife's mother. If you marry Millamant, you must call cousins too.

MIR. I had rather be his relation than his acquaintance.

FAIN. He comes to town in order to equip himself for travel.

MIR. For travel! Why the man that I mean is above forty.[18]

FAIN. No matter for that; 'tis for the honour of England that all Europe should know we have blockheads of all ages.

---

[16] accustomed.

[17] somewhat eccentric.

[18] It was customary for a gentleman of quality to make a Grand Tour of Continental capitals in his early twenties.

MIR. I wonder there is not an act of parliament to save the credit of the nation, and prohibit the exportation of fools.

FAIN. By no means; 'tis better as 'tis. 'Tis better to trade with a little loss than to be quite eaten up with being overstocked.

MIR. Pray, are the follies of this knight-errant and those of the squire his brother anything related?

FAIN. Not at all; Witwoud grows by the knight, like a medlar grafted on a crab.[19] One will melt in your mouth, and t'other set your teeth on edge; one is all pulp, and the other all core.

MIR. So one will be rotten before he be ripe, and the other will be rotten without ever being ripe at all.

FAIN. Sir Wilfull is an odd mixture of bashfulness and obstinacy. But when he's drunk, he's as loving as the monster in *The Tempest*,[20] and much after the same manner. To give t'other his due, he has something of good nature and does not always want wit.

MIR. Not always; but as often as his memory fails him, and his commonplace[21] of comparisons. He is a fool with a good memory and some few scraps of other folks' wit. He is one whose conversation can never be approved, yet it is now and then to be endured. He has indeed one good quality, he is not exceptious;[22] for he so passionately affects the reputation of understanding raillery that he will construe an affront into a jest and call downright rudeness and ill language, satire and fire.

FAIN. If you have a mind to finish his picture, you have an opportunity to do it at full length. Behold the original!

Enter WITWOUD

WIT. Afford me your compassion, my dears! Pity me, Fainall! Mirabell, pity me!

MIR. I do from my soul.

---

[19] The medlar is like a crab apple and is edible only when it begins to decay. The crab apple is always sour.

[20] Caliban (or Sycorax) in the adap-

tation of Shakespeare's play by Dryden and Sir William Davenant (1667).

[21] commonplace book; scrapbook.

[22] inclined to take exceptions.

FAIN. Why, what's the matter?

WIT. No letters for me, Betty?

BET. Did not a messenger bring you one but now, sir?

WIT. Aye, but no other?

BET. No, sir.

WIT. That's hard, that's very hard. A messenger, a mule, a beast of burden! He has brought me a letter from the fool my brother, as heavy as a panegyric in a funeral sermon, or a copy of commendatory verses from one poet to another. And what's worse, 'tis as sure a forerunner of the author as an epistle dedicatory.

MIR. A fool, and your brother, Witwoud!

WIT. Aye, aye, my half brother. My half brother he is, no nearer upon honour.

MIR. Then 'tis possible he may be but half a fool.

WIT. Good, good, Mirabell, *le drôle*![23] Good, good; hang him, don't let's talk of him. Fainall, how does your lady? Gad, I say anything in the world to get this fellow out of my head. I beg pardon that I should ask a man of pleasure and the town a question at once so foreign and domestic.[24] But I talk like an old maid at a marriage, I don't know what I say; but she's the best woman in the world.[25]

FAIN. 'Tis well you don't know what you say, or else your commendation would go near to make me either vain or jealous.

WIT. No man in town lives well with a wife but Fainall. Your judgment, Mirabell?

MIR. You had better step and ask his wife, if you would be credibly informed.

WIT. Mirabell.

MIR. Aye.

WIT. My dear, I ask ten thousand pardons; gad, I have forgot what I was going to say to you!

MIR. I thank you heartily, heartily.

---

[23] the wag!

[24] Since he knows (by gossip) that the Fainall marriage is not working out very well, Witwoud plays on the words "foreign and domestic".

[25] i.e., Mrs. Fainall. Witwoud realizes that he has blundered into a rather delicate situation.

WIT. No, but prithee excuse me; my memory is such a memory.

MIR. Have a care of such apologies, Witwoud; for I never knew a fool but he affected to complain, either of the spleen[26] or his memory.

FAIN. What have you done with Petulant?

WIT. He's reckoning his money – my money it was. I have no luck to-day.

FAIN. You may allow him to win of you at play, for you are sure to be too hard for him at repartee; since you monopolize the wit that is between you, the fortune must be his, of course.

MIR. I don't find that Petulant confesses the superiority of wit to be your talent, Witwoud.

WIT. Come, come, you are malicious now, and would breed debates. Petulant's my friend, and a very honest fellow, and a very pretty fellow, and has a smattering – faith and troth, a pretty deal of an odd sort of a small wit; nay, I'll do him justice. I'm his friend, I won't wrong him. And if he had any judgment in the world, he would not be altogether contemptible. Come, come, don't detract from the merits of my friend.

FAIN. You don't take your friend to be over-nicely bred?

WIT. No, no, hang him, the rogue has no manners at all, that I must own. No more breeding than a bum-baily,[27] that I grant you. 'Tis pity, faith; the fellow has fire and life.

MIR. What, courage?

WIT. Hum, faith I don't know as to that; I can't say as to that. Yes, faith, in a controversy he'll contradict anybody.

MIR. Though 'twere a man whom he feared, or a woman whom he loved.

WIT. Well, well, he does not always think before he speaks; we have all our failings. You are too hard upon him, you are, faith. Let me excuse him. I can defend most of his faults, except one or two. One he has, that's the truth on't; if he were my brother, I could not acquit him. That indeed I could wish were otherwise.

26 ill-humour; peevishness.
27 an under-bailiff.

MIR. Aye, marry, what's that, Witwoud?

WIT. Oh, pardon me! Expose the infirmities of my friend? No, my dear, excuse me there.

FAIN. What, I warrant he's unsincere, or 'tis some such trifle.

WIT. No, no, what if he be? 'Tis no matter for that; his wit will excuse that. A wit should no more be sincere than a woman constant; one argues a decay of parts,[28] as t'other of beauty.

MIR. Maybe you think him too positive?

WIT. No, no, his being positive is an incentive to argument, and keeps up conversation.

FAIN. Too illiterate?

WIT. That! that's his happiness; his want of learning gives him the more opportunities to show his natural parts.

MIR. He wants words?

WIT. Aye, but I like him for that now; for his want of words gives me the pleasure very often to explain his meaning.

FAIN. He's impudent?

WIT. No, that's not it.

MIR. Vain?

WIT. No.

MIR. What! he speaks unseasonable truths sometimes, because he has not wit enough to invent an evasion?

WIT. Truths! ha! ha! ha! No, no; since you will have it, I mean he never speaks truth at all, that's all. He will lie like a chambermaid, or a woman of quality's porter. Now that is a fault.

Enter a COACHMAN

COACH. Is Master Petulant here, mistress?

BET. Yes.

COACH. Three gentlewomen in a coach would speak with him.

FAIN. O brave Petulant! Three!

BET. I'll tell him.

28 personal endowments.

COACH. You must bring two dishes of chocolate and a glass of cinnamon-water.[29]

(Exeunt BETTY *and* COACHMAN.*)*

WIT. That should be for two fasting strumpets, and a bawd troubled with wind.[30] Now you may know what the three are.

MIR. You are very free with your friend's acquaintance.

WIT. Aye, aye, friendship without freedom is as dull as love without enjoyment, or wine without toasting. But to tell you a secret, these are trulls[31] whom he allows coach-hire, and something more, by the week, to call on him once a day at public places.

MIR. How!

WIT. You shall see how he won't go to 'em, because there's no more company here to take notice of him. Why, this is nothing to what he used to do; before he found out this way, I have known him call for himself.

FAIN. Call for himself? What dost thou mean?

WIT. Mean! Why, he would slip you out[32] of this chocolate-house, just when you had been talking to him; as soon as your back was turned, whip, he was gone! Then trip to his lodging, clap on a hood and scarf, and a mask, slap into a hackney-coach, and drive hither to the door again in a trice, where he would send in for himself; that I mean, call for himself, wait for himself. Nay, and what's more, not finding himself, sometimes leave a letter for himself.

MIR. I confess this is something extraordinary. I believe he waits for himself now, he is so long a-coming. Oh! I ask his pardon.

Enter PETULANT *and* BETTY

BET. Sir, the coach stays.

PET. Well, well; I come. 'Sbud,[33] a man had as good be a pro-

---

[29] a cordial of spirits, cinnamon, and hot water, prescribed to aid digestion.
[30] air in the stomach or bowels.
[31] women of easy virtue.

[32] an example of ethical dative. The meaning is simply "slip out".
[33] a mild oath: "God's blood".

fessed midwife as a professed whoremaster, at this rate! To
be knocked up and raised at all hours, and in all places!
Pox on 'em, I won't come! D'ye hear, tell 'em I won't come.
Let 'em snivel and cry their hearts out.

FAIN. You are very cruel, Petulant.

PET. All's one, let it pass. I have a humour to be cruel.

MIR. I hope they are not persons of condition[34] that you use at
this rate.

PET. Condition! Condition's a dried fig, if I am not in humour!
By this hand, if they were your – a – a – your what-d'ye-call-
'ems themselves, they must wait or rub off,[35] if I want appetite.

MIR. What-d'ye-call-'ems! What are they, Witwoud?

WIT. Empresses, my dear; by your what-d'ye-call-'ems he means
sultana queens.

PET. Aye, Roxolanas.[36]

MIR. Cry you mercy!

FAIN. Witwoud says they are —

PET. What does he say th'are?

WIT. I? Fine ladies, I say.

PET. Pass on, Witwoud. Harkee, by this light his relations: two
co-heiresses his cousins, and an old aunt, who loves cater-
wauling better than a conventicle.[37]

WIT. Ha! ha! ha! I had a mind to see how the rogue would come
off. Ha! ha! ha! Gad, I can't be angry with him, if he had
said they were my mother and my sisters.

MIR. No!

WIT. No; the rogue's wit and readiness of invention charm me.
Dear Petulant!

BET. They are gone, sir, in great anger.

PET. Enough, let 'em trundle. Anger helps complexion, saves
paint.

FAIN. This continence is all dissembled; this is in order to have

---

[34] social distinction.

[35] go away.

[36] Roxolana is the name of the Turk-
ish sultana in Davenant's *The Siege*

of Rhodes (1656), one of the first
"heroic plays".

[37] a meeting-house of nonconformist
sects, especially Presbyterians.

Uncles & nephews as rivals.

something to brag of the next time he makes court to Millamant, and swear he has abandoned the whole sex for her sake.

MIR. Have you not left off your impudent pretensions there yet? I shall cut your throat some time or other, Petulant, about that business.

PET. Aye, aye, let that pass. There are other throats to be cut.

MIR. Meaning mine, sir?

PET. Not I. I mean nobody; I know nothing. But there are uncles and nephews in the world, and they may be rivals. What then? All's one for that. *Rivals.*

MIR. How! harkee Petulant, come hither. Explain, or I shall call your interpreter.[38]

PET. Explain! I know nothing. Why, you have an uncle, have you not, lately come to town, and lodges by my Lady Wishfort's?

MIR. True.

PET. Why, that's enough. You and he are not friends; and if he should marry and have a child, you may be disinherited, ha?

MIR. Where hast thou stumbled upon all this truth?

PET. All's one for that; why, then say I know something.

MIR. Come, thou art an honest fellow, Petulant, and shalt make love to my mistress, thou sha't,[39] faith. What hast thou heard of my uncle?

PET. I? Nothing I. If throats are to be cut, let swords clash! Snug's the word;[40] I shrug and am silent.

MIR. Oh, raillery, raillery! Come, I know thou art in the women's secrets. What, you're a cabalist; I know you stayed at Millamant's last night, after I went. Was there any mention made of my uncle or me? Tell me. If thou hadst but good nature equal to thy wit, Petulant, Tony Witwoud, who is now thy competitor in fame, would show as dim by thee as a dead whiting's[41] eye by a pearl of orient;[42] he would no more be

---

[38] possibly a second, as in a duel.
[39] a slangy contraction for "shalt".
[40] in modern slang, "Mum's the word."
[41] A whiting is a kind of codfish.
[42] said to be particularly brilliant.

seen by thee than Mercury is by the sun.[43] Come, I'm sure
thou wo't[44] tell me.

PET. If I do, will you grant me common sense then for the
future?

MIR. Faith, I'll do what I can for thee, and I'll pray that Heaven
may grant it thee in the meantime.

PET. Well, harkee.

(MIRABELL and PETULANT talk apart.)

FAIN. Petulant and you both will find Mirabell as warm a rival
as a lover.

WIT. Pshaw! pshaw! That she laughs at Petulant is plain. And
for my part, but that it is almost a fashion to admire her,
I should – Harkee, to tell you a secret, but let it go no
further; between friends, I shall never break my heart for
her.

FAIN. How!

WIT. She's handsome; but she's a sort of an uncertain woman.

FAIN. I thought you had died for her.

WIT. Umh – no —

FAIN. She has wit.

WIT. 'Tis what she will hardly allow anybody else. Now, dem-
me,[45] I should hate that, if she were as handsome as Cleo-
patra. Mirabell is not so sure of her as he thinks for.

FAIN. Why do you think so?

WIT. We stayed pretty late there last night, and heard something of an uncle to Mirabell, who is lately come to town,
and is between him and the best part of his estate. Mirabell
and he are at some distance, as my Lady Wishfort has been
told; and you know she hates Mirabell worse than a Quaker
hates a parrot,[46] or than a fishmonger hates a hard frost.[47]
Whether this uncle has seen Mrs. Millamant or not, I cannot say; but there were items of such a treaty being in

---

[43] the planet nearest the sun, and of
very low magnitude.

[44] wilt.

[45] a contraction of "damn me".

[46] Parrots are proverbially known to
swear.

[47] Fishmongers peddled fish and consequently hated very cold weather.

embryo, and if it should come to life, poor Mirabell would be in some sort unfortunately fobbed,[48] i'faith.

FAIN. 'Tis impossible Millamant should hearken to it.

WIT. Faith, my dear, I can't tell; she's a woman, and a kind of a humourist.[49]

MIR. And this[50] is the sum of what you could collect last night?

PET. The quintessence. Maybe Witwoud knows more; he stayed longer. Besides, they never mind him; they say anything before him.

MIR. I thought you had been the greatest favourite.

PET. Aye, tête à tête, but not in public, because I make remarks.

MIR. You do?

PET. Aye, aye, pox, I'm malicious, man! Now he's soft, you know; they are not in awe of him. The fellow's well-bred; he's what you call a what-d'ye-call-'em, a fine gentleman; but he's silly withal.

MIR. I thank you. I know as much as my curiosity requires. Fainall, are you for the Mall?[51]

FAIN. Aye, I'll take a turn before dinner.

WIT. Aye, we'll walk in the Park; the ladies talked of being there.

MIR. I thought you were obliged to watch for your brother Sir Wilfull's arrival.

WIT. No, no, he comes to his aunt's, my Lady Wishfort. Pox on him! I shall be troubled with him too; what shall I do with the fool?

PET. Beg him for his estate, that I may beg you afterwards; and so have but one trouble with you both.

WIT. O rare Petulant! Thou art as quick as fire in a frosty morning; thou shalt to the Mall with us, and we'll be very severe.

PET. Enough, I'm in a humour to be severe.

MIR. Are you? Pray then walk by yourselves: let us not be accessory to your putting the ladies out of countenance with

---

[48] cheated.
[49] a moody or capricious person; hence unreliable.
[50] During the dialogue of Fainall and Witwoud, Mirabell and Petulant have been talking "apart". They now re-enter the general dialogue.
[51] a fashionable walk in St. James's Park.

Epicæne

your senseless ribaldry, which you roar out aloud as often as they pass by you; and when you have made a handsome woman blush, then you think you have been severe.

PET. What, what? Then let 'em either show their innocence by not understanding what they hear, or else show their discretion by not hearing what they would not be thought to understand.

MIR. But hast not thou then sense enough to know that thou oughtest to be most ashamed thyself, when thou hast put another out of countenance?

PET. Not I, by this hand! I always take blushing either for a sign of guilt or ill breeding.

MIR. I confess you ought to think so. You are in the right, that you may plead the error of your judgment in defence of your practice.

Where modesty's ill manners, 'tis but fit
That impudence and malice pass for wit.

(Exeunt.)

Act II

St. James's Park

Enter MRS. FAINALL *and* MRS. MARWOOD

MRS. FAIN. Aye, aye, dear Marwood, if we will be happy, we must find the means in ourselves, and among ourselves. Men are ever in extremes, either doting or averse. While they are lovers, if they have fire and sense, their jealousies are insupportable. And when they cease to love (we ought to think at least) they loathe; they look upon us with horror and distaste; they meet us like the ghosts of what we were, and as from such, fly from us.

MRS. MAR. True, 'tis an unhappy circumstance of life that love should ever die before us; and that the man so often should outlive the lover. But say what you will, 'tis better to be left than never to have been loved. To pass our youth in dull indifference, to refuse the sweets of life because they once must leave us, is as preposterous as to wish to have been born old, because we one day must be old. For my part, my youth may wear and waste, but it shall never rust in my possession.

MRS. FAIN. Then it seems you dissemble an aversion to mankind, only in compliance to my mother's humour?

MRS. MAR. Certainly. To be free,[1] I have no taste of those insipid dry discourses with which our sex of force must entertain themselves, apart from men. We may affect endearments to each other, profess eternal friendships, and seem to dote like lovers; but 'tis not in our natures long to persevere. Love will resume his empire in our breasts; and every heart,

[1] frank.

or soon or late, receive and readmit him as its lawful tyrant.

MRS. FAIN. Bless me, how have I been deceived! Why, you profess[2] a libertine!

MRS. MAR. You see my friendship by my freedom. Come, be as sincere, acknowledge that your sentiments agree with mine.

MRS. FAIN. Never!

MRS. MAR. You hate mankind?

MRS. FAIN. Heartily, inveterately.

MRS. MAR. Your husband?

MRS. FAIN. Most transcendently; aye, though I say it, meritoriously.

MRS. MAR. Give me your hand upon it.

MRS. FAIN. There.

MRS. MAR. I join with you; what I have said has been to try you.

MRS. FAIN. Is it possible? Dost thou hate those vipers, men?

MRS. MAR. I have done hating 'em; and am now come to despise 'em; the next thing I have to do, is eternally to forget 'em.

MRS. FAIN. There spoke the spirit of an Amazon, a Penthesilea![3]

MRS. MAR. And yet I am thinking sometimes to carry my aversion further.

MRS. FAIN. How?

MRS. MAR. Faith, by marrying; if I could but find one that loved me very well and would be thoroughly sensible of ill usage, I think I should do myself the violence of undergoing the ceremony.

MRS. FAIN. You would not make him a cuckold?

MRS. MAR. No, but I'd make him believe I did, and that's as bad.

MRS. FAIN. Why had not you as good do it?

MRS. MAR. Oh, if he should ever discover it, he would then know the worst, and be out of his pain; but I would have him ever to continue upon the rack of fear and jealousy.

MRS. FAIN. Ingenious mischief! Would thou wert married to Mirabell.

[2] talk like.

[3] Queen of the Amazons. After befriending Priam following the death of Hector, she was killed by Achilles, who fell in love with her as she lay dying. See Quintus Smyrnaeus, *Post-homerica*, or *The Fall of Troy*, I, lines 654 ff.

Mrs. F. waits to hear from Miss about Lady W. the previous night.

THE WAY OF THE WORLD / ACT II / 175

MRS. MAR. Would I were!

MRS. FAIN. You change colour.

MRS. MAR. Because I hate him.

MRS. FAIN. So do I; but I can hear him named. But what reason have you to hate him in particular?

MRS. MAR. I never loved him; he is, and always was, insufferably proud.

MRS. FAIN. By the reason you give for your aversion, one would think it dissembled; for you have laid a fault to his charge of which his enemies must acquit him.

MRS. MAR. Oh, then it seems you are one of his favourable enemies. Methinks you look a little pale, and now you flush again.

MRS. FAIN. Do I? I think I am a little sick o' the sudden.

MRS. MAR. What ails you?

MRS. FAIN. My husband. Don't you see him? He turned short upon me unawares, and has almost overcome me.

Enter FAINALL *and* MIRABELL

MRS. MAR. Ha! ha! ha! He comes opportunely for you.

MRS. FAIN. For you, for he has brought Mirabell with him.

FAIN. My dear!

MRS. FAIN. My soul!

FAIN. You don't look well to-day, child.

MRS. FAIN. D'ye think so?

MIR. He is the only man that does, madam.

MRS. FAIN. The only man that would tell me so at least; and the only man from whom I could hear it without mortification.

FAIN. O my dear, I am satisfied of your tenderness; I know you cannot resent anything from me, especially what is in effect of my concern.

MRS. FAIN. Mr. Mirabell, my mother interrupted you in a pleasant relation last night; I would fain hear it out.

MIR. The persons concerned in that affair have yet a tolerable reputation. I am afraid Mr. Fainall will be censorious.

MRS. FAIN. He has a humour more prevailing than his curiosity and will willingly dispense with the hearing of one scandalous story, to avoid giving an occasion to make another by being seen to walk with his wife. This way, Mr. Mirabell, and I dare promise you will oblige us both.

(Exeunt MRS. FAINALL *and* MIRABELL.*)*

FAIN. Excellent creature! Well, sure if I should live to be rid of my wife, I should be a miserable man.

MRS. MAR. Aye!

FAIN. For having only that one hope, the accomplishment of it, of consequence, must put an end to all my hopes; and what a wretch is he who must survive his hopes! Nothing remains when that day comes, but to sit down and weep like Alexander,[4] when he wanted other worlds to conquer.

MRS. MAR. Will you not follow 'em?

FAIN. Faith, I think not.

MRS. MAR. Pray let us; I have a reason.

FAIN. You are not jealous?

MRS. MAR. Of whom?

FAIN. Of Mirabell.

MRS. MAR. If I am, is it inconsistent with my love to you that I am tender of your honour?

FAIN. You would intimate, then, as if there were a fellow-feeling between my wife and him.

MRS. MAR. I think she does not hate him to that degree she would be thought.

FAIN. But he, I fear, is too insensible.

MRS. MAR. It may be you are deceived.

FAIN. It may be so. I do now begin to apprehend it.

MRS. MAR. What?

FAIN. That I have been deceived, madam, and you are false.

MRS. MAR. That I am false! What mean you?

FAIN. To let you know I see through all your little arts. Come, you both love him; and both have equally dissembled your aversion. Your mutual jealousies of one another have made you clash till you have both struck fire. I have seen the warm

[4] Alexander the Great, King of Macedon.

confession reddening on your cheeks and sparkling from
your eyes.

MRS. MAR. You do me wrong.

FAIN. I do not. 'Twas for my ease to oversee[5] and wilfully neglect
the gross advances made him by my wife; that by permitting
her to be engaged, I might continue unsuspected in my
pleasures, and take you oftener to my arms in full security.
But could you think, because the nodding husband would
not awake, that e'er the watchful lover slept?

MRS. MAR. And wherewithal can you reproach me?

FAIN. With infidelity, with loving another, with love of Mirabell.

MRS. MAR. 'Tis false! I challenge you to show an instance that
can confirm your groundless accusation. I hate him.

FAIN. And wherefore do you hate him? He is insensible, and
your resentment follows his neglect. An instance? The injuries you have done him are a proof, your interposing in
his love. What cause had you to make discoveries of his
pretended passion? to undeceive the credulous aunt, and
be the officious obstacle of his match with Millamant?

MRS. MAR. My obligations to my lady urged me; I had professed
a friendship to her, and could not see her easy nature so
abused by that dissembler.

FAIN. What, was it conscience then? Professed a friendship! Oh,
the pious friendships of the female sex!

MRS. MAR. More tender, more sincere, and more enduring, than
all the vain and empty vows of men, whether professing
love to us, or mutual faith to one another.

FAIN. Ha! ha! ha! You are my wife's friend too.

MRS. MAR. Shame and ingratitude! Do you reproach me? You,
you upbraid me? Have I been false to her, through strict
fidelity to you, and sacrificed my friendship to keep my love
inviolate? And have you the baseness to charge me with the
guilt, unmindful of the merit? To you it should be meritor-
ious, that I have been vicious; and do you reflect that guilt
upon me, which should lie buried in your bosom?

[5] overlook.

FAIN. You misinterpret my reproof. I meant but to remind you of the slight account you once could make of strictest ties, when set in competition with your love to me.

MRS. MAR. 'Tis false; you urged it with deliberate malice! 'Twas spoke in scorn, and I never will forgive it.

FAIN. Your guilt, not your resentment, begets your rage. If yet you loved, you could forgive a jealousy; but you are stung to find that you are discovered.

MRS. MAR. It shall be all discovered. You too shall be discovered; be sure you shall. I can but be exposed. If I do it myself, I shall prevent[6] your baseness.

FAIN. Why, what will you do?

MRS. MAR. Disclose it to your wife; own what has passed between us.

FAIN. Frenzy!

MRS. MAR. By all my wrongs I'll do't! I'll publish to the world the injuries you have done me, both in my fame and fortune! With both I trusted you, you bankrupt in honour, as indigent of wealth.

FAIN. Your fame I have preserved. Your fortune has been bestowed as the prodigality of your love would have it, in pleasures which we both have shared. Yet, had not you been false, I had ere this repaid it. 'Tis true, had you permitted Mirabell with Millamant to have stolen their marriage, my lady had been incensed beyond all means of reconcilement; Millamant had forfeited the moiety[7] of her fortune, which then would have descended to my wife. And wherefore did I marry, but to make lawful prize of a rich widow's wealth, and squander it on love and you?

MRS. MAR. Deceit and frivolous pretence!

FAIN. Death, am I not married! What's pretence? Am I not imprisoned, fettered? Have I not a wife? nay a wife that was a widow, a young widow, a handsome widow; and would be again a widow, but that I have a heart of proof,[8] and something of a constitution to bustle through the ways of

---

[6] anticipate.
[7] half.

[8] i.e., a heart that is proof against such wishes.

wedlock and this world! Will you yet be reconciled to truth
and me?

MRS. MAR. Impossible. Truth and you are inconsistent. I hate
you, and shall for ever.

FAIN. For loving you?

MRS. MAR. I loathe the name of love after such usage; and next
to the guilt with which you would asperse me, I scorn you
most. Farewell!

FAIN. Nay, we must not part thus.

MRS. MAR. Let me go.

FAIN. Come, I'm sorry.

MRS. MAR. I care not, let me go, break my hands, do! I'd leave
'em to get loose.

FAIN. I would not hurt you for the world. Have I no other hold
to keep you here?

MRS. MAR. Well, I have deserved it all.

FAIN. You know I love you.

MRS. MAR. Poor dissembling! Oh, that – well, it is not yet —

FAIN. What? what is it not? what is it not yet? It is not yet too
late —

MRS. MAR. No, it is not yet too late; I have that comfort.

FAIN. It is, to love another.

MRS. MAR. But not to loathe, detest, abhor mankind, myself, and
the whole treacherous world.

FAIN. Nay, this is extravagance. Come, I ask your pardon. No
tears. I was to blame; I could not love you and be easy in
my doubts. Pray, forbear. I believe you. I'm convinced I've
done you wrong; and any way, every way will make amends.
I'll hate my wife yet more, damn her! I'll part with her,
rob her of all she's worth, and we'll retire somewhere, any-
where, to another world. I'll marry thee; be pacified.
'Sdeath,[9] they come; hide your face, your tears. You have
a mask;[10] wear it a moment. This way, this way. Be persuaded. *(Exeunt.)*

[9] an oath: "God's death".

[10] Ladies' masks were fashionable, and reputable except when worn at the theatre where they were con-strued as the mark of the loose woman.

Re-enter MIRABELL *and* MRS. FAINALL

MRS. FAIN. They are here yet.

MIR. They are turning into the other walk.

MRS. FAIN. While I only hated my husband, I could bear to see him; but since I have despised him, he's too offensive.

MIR. Oh, you should hate with prudence.

MRS. FAIN. Yes, for I have loved with indiscretion.

MIR. You should have just so much disgust for your husband as may be sufficient to make you relish your lover.

MRS. FAIN. You have been the cause that I have loved without bounds, and would you set limits to that aversion of which you have been the occasion? Why did you make me marry this man?

MIR. Why do we daily commit disagreeable and dangerous actions? To save that idol, reputation. If the familiarities of our loves had produced that consequence of which you were apprehensive, where could you have fixed a father's name with credit, but on a husband?[11] I knew Fainall to be a man lavish of his morals, an interested and professing[12] friend, a false and a designing lover; yet one whose wit and outward fair behaviour have gained a reputation with the town enough to make that woman stand excused who has suffered herself to be won by his addresses. A better man ought not to have been sacrificed to the occasion; a worse had not answered to the purpose. When you are weary of him, you know your remedy.

MRS. FAIN. I ought to stand in some degree of credit with you, Mirabell.

MIR. In justice to you, I have made you privy to my whole design, and put it in your power to ruin or advance my fortune.

MRS. FAIN. Whom have you instructed to represent your pretended uncle?

[11] Mirabell refers to the period of his affair with Mrs. Fainall, after the death of her first husband, Mr. Languish, and prior to her marriage to Fainall. She feared that she was pregnant by Mirabell, and as a result Mirabell urged her marriage to Fainall.

[12] i.e., self-interested and dissembling.

The plot (M. & mrs F.)

MIR. Waitwell, my servant.

MRS. FAIN. He is an humble servant[13] to Foible, my mother's woman, and may win her to your interest.

MIR. Care is taken for that. She is won and worn by this time. They were married this morning.

MRS. FAIN. Who?

MIR. Waitwell and Foible. I would not tempt my servant to betray me by trusting him too far. If your mother, in hopes to ruin me, should consent to marry my pretended uncle, he might, like Mosca in *The Fox*,[14] stand upon terms;[15] so I made him sure beforehand.

MRS. FAIN. So if my poor mother is caught in a contract, you will discover the imposture betimes, and release her by producing a certificate of her gallant's former marriage?

MIR. Yes, upon condition that she consent to my marriage with her niece, and surrender the moiety of her fortune in her possession.[16]

MRS. FAIN. She talked last night of endeavouring at a match between Millamant and your uncle.

MIR. That was by Foible's direction, and my instruction, that she might seem to carry it more privately.[17]

MRS. FAIN. Well, I have an opinion of your success, for I believe my lady will do anything to get a husband; and when she has this, which you have provided for her, I suppose she will submit to anything to get rid of him.

MIR. Yes, I think the good lady would marry anything that resembled a man, though 'twere no more than what a butler could pinch out of a napkin.[18]

[13] suitor.

[14] Mosca, the crafty servant in Jonson's play *Volpone: or, The Fox* (1606).

[15] i.e., insist upon the proper terms of a binding contract, as Mosca does in the denouement of the Jonson play.

[16] Lady Wishfort has control of half of Mrs. Millamant's (her niece's) fortune, which Millamant will ac-quire upon her marriage, provided Lady Wishfort approves of the match; should Millamant marry without her aunt's approval, she forfeits the half of her fortune in trust.

[17] i.e., to allay any suspicions Lady Wishfort might have about the validity of Mirabell's "uncle".

[18] It was fashionable to "pinch" table napkins into curious and fancy shapes.

An old woman's attitude.

MRS. FAIN. Female frailty! We must all come to it, if we live to be old and feel the craving of a false appetite when the true is decayed.

MIR. An old woman's appetite is depraved like that of a girl. 'Tis the green sickness[19] of a second childhood; and, like the faint offer of a latter spring, serves but to usher in the fall, and withers in an affected bloom.

MRS. FAIN. Here's your mistress.

Enter MRS. MILLAMANT, WITWOUD, *and* MINCING

MIR. Here she comes, i'faith, full sail, with her fan spread and streamers[20] out, and a shoal of fools for tenders.[21] Ha, no, I cry her mercy!

MRS. FAIN. I see but one poor empty sculler;[22] and he tows her woman after him.

MIR. *(to* MRS. MILLAMANT*)* You seem to be unattended, madam. You used to have the *beau monde*[23] throng after you, and a flock of gay, fine perukes hovering round you.

WIT. Like moths about a candle. I had like to have lost my comparison for want of breath.

MRS. MIL. Oh, I have denied myself airs to-day. I have walked as fast through the crowd —

WIT. As a favourite just disgraced, and with as few followers.

MRS. MIL. Dear Mr. Witwoud, truce with your similitudes;[24] for I'm as sick of 'em —

WIT. As a physician of a good air. I cannot help it, madam, though 'tis against myself.

MRS. MIL. Yet again! Mincing, stand between me and his wit.

WIT. Do, Mrs. Mincing, like a screen before a great fire. I confess I do blaze to-day; I am too bright.

[19] an anaemia prevalent in adolescent girls, marked by a sallow yellow-green complexion.

[20] Cf. entrance of Dalila in Milton, *Samson Agonistes,* lines 710ff., especially:
Like a stately ship . . .
With all her bravery on, and tackle trim,
Sails fill'd and streamers flying.

[21] small boats that attend on larger ships.

[22] a man operating a row-boat: i.e., Witwoud.

[23] people of fashion.

[24] Witwoud is a tireless (and tiresome) maker of comparisons, or similes. Cf. "his commonplace [book] of comparisons", Act I.

MRS. FAIN. But, dear Millamant, why were you so long?

MRS. MIL. Long! Lord, have I not made violent haste? I have asked every living thing I met for you; I have inquired after you, as after a new fashion.

WIT. Madam, truce with your similitudes. No, you met her husband, and did not ask him for her.

MIR. By your leave, Witwoud, that were like inquiring after an old fashion, to ask a husband for his wife.

WIT. Hum, a hit! a hit! a palpable hit![25] I confess it.

MRS. FAIN. You were dressed before I came abroad.

MRS. MIL. Aye, that's true. Oh, but then I had – Mincing, what had I? Why was I so long?

MIN. O mem,[26] your laship[27] stayed to peruse a pecket[28] of letters.

MRS. MIL. Oh, aye, letters; I had letters. I am persecuted with letters. I hate letters. Nobody knows how to write letters, and yet one has 'em, one does not know why. They serve one to pin up one's hair.

WIT. Is that the way? Pray, madam, do you pin up your hair with all your letters? I find I must keep copies.

MRS. MIL. Only with those in verse, Mr. Witwoud. I never pin up my hair with prose. I think I tried once, Mincing.

MIN. O mem, I shall never forget it.

MRS. MIL. Aye, poor Mincing tiffed[29] and tiffed all the morning.

MIN. Till I had the cremp in my fingers, I'll vow, mem. And all to no purpose. But when your laship pins it up with poetry, it sits so pleasant the next day as anything, and is so pure and so crips.

WIT. Indeed, so crips?

MIN. You're such a critic, Mr. Witwoud.

MRS. MIL. Mirabell, did you take exceptions last night? Oh, aye, and went away. Now I think on't, I'm angry. No, now I think on't, I'm pleased; for I believe I gave you some pain.

---

[25] Cf. Osric in *Hamlet*, V, ii: "A hit, a very palpable hit."

[26] madam.

[27] ladyship.

[28] packet. (Mincing's eccentric pronunciations are part of her characterization.)

[29] arranged.

MIR. Does that please you?

MRS. MIL. Infinitely; I love to give pain.

MIR. You would affect a cruelty which is not in your nature; your true vanity is in the power of pleasing.

MRS. MIL. Oh, I ask your pardon for that. One's cruelty is one's power; and when one parts with one's cruelty, one parts with one's power; and when one has parted with that, I fancy one's old and ugly.

MIR. Aye, aye, suffer your cruelty to ruin the object of your power, to destroy your lover, and then how vain, how lost a thing you'll be! Nay, 'tis true: you are no longer handsome when you've lost your lover; your beauty dies upon the instant. For beauty is the lover's gift; 'tis he bestows your charms, your glass is all a cheat. The ugly and the old, whom the looking-glass mortifies, yet after commendation[30] can be flattered by it, and discover beauties in it; for that reflects our praises, rather than your face.

MRS. MIL. Oh, the vanity of these men! Fainall, d'ye hear him? If they did not commend us, we were not handsome! Now, you must know they could not commend one, if one was not handsome. Beauty the lover's gift! Lord, what is a lover, that it can give? Why, one makes lovers as fast as one pleases, and they live as long as one pleases, and they die as soon as one pleases; and then, if one pleases, one makes more.

WIT. Very pretty. Why, you make no more of making of lovers, madam, than of making so many card-matches.[31]

MRS. MIL. One no more owes one's beauty to a lover than one's wit to an echo. They can but reflect what we look and say; vain empty things if we are silent or unseen, and want a being.

MIR. Yet to those two vain empty things you owe two[32] the greatest pleasures of your life.

MRS. MIL. How so?

MIR. To your lover you owe the pleasure of hearing yourselves

---

[30] praise.

[31] matches made from pieces of heavy paper tipped with sulphur.

[32] Read "two of".

praised; and to an echo the pleasure of hearing yourselves talk.

WIT. But I know a lady that loves talking so incessantly, she won't give an echo fair play; she has that everlasting rotation of tongue, that an echo must wait till she dies, before it can catch her last words.

MRS. MIL. Oh, fiction! Fainall, let us leave these men.

MIR. *(aside to MRS. FAINALL)* Draw off Witwoud.

MRS. FAIN. Immediately. I have a word or two for Mr. Witwoud.

                              (Exeunt WITWOUD and MRS. FAINALL.)

MIR. I would beg a little private audience too. You had the tyranny to deny me last night, though you knew I came to impart a secret to you that concerned my love.

MRS. MIL. You saw I was engaged.

MIR. Unkind! You had the leisure to entertain a herd of fools; things who visit you from their excessive idleness, bestowing on your easiness that time which is the encumbrance of their lives. How can you find delight in such society? It is impossible they should admire you; they are not capable. Or if they were, it should be to you as a mortification, for sure to please a fool is some degree of folly.

MRS. MIL. I please myself. Besides, sometimes to converse with fools is for my health.

MIR. Your health! Is there a worse disease than the conversation of fools?

MRS. MIL. Yes, the vapours; fools are physic[33] for it, next to assafœtida.[34]

MIR. You are not in a course of fools?[35]

MRS. MIL. Mirabell, if you persist in this offensive freedom, you'll displease me. I think I must resolve, after all, not to have you; we shan't agree.

MIR. Not in our physic, it may be.

MRS. MIL. And yet our distemper,[36] in all likelihood, will be the same; for we shall be sick of one another. I shan't endure

---

[33] medicine.
[34] a gum resin prescribed by doctors as an antidote to "the vapours".

[35] "course" in the sense of a series of treatments.
[36] illness.

to be reprimanded nor instructed; 'tis so dull to act always by advice, and so tedious to be told of one's faults – I can't bear it. Well, I won't have you, Mirabell. I'm resolved – I think – you may go. Ha! ha! ha! What would you give that you could help loving me?

MIR. I would give something that you did not know I could not help it.

MRS. MIL. Come, don't look grave then. Well, what do you say to me?

MIR. I say that a man may as soon make a friend by his wit, or a fortune by his honesty, as win a woman with plain-dealing[37] and sincerity.

MRS. MIL. Sententious Mirabell! Prithee, don't look with that violent and inflexible wise face, like Solomon at the dividing of the child[38] in an old tapestry hanging.[39]

MIR. You are merry, madam, but I would persuade you for a moment to be serious.

MRS. MIL. What, with that face? No, if you keep your countenance, 'tis impossible I should hold mine. Well, after all, there is something very moving in a love-sick face. Ha! ha! ha! Well, I won't laugh; don't be peevish. Heigho! now I'll be melancholy, as melancholy as a watch-light.[40] Well, Mirabell, if ever you will win me, woo me now. Nay, if you are so tedious, fare you well; I see they are walking away.

MIR. Can you not find in the variety of your disposition one moment —

MRS. MIL. To hear you tell me Foible's married, and your plot like to speed? No.

MIR. But how you came to know it —

MRS. MIL. Without the help of the devil, you can't imagine; unless she should tell me herself. Which of the two it may have been, I will leave you to consider; and when you have done thinking of that, think of me.

(Exeunt MRS. MILLAMANT *with* MINCING.)

---

[37] honesty, frankness.
[38] Refer I Kings, 3, verses 16-28.
[39] Such Old-Testament subjects were common in the tapestries of the day.
[40] a small night-candle.

MIR. I have something more – Gone! Think of you! To think
of a whirlwind, though 'twere in a whirlwind, were a case
of more steady contemplation; a very tranquillity of mind
and mansion. A fellow that lives in a windmill has not a
more whimsical dwelling than the heart of a man that is
lodged in a woman. There is no point of the compass to
which they cannot turn, and by which they are not turned;
and by one as well as another; for motion, not method, is
their occupation. To know this, and yet continue to be in
love, is to be made wise from the dictates of reason, and yet
persevere to play the fool by the force of instinct. Oh, here
come my pair of turtles![41] What, billing so sweetly? Is not
Valentine's Day over with you yet?

Enter WAITWELL *and* FOIBLE

Sirrah, Waitwell, why, sure you think you were married for
your own recreation, and not for my conveniency.

WAIT. Your pardon, sir. With submission, we have indeed been
solacing[42] in lawful delights; but still with an eye to business, sir. I have instructed her as well as I could. If she can
take your directions as readily as my instructions, sir, your
affairs are in a prosperous way.

MIR. Give you joy, Mrs. Foible.

FOIB. O las, sir, I'm so ashamed! I'm afraid my lady has been in
a thousand inquietudes for me. But I protest, sir, I made
as much haste as I could.

WAIT. That she did indeed, sir. It was my fault that she did not
make more.

MIR. That I believe.

FOIB. But I told my lady as you instructed me, sir, that I had a
prospect of seeing Sir Rowland, your uncle; and that I
would put her ladyship's picture in my pocket to show him,
which I'll be sure to say has made him so enamoured of her
beauty, that he burns with impatience to lie at her ladyship's feet and worship the original.

MIR. Excellent Foible! Matrimony has made you eloquent in
love.

[41] turtle-doves; lovers.   [42] taking pleasure.

WAIT. I think she has profited, sir. I think so.

FOIB. You have seen Madam Millamant, sir?

MIR. Yes.

FOIB. I told her, sir, because I did not know that you might find an opportunity; she had so much company last night.

MIR. Your diligence will merit more. In the meantime —

(Gives money.)

FOIB. O dear sir, your humble servant!

WAIT. Spouse.

MIR. Stand off, sir, not a penny! Go on and prosper, Foible; the lease shall be made good and the farm stocked, if we succeed.[43]

FOIB. I don't question your generosity, sir; and you need not doubt of success. If you have no more commands, sir, I'll be gone; I'm sure my lady is at her toilet and can't dress till I come. Oh, dear, I'm sure that *(looking out)* was Mrs. Marwood that went by in a mask; if she has seen me with you, I'm sure she'll tell my lady. I'll make haste home and prevent her. Your servant, sir. B'w'y,[44] Waitwell.   *(Exit.)*

WAIT. Sir Rowland, if you please. The jade's so pert upon her preferment[45] she forgets herself.

MIR. Come, sir, will you endeavour to forget yourself, and transform into Sir Rowland?

WAIT. Why, sir, it will be impossible I should remember myself. Married, knighted, and attended[46] all in one day! 'Tis enough to make any forget himself. The difficulty will be how to recover my acquaintance and familiarity with my former self, and fall from my transformation to a reformation into Waitwell. Nay, I shan't be quite the same Waitwell neither; for, now I remember me, I'm married and can't be my own man again.

> Aye, there's my grief; that's the sad change of life,
> To lose my title, and yet keep my wife.

(Exeunt.)

[43] i.e., "If our little plot succeeds, I'll be even more generous."

[44] a slurred form of "God be with you".

[45] her advancement in the world; her new status as a wife.

[46] waited upon.

Act III

A Room in LADY WISHFORT's *House*

LADY WISHFORT *at her toilet,* PEG *waiting*

LADY WISH. Merciful! no news of Foible yet?

PEG. No, madam.

LADY WISH. I have no more patience. If I have not fretted myself till I am pale again, there's no veracity in me! Fetch me the red; the red, do you hear, sweetheart? An arrant ash-colour, as I'm a person! Look you how this wench stirs! Why dost thou not fetch me a little red? Didst thou not hear me, mopus?[1]

PEG. The red ratafia does your ladyship mean, or the cherry-brandy?

LADY WISH. Ratafia, fool! No, fool! Not the ratafia, fool. Grant me patience! I mean the Spanish paper,[2] idiot; complexion, darling. Paint, paint, paint; dost thou understand that, changeling,[3] dangling thy hands like bobbins[4] before thee? Why dost thou not stir, puppet? thou wooden thing upon wires!

PEG. Lord, madam, your ladyship is so impatient! I cannot come at the paint, madam; Mrs. Foible has locked it up and carried the key with her.

LADY WISH. A pox take you both! Fetch me the cherry-brandy then. *(Exit* PEG.*)* I'm as pale and as faint, I look like Mrs. Qualmsick, the curate's wife, that's always breeding. Wench,

---

[1] idiot; dull-witted girl.

[2] cosmetic rouge.

[3] simpleton.

[4] cylinders or spools (used in spinning) upon which yarn or thread is wound.

come, come, wench, what art thou doing? sipping? tasting? Save thee, dost thou not know the bottle?

Re-enter PEG *with a bottle and china cup*

PEG. Madam, I was looking for a cup.

LADY WISH. A cup, save thee! and what a cup hast thou brought! Dost thou take me for a fairy, to drink out of an acorn? Why didst thou not bring thy thimble? Hast thou ne'er a brass thimble clinking in thy pocket with a bit of nutmeg? I warrant thee. Come, fill, fill! So; again. *(One knocks.)* See who that is. Set down the bottle first. Here, here, under the table. What, wouldst thou go with the bottle in thy hand, like a tapster? As I'm a person, this wench has lived in an inn upon the road, before she came to me, like Maritornes the Asturian in *Don Quixote*![5] No Foible yet?

PEG. No, madam; Mrs. Marwood.

LADY WISH. Oh, Marwood; let her come in. Come in, good Marwood.

Enter MRS. MARWOOD

MRS. MAR. I'm surprised to find your ladyship in *déshabillé*[6] at this time of day.

LADY WISH. Foible's a lost thing; has been abroad since morning, and never heard of since.

MRS. MAR. I saw her but now, as I came masked through the park, in conference with Mirabell.

LADY WISH. With Mirabell! You call my blood into my face, with mentioning that traitor. She durst not have the confidence! I sent her to negotiate an affair in which, if I'm detected, I'm undone. If that wheedling villain has wrought upon Foible to detect me, I'm ruined. O my dear friend, I'm a wretch of wretches if I'm detected.

MRS. MAR. O madam, you cannot suspect Mrs. Foible's integrity.

LADY WISH. Oh, he carries poison in his tongue that would corrupt integrity itself! If she has given him an opportunity,

---

[5] In Cervantes' *Don Quixote* (Part I, chapter xvi), Maritornes is an Asturian chambermaid with whom the Don fancies himself in love.

[6] casual attire; *en négligé*.

she has as good as put her integrity into his hands. Ah, dear
Marwood, what's integrity to an opportunity? Hark! I hear
her! Go, you thing, and send her in. *(Exit* PEG.*)* Dear friend,
retire into my closet,[7] that I may examine her with more
freedom. You'll pardon me, dear friend; I can make bold
with you. There are books over the chimney, Quarles[8] and
Prynne,[9] and the *Short View of the Stage*,[10] with Bunyan's
works,[11] to entertain you.

(Exit MRS. MARWOOD.*)*

Enter FOIBLE

O Foible, where hast thou been? What hast thou been doing?

FOIB. Madam, I have seen the party.

LADY WISH. But what hast thou done?

FOIB. Nay, 'tis your ladyship has done, and are to do; I have
only promised. But a man so enamoured, so transported!
Well, if worshipping of pictures be a sin, poor Sir Rowland,
I say.

LADY WISH. The miniature has been counted like. But hast thou
not betrayed me, Foible? Hast thou not detected me to that
faithless Mirabell? What hadst thou to do with him in the
Park? Answer me, has he got nothing out of thee?

FOIB. *(aside)* So the devil has been beforehand with me. What
shall I say? *(aloud)* Alas, madam, could I help it, if I met
that confident thing? Was I in fault? If you had heard how
he used me, and all upon your ladyship's account, I'm sure
you would not suspect my fidelity. Nay, if that had been
the worst, I could have borne; but he had a fling at your

---

[7] private sitting-room.

[8] Francis Quarles, devotional poet, author of *Emblems, Divine and Moral* (1635).

[9] William Prynne, Puritan author of *Histrio-Mastix* (1633), an attack upon the immorality of the stage.

[10] by Jeremy Collier; an attack upon "the Immorality and Profaneness of the English Stage" (1698), directly aimed at the earlier plays of Congreve. Dryden answered the censures of Collier in his Preface to the *Fables* (1700).

[11] John Bunyan, the great Puritan writer and preacher. A one-volume edition of the *Works of that Eminent Servant of Christ, Mr. John Bunyan* had appeared in 1692.

ladyship too. And then I could not hold; but i'faith I gave him his own.

LADY WISH. Me? what did the filthy fellow say?

FOIB. O madam! 'tis a shame to say what he said, with his taunts and his fleers, tossing up his nose. "Humh!" says he. "What, you are a-hatching some plot," says he, "you are so early abroad, or catering," says he. "Ferreting for some disbanded[12] officer, I warrant. Half-pay is but thin subsistence," says he. "Well, what pension does your lady propose? Let me see," says he. "What, she must come down pretty deep now, she's superannuated," says he, "and —"

LADY WISH. Ods[13] my life, I'll have him, I'll have him murdered! I'll have him poisoned! Where does he eat? I'll marry a drawer[14] to have him poisoned in his wine! I'll send for Robin[15] from Locket's[16] immediately.

FOIB. Poison him? Poisoning's too good for him. Starve him, madam, starve him; marry Sir Rowland, and get him disinherited. Oh, you would bless yourself to hear what he said!

LADY WISH. A villain! "superannuated!"

FOIB. "Humh," says he. "I hear you are laying designs against me too," says he, "and Mrs. Millamant is to marry my uncle" (he does not suspect a word of your ladyship); "but," says he, "I'll fit you for that." "I warrant you," says he. "I'll hamper you for that," says he. "You and your old frippery[17] too," says he. "I'll handle you —"

LADY WISH. Audacious villain! "handle" me; would he durst! "Frippery! old frippery!" Was there ever such a foulmouthed fellow? I'll be married to-morrow; I'll be contracted to-night.

FOIB. The sooner the better, madam.

LADY WISH. Will Sir Rowland be here, sayest thou? When, Foible?

---

[12] discharged.
[13] "God's".
[14] one who draws wine or ale; a waiter.
[15] common name for a waiter.

[16] a fashionable ordinary (restaurant) in Charing Cross.
[17] old clothes; as applied to Lady Wishfort, "old clotheshorse".

FOIB. Incontinently,[18] madam. No new sheriff's wife expects the return of her husband after knighthood with that impatience in which Sir Rowland burns for the dear hour of kissing your ladyship's hands after dinner.

LADY WISH. "Frippery! superannuated! frippery!" I'll frippery the villain; I'll reduce him to frippery and rags! A tatterdemalion![19] I hope to see him hung with tatters, like a Long-Lane penthouse[20] or a gibbet thief. A slander-mouthed railer! I warrant the spend-thrift prodigal's in debt as much as the million lottery,[21] or the whole court upon a birthday.[22] I'll spoil his credit with his tailor. Yes, he shall have my niece with her fortune, he shall!

FOIB. He! I hope to see him lodge in Ludgate[23] first, and angle into Blackfriars[24] for brass farthings with an old mitten.[25]

LADY WISH. Aye, dear Foible; thank thee for that, dear Foible. He has put me out of all patience. I shall never recompose my features to receive Sir Rowland with any economy of face.[26] This wretch has fretted me that I am absolutely decayed. Look, Foible.

FOIB. Your ladyship has frowned a little too rashly, indeed, madam. There are some cracks discernible in the white varnish.

LADY WISH. Let me see the glass. "Cracks," sayest thou? Why I am arrantly fleaed;[27] I look like an old peeled wall. Thou

---

[18] immediately, and with the added suggestion of passionate impatience.
[19] a tattered fellow.
[20] a shed with a sloping roof in Long Lane, a district famous for its shops of old and second-hand clothes.
[21] a wild scheme to raise a million pounds by the sale of lottery tickets.
[22] Since custom demanded gifts on such an occasion, a royal birthday was an expensive event.
[23] the debtors' prison.
[24] Ludgate Prison abutted on the precinct of Blackfriars, the area of London between Ludgate Hill and the river.
[25] The statement refers to the practice of Ludgate prisoners of begging money from passers-by, probably by lowering an old mitten on a string from a high window.
[26] The sense is, that Lady Wishfort has been so distressed by Foible's account of Mirabell's words that her make-up has been ruined, and the cosmetics necessary to make her face presentable to Sir Rowland will be very expensive.
[27] flayed.

must repair me, Foible, before Sir Rowland comes, or I shall never keep up to my picture.[28]

FOIB. I warrant you, madam, a little art once made your picture like you; and now a little of the same art must make you like your picture. Your picture must sit for you, madam.

LADY WISH. But art thou sure Sir Rowland will not fail to come? Or will 'a not fail when he does come? Will he be importunate, Foible, and push? For if he should not be importunate, I shall never break decorums. I shall die with confusion, if I am forced to advance. Oh no, I can never advance! I shall swoon if he should expect advances. No, I hope Sir Rowland is better bred than to put a lady to the necessity of breaking her forms. I won't be too coy neither. I won't give him despair; but a little disdain is not amiss, a little scorn is alluring.

FOIB. A little scorn becomes your ladyship.

LADY WISH. Yes, but tenderness becomes me best, a sort of dyingness. You see that picture has a sort of a – ha, Foible? a swimmingness in the eyes. Yes, I'll look so. My niece affects it; but she wants features. Is Sir Rowland handsome? Let my toilet be removed. I'll dress above. I'll receive Sir Rowland here. Is he handsome? Don't answer me. I won't know; I'll be surprised, I'll be taken by surprise.

FOIB. By storm, madam. Sir Rowland's a brisk man.

LADY WISH. Is he! Oh, then he'll importune, if he's a brisk man. I shall save decorums if Sir Rowland importunes. I have a mortal terror at the apprehension of offending against decorums. Oh, I'm glad he's a brisk man. Let my things be removed, good Foible. *(Exit.)*

Enter MRS. FAINALL

MRS. FAIN. O Foible, I have been in a fright, lest I should come too late! That devil Marwood saw you in the Park with Mirabell, and I'm afraid will discover it to my lady.

FOIB. Discover what, madam?

28 i.e., "look as lovely as I do in my picture".

MRS. FAIN. Nay, nay, put not on that strange face. I am privy to the whole design, and know that Waitwell, to whom thou wert this morning married, is to personate Mirabell's uncle, and as such, winning my lady, to involve her in those difficulties from which Mirabell only must release her, by his making his conditions to have my cousin and her fortune left to her own disposal.

FOIB. O dear madam, I beg your pardon. It was not my confidence in your ladyship that was deficient; but I thought the former good correspondence between your ladyship and Mr. Mirabell might have hindered his communicating this secret.

MRS. FAIN. Dear Foible, forget that.

FOIB. O dear madam, Mr. Mirabell is such a sweet, winning gentleman, but your ladyship is the pattern of generosity. Sweet lady, to be so good! Mr. Mirabell cannot choose but be grateful. I find your ladyship has his heart still. Now, madam, I can safely tell your ladyship our success. Mrs. Marwood had told my lady; but I warrant I managed myself. I turned it all for the better. I told my lady that Mr. Mirabell railed at her. I laid horrid things to his charge, I'll vow; and my lady is so incensed that she'll be contracted to Sir Rowland to-night, she says. I warrant I worked her up, that he may have her for asking for, as they say of a Welsh maidenhead.

MRS. FAIN. O rare Foible!

FOIB. I beg your ladyship to acquaint Mr. Mirabell of his success. I would be seen as little as possible to speak to him; besides, I believe Madam Marwood watches me. She has a month's mind;[29] but I know Mr. Mirabell can't abide her. *(calls)* John! Remove my lady's toilet. Madam, your servant. My lady is so impatient, I fear she'll come for me if I stay.

MRS. FAIN. I'll go with you up the back stairs, lest I should meet her.   *(Exeunt.)*

Re-enter MRS. MARWOOD *alone*

[29] a longing, desire.

MRS. MAR. Indeed, Mrs. Engine,[30] is it thus with you? Are you become a go-between of this importance? Yes, I shall watch you. Why, this wench is the *passe-partout*, a very master-key to everybody's strong-box. My friend Fainall,[31] have you carried it so swimmingly? I thought there was something in it; but it seems it's over with you.[32] Your loathing is not from a want of appetite then, but from a surfeit. Else you could never be so cool to fall from a principal to be an assistant; to procure for him! "A pattern of generosity," that I confess. Well, Mr. Fainall, you have met with your match. O man, man! woman, woman! the devil's an ass; if I were a painter, I would draw him like an idiot, a driveller with a bib and bells. Man should have his head and horns,[33] and woman the rest of him. Poor simple fiend! "Madam Marwood has a month's mind, but he can't abide her." 'Twere better for him you had not been his confessor in that affair, without[34] you could have kept his counsel closer. I shall not prove another "pattern of generosity". He has not obliged me to that with those excesses of himself; and now I'll have none of him. Here comes the good lady, panting ripe; with a heart full of hope, and a head full of care, like any chemist upon the day of projection.[35]

Re-enter LADY WISHFORT

LADY WISH. O dear Marwood, what shall I say for this rude forgetfulness? But my dear friend is all goodness.

MRS. MAR. No apologies, dear madam. I have been very well entertained.

LADY WISH. As I'm a person, I am in a very chaos to think I

---

[30] i.e., Foible, the agent of the plot, which Mrs. Marwood has discovered by eavesdropping on the discourse between Foible and Mrs. Fainall.

[31] i.e., Mrs. Fainall.

[32] Among other things, Mrs. Marwood has learned of Mrs. Fainall's affair with Mirabell before her marriage to Fainall.

[33] referring to the proverbial horns of the cuckold.

[34] unless.

[35] The comparison refers to the attempts of the alchemists to transmute base metals into gold. The "day of projection" is the last day of the experiment, when success or failure will be known.

should so forget myself; but I have such an olio of affairs,[36] really I know not what to do. *(calls)* Foible! I expect my nephew, Sir Wilfull, every moment too. *(calls)* Why, Foible! He means to travel for improvement.

MRS. MAR. Methinks Sir Wilfull should rather think of marrying than travelling at his years. I hear he is turned of forty.

LADY WISH. Oh, he's in less danger of being spoiled by his travels. I am against my nephew's marrying too young. It will be time enough when he comes back and has acquired discretion to choose for himself.

MRS. MAR. Methinks Mrs. Millamant and he would make a very fit match. He may travel afterwards. 'Tis a thing very usual with young gentlemen.

LADY WISH. I promise you I have thought on't; and since 'tis your judgment, I'll think on't again. I assure you I will; I value your judgment extremely. On my word, I'll propose it.

Re-enter FOIBLE

Come, come, Foible, I had forgot my nephew will be here before dinner. I must make haste.

FOIB. Mr. Witwoud and Mr. Petulant are come to dine with your ladyship.

LADY WISH. Oh, dear, I can't appear till I am dressed. Dear Marwood, shall I be free with you again, and beg you to entertain 'em? I'll make all imaginable haste. Dear friend, excuse me.

(Exeunt LADY WISHFORT *and* FOIBLE.*)*

Enter MRS. MILLAMANT *and* MINCING

MRS. MIL. Sure never anything was so unbred as that odious man! Marwood, your servant.

MRS. MAR. You have a colour; what's the matter?

MRS. MIL. That horrid fellow, Petulant, has provoked me into a flame. I have broke my fan. Mincing, lend me yours; is not all the powder out of my hair?

[36] i.e., "such a number of things on my mind".

MRS. MAR. No. What has he done?

MRS. MIL. Nay, he has done nothing; he has only talked. Nay, he has said nothing neither; but he has contradicted everything that has been said. For my part, I thought Witwoud and he would have quarrelled.

MIN. I vow, mem, I thought once they would have fit.[37]

MRS. MIL. Well, 'tis a lamentable thing, I swear, that one has not the liberty of choosing one's acquaintance as one does one's clothes.

MRS. MAR. If we had that liberty, we should be as weary of one set of acquaintance, though never so good, as we are of one suit, though never so fine. A fool and a doily stuff[38] would now and then find days of grace, and be worn for variety.

MRS. MIL. I could consent to wear 'em, if they would wear alike; but fools never wear out, they are such *drap-de-Berry*[39] things! without one could give 'em to one's chambermaid after a day or two.

MRS. MAR. 'Twere better so indeed. Or what think you of the playhouse? A fine, gay, glossy fool should be given there, like a new masking habit, after the masquerade is over, and we have done with the disguise. For a fool's visit is always a disguise, and never admitted by a woman of wit, but to blind[40] her affair with a lover of sense. If you would but appear barefaced now, and own Mirabell, you might as easily put off Petulant and Witwoud as your hood and scarf. And indeed 'tis time, for the town has found it; the secret is grown too big for the pretence. 'Tis like Mrs. Primly's great belly; she may lace it down before, but it burnishes[41] on her hips. Indeed, Millamant, you can no more conceal it than my Lady Strammel can her face, that goodly face, which, in defiance of her Rhenish-wine tea,[42] will not be comprehended in a mask.[43]

---

[37] fought; another of Mincing's provincialisms.

[38] a coarse woollen material.

[39] woollen cloth, probably coarse, from the French province of Berry.

[40] camouflage.

[41] is all the more evident.

[42] Rhenish white wine was supposed to reduce corpulence.

[43] The sense is that the lady's face was so fat that no mask would fit it.

MRS. MIL. I'll take my death, Marwood, you are more censorious than a decayed beauty, or a discarded toast. Mincing, tell the men they may come up. My aunt is not dressing here; their folly is less provoking than your malice. (*Exit* MINCING.) "The town has found it!" What has it found? That Mirabell loves me is no more a secret than it is a secret that you discovered it to my aunt, or than the reason why you discovered it is a secret.

MRS. MAR. You are nettled.[44]

MRS. MIL. You're mistaken. Ridiculous!

MRS. MAR. Indeed, my dear, you'll tear another fan, if you don't mitigate those violent airs.

MRS. MIL. O silly! ha! ha! ha! I could laugh immoderately. Poor Mirabell! His constancy to me has quite destroyed his complaisance for all the world beside. I swear, I never enjoined it him to be so coy. If I had the vanity to think he would obey me, I would command him to show more gallantry. 'Tis hardly well-bred to be so particular[45] on one hand, and so insensible on the other. But I despair to prevail, and so let him follow his own way, ha! ha! ha! Pardon me, dear creature, I must laugh, ha! ha! ha! though I grant you 'tis a little barbarous, ha! ha! ha!

MRS. MAR. What pity 'tis, so much fine raillery, and delivered with so significant gesture, should be so unhappily directed to miscarry!

MRS. MIL. Ha? Dear creature, I ask your pardon. I swear I did not mind you.[46]

MRS. MAR. Mr. Mirabell and you both may think it a thing impossible, when I shall tell him by telling you —

MRS. MIL. Oh, dear, what? For it is the same thing if I hear it, ha! ha! ha!

MRS. MAR. That I detest him, hate him, madam.

MRS. MIL. O madam, why so do I. And yet the creature loves me, ha! ha! ha! How can one forbear laughing to think of it!

[44] annoyed.
[45] attentive to one lady (i.e., Millamant).
[46] "I did not have you in mind."

I am a sibyl[47] if I am not amazed to think what he can see in me. I'll take my death, I think you are handsomer and, within a year or two as young; if you could but stay for me, I should overtake you, but that cannot be. Well, that thought makes me melancholic. Now, I'll be sad.

MRS. MAR. Your merry note may be changed sooner than you think.

MRS. MIL. D'ye say so? Then I'm resolved I'll have a song to keep up my spirits.

Re-enter MINCING

MIN. The gentlemen stay but to comb,[48] madam, and will wait on you.

MRS. MIL. Desire Mrs. —, that is in the next room, to sing the song I would have learnt yesterday. You shall hear it, madam, not that there's any great matter in it, but 'tis agreeable to my humour.

SONG
[*Set by* MR. JOHN ECCLES]

I

Love's but the frailty of the mind,
When 'tis not with ambition join'd;
A sickly flame, which, if not fed, expires,
And feeding, wastes in self-consuming fires.

II

'Tis not to wound a wanton boy
Or am'rous youth, that gives the joy;
But 'tis the glory to have pierc'd a swain,
For whom inferior beauties sigh'd in vain.

---

[47] seeress.
[48] i.e., comb their wigs.

Wit of Petulant & Witwoud.

III

Pet. contradicts

Then I alone the conquest prize,
When I insult a rival's eyes;
If there's delight in love, 'tis when I see
That heart, which others bleed for, bleed for me.

Cruelty?

Enter PETULANT *and* WITWOUD

MRS. MIL. Is your animosity composed, gentlemen?

WIT. Raillery, raillery, madam; we have no animosity. We hit off a little wit now and then, but no animosity. The falling-out of wits is like the falling-out of lovers; we agree in the main, like treble and bass. Ha, Petulant?

PET. Aye, in the main, but when I have a humour to contradict.

WIT. Aye, when he has a humour to contradict, then I contradict too. What, I know my cue. Then we contradict one another like two battledores; for contradictions beget one another like Jews.

Wit?

PET. If he says black's black, if I have a humour to say 'tis blue, let that pass; all's one for that. If I have a humour to prove it, it must be granted.

WIT. Not positively must, but it may, it may.

PET. Yes, it positively must, upon proof positive.

WIT. Aye, upon proof positive it must; but upon proof presumptive it only may. That's a logical distinction now, madam.

MRS. MAR. I perceive your debates are of importance and very learnedly handled.

PET. Importance is one thing, and learning's another; but a debate's a debate, that I assert.

WIT. Petulant's an enemy to learning; he relies altogether on his parts.

PET. No, I'm no enemy to learning; it hurts not me.

MRS. MAR. That's a sign indeed it's no enemy to you.

PET. No, no, it's no enemy to anybody but them that have it.

MRS. MIL. Well, an illiterate man's my aversion; I wonder at the impudence of any illiterate man to offer to make love.

WIT. That I confess I wonder at too.

MRS. MIL. Ah! to marry an ignorant that can hardly read or write!

PET. Why should a man be any further from being married, though he can't read, than he is from being hanged? The ordinary's[49] paid for setting the psalm, and the parish-priest for reading the ceremony. And for the rest which is to follow in both cases, a man may do it without book; so all's one for that.

MRS. MIL. D'ye hear the creature? Lord, here's company; I'll be gone.

(*Exeunt* MRS. MILLAMANT *and* MINCING.)

Enter SIR WILFULL WITWOUD *in a riding dress, and a* FOOTMAN *to* LADY WISHFORT

WIT. In the name of Bartlemew and his fair,[50] what have we here?

MRS. MAR. 'Tis your brother, I fancy. Don't you know him?

WIT. Not I. Yes, I think it is he. I've almost forgot him; I have not seen him since the Revolution.[51]

FOOT. (*to* SIR WILFULL) Sir, my lady's dressing. Here's company; if you please to walk in, in the meantime.

SIR WIL. Dressing! What, it's but morning here, I warrant, with you in London; we should count it towards afternoon in our parts, down in Shropshire. Why then, belike my aunt han't dined yet, ha, friend?

FOOT. Your aunt, sir?

SIR WIL. My aunt, sir! Yes, my aunt, sir, and your lady, sir; your lady is my aunt, sir. Why, what, dost thou not know me, friend? Why, then send somebody hither that does. How long hast thou lived with thy lady, fellow, ha?

FOOT. A week, sir; longer than anybody else in the house, except my lady's woman.

[49] The ordinary was the chaplain of a prison, who prepared criminals for death.

[50] Bartholomew Fair was held in August of each year at Smithfield. Since it was specially renowned for its sale of country cloths, Witwoud may here be referring to the inappropriateness of his brother's riding-habit in a London drawing-room.

[51] the bloodless Revolution of 1688, which marked the defeat of James II and the accession to the throne of William and Mary.

Sir Wilful

SIR WIL. Why then, belike thou dost not know thy lady, if thou seest her, ha, friend?

FOOT. Why truly, sir, I cannot safely swear to her face in a morning, before she is dressed. 'Tis like I may give a shrewd guess at her by this time.

SIR WIL. Well, prithee try what thou canst do; if thou canst not guess, inquire her out, dost hear, fellow? And tell her, her nephew, Sir Wilfull Witwoud, is in the house.

FOOT. I shall, sir.

SIR WIL. Hold ye, hear me, friend; a word with you in your ear. Prithee who are these gallants?

FOOT. Really, sir, I can't tell; here come so many here, 'tis hard to know 'em all. *(Exit.)*

SIR WIL. Oons,[52] this fellow knows less than a starling;[53] I don't think 'a knows his own name.

MRS. MAR. Mr. Witwoud, your brother is not behind-hand in forgetfulness; I fancy he has forgot you too.

WIT. I hope so. The devil take him that remembers first, I say.

SIR WIL. Save you, gentlemen and lady!

MRS. MAR. For shame, Mr. Witwoud; why won't you speak to him? And you, sir.

WIT. Petulant, speak.

PET. And you, sir.

SIR WIL. No offence, I hope. *(Salutes MRS. MARWOOD.)*

MRS. MAR. No sure, sir.

WIT. This is a vile dog; I see that already. No offence! Ha! ha! ha! to him; to him, Petulant, smoke[54] him.

PET. It seems as if you had come a journey, sir; hem, hem.

(Surveying him round.)

SIR. WIL. Very likely, sir, that it may seem so.

PET. No offence, I hope, sir.

WIT. Smoke the boots, the boots; Petulant, the boots, ha! ha! ha!

SIR WIL. May be not, sir; thereafter as 'tis meant,[55] sir.

---

[52] an oath: "God's wounds".
[53] proverbially a stupid bird.
[54] According to Summers, *Dictionary of the Canting Crew*, "smoke" meant

"to affront a stranger at his coming in".
[55] "according to the way it is meant".

PET. Sir, I presume upon the information of your boots.

SIR WIL. Why, 'tis like you may, sir. If you are not satisfied with the information of my boots, sir, if you will step to the stable, you may inquire further of my horse, sir.

PET. Your horse, sir! Your horse is an ass, sir!

SIR WIL. Do you speak by way of offence, sir?

MRS. MAR. The gentleman's merry, that's all sir. *(aside)* 'Slife,[56] we shall have a quarrel betwixt an horse and an ass, before they find one another out. *(aloud)* You must not take anything amiss from your friends, sir. You are among your friends here, though it may be you don't know it. If I am not mistaken, you are Sir Wilfull Witwoud.

SIR WIL. Right, lady; I am Sir Wilfull Witwoud, so I write myself; no offence to anybody, I hope; and nephew to the Lady Wishfort of this mansion.

MRS. MAR. Don't you know this gentleman, sir?

SIR WIL. Hum! What, sure 'tis not – yea by'r Lady, but 'tis. 'Sheart[57] I know not whether 'tis or no. Yea, but 'tis, by the Wrekin.[58] Brother Antony! What, Tony, i'faith! What, dost thou not know me? By'r Lady, nor I thee, thou art so becravated and so beperiwigged. 'Sheart, why dost not speak? Art thou o'erjoyed?

WIT. Odso, brother, is it you? Your servant, brother.

SIR WIL. Your servant! Why, yours, sir. Your servant again, 'sheart, and your friend and servant to that, and a – *(puff)* and a flapdragon[59] for your service, sir! and a hare's foot, and a hare's scut[60] for your service, sir, an you be so cold and so courtly!

WIT. No offence, I hope, brother.

SIR WIL. 'Sheart, sir, but there is, and much offence! A pox, is this your Inns o' Court[61] breeding, not to know your friends and your relations, your elders and your betters?

---

[56] i.e., "God's life".

[57] i.e., "God's heart".

[58] a hill in his native Shropshire.

[59] derived from the game of catching raisins out of burning brandy; meaning, "a fig for your service".

[60] tail.

[61] the centre of the legal world of London; synecdoche for the city itself. Sir Wilfull, the country squire, simply asks if Witwoud's rudeness is a mark of city manners.

WIT. Why, brother Wilfull of Salop,[62] you may be as short as a Shrewsbury[63] cake, if you please. But I tell you 'tis not modish to know relations in town. You think you're in the country, where great lubberly[64] brothers slabber[65] and kiss one another when they meet, like a call of serjeants.[66] 'Tis not the fashion here; 'tis not indeed, dear brother.

SIR WIL. The fashion's a fool; and you're a fop, dear brother. 'Sheart, I've suspected this. By'r Lady, I conjectured you were a fop, since you began to change the style of your letters, and write in a scrap of paper, gilt round the edges, no broader than a *subpœna*.[67] I might expect this when you left off, "Honoured brother," and "hoping you are in good health," and so forth, to begin with a "Rat me,[68] knight, I'm so sick of a last night's debauch," ods heart, and then tell a familiar tale of a cock and a bull,[69] and a whore and a bottle, and so conclude. You could write news before you were out of your time,[70] when you lived with honest Pumple Nose, the attorney of Furnival's Inn;[71] you could entreat to be remembered then to your friends round the Wrekin. We could have gazettes, then, and *Dawks's Letter*,[72] and the *Weekly Bill*,[73] till of late days.

PET. 'Slife, Witwoud, were you ever an attorney's clerk? of the family of the Furnivals? Ha! ha! ha!

WIT. Aye, aye, but that was but for a while, not long, not long. Pshaw! I was not in my own power then; an orphan, and this fellow was my guardian. Aye, aye, I was glad to consent to that man to come to London. He had the disposal of me then. If I had not agreed to that, I might have been bound

---

[62] another name for Shropshire.

[63] the capital of Shropshire.

[64] loutish.

[65] slobber.

[66] when sergeants-at-law are admitted to the bar.

[67] a legal summons.

[68] contraction of the oath, "May God rot me."

[69] a wildly exaggerated tale.

[70] i.e., before he had finished his legal apprenticeship.

[71] one of the Inns of Court (Chancery) attached to Lincoln's Inn.

[72] a newsletter with a wide circulation in the provinces.

[73] It reported all deaths in and around London.

prentice to a felt-maker in Shrewsbury; this fellow would have bound me to a maker of felts.

SIR WIL. 'Sheart, and better than to be bound to a maker of fops, where, I suppose, you have served your time; and now you may set up for yourself.

MRS. MAR. You intend to travel, sir, as I'm informed.

SIR WIL. Belike I may, madam. I may chance to sail upon the salt seas, if my mind hold.

PET. And the wind serve.

SIR WIL. Serve or not serve, I shan't ask licence of you, sir; nor the weathercock your companion. I direct my discourse to the lady, sir. 'Tis like my aunt may have told you, madam. Yes, I have settled my concerns, I may say now, and am minded to see foreign parts. If an how that the peace[74] holds, whereby, that is, taxes abate.

MRS. MAR. I thought you had designed for France at all adventures.[75]

SIR WIL. I can't tell that; 'tis like I may, and 'tis like I may not. I am somewhat dainty in making a resolution, because when I make it, I keep it. I don't stand shill I, shall I,[76] then; if I say't, I'll do't. But I have thoughts to tarry a small matter in town, to learn somewhat of your lingo first, before I cross the seas. I'd gladly have a spice of your French, as they say, whereby to hold discourse in foreign countries.

MRS. MAR. Here's an academy in town for that use.

SIR WIL. There is? 'Tis like there may.

MRS. MAR. No doubt you will return very much improved.

WIT. Yes, refined, like a Dutch skipper from a whale-fishing.

Re-enter LADY WISHFORT *with* FAINALL

LADY WISH. Nephew, you are welcome.

SIR WIL. Aunt, your servant.

---

[74] the Treaty of Ryswick (1697), which temporarily terminated the war between France on the one hand, and England and her Continental allies on the other.

[75] in any case.

[76] shilly-shally. Sir Wilfull is saying that he is not an indecisive man.

FAIN. Sir Wilfull, your most faithful servant.

SIR WIL. Cousin Fainall, give me your hand.

LADY WISH. Cousin Witwoud, your servant; Mr. Petulant, your servant. Nephew, you are welcome again. Will you drink anything after your journey, nephew, before you eat? Dinner's almost ready.

SIR WIL. I'm very well, I thank you, aunt; however, I thank you for your courteous offer. 'Sheart I was afraid you would have been in the fashion too, and have remembered to have forgot your relations. Here's your cousin Tony; belike I mayn't call him brother for fear of offence.

LADY WISH. O, he's a railer,[77] nephew. My cousin's a wit; and your great wits always rally their best friends to choose.[78] When you have been abroad, nephew, you'll understand raillery better.

(FAINALL *and* MRS. MARWOOD *talk apart.*)

SIR WIL. Why then, let him hold his tongue in the meantime, and rail when that day comes.

Re-enter MINCING

MIN. Mem, I come to acquaint your laship that dinner is impatient.

SIR WIL. Impatient? Why then, belike it won't stay till I pull off my boots. Sweetheart, can you help me to a pair of slippers? My man's with the horses, I warrant.

LADY WISH. Fie, fie, nephew, you would not pull off your boots here. Go down into the hall; dinner shall stay for you. My nephew's a little unbred; you'll pardon him, madam. Gentlemen, will you walk? Marwood?

MRS. MAR. I'll follow you, madam, before Sir Wilfull is ready.

(*Exeunt all but* MRS. MARWOOD *and* FAINALL.)

FAIN. Why then, Foible's a bawd, an arrant, rank, match-making bawd. And I, it seems, am a husband, a rank husband; and my wife a very arrant, rank wife, all in the way of the world.

---

[77] a railer; one who delights in raillery, in gentle mockery.

[78] as they like.

'Sdeath, to be a cuckold by anticipation, a cuckold in embryo![79] Sure I was born with budding antlers, like a young satyr, or a citizen's child.[80] 'Sdeath! to be out-witted, to be out-jilted, out-matrimonied! If I had kept my speed like a stag, 'twere somewhat; but to crawl after, with my horns, like a snail, and be outstripped by my wife, 'tis scurvy wedlock.

MRS. MAR. Then shake it off. You have often wished for an opportunity to part; and now you have it. But first prevent their plot; the half of Millamant's fortune is too considerable to be parted with, to a foe, to Mirabell.

FAIN. Damn him! that had been mine, had you not made that fond[81] discovery. That had been forfeited, had they been married. My wife had added lustre to my horns by that increase of fortune; I could have worn 'em tipped with gold, though my forehead had been furnished like a deputy-lieutenant's hall.[82]

MRS. MAR. They may prove a cap of maintenance[83] to you still, if you can away with[84] your wife. And she's no worse than when you had her. I dare swear she had given up her game before she was married.

FAIN. Hum! that may be.

MRS. MAR. You married her to keep you; and if you can contrive to have her keep you better than you expected, why should you not keep her longer than you intended?

FAIN. The means, the means.

MRS. MAR. Discover to my lady your wife's conduct; threaten to

---

[79] In their "talk apart" (above), Mrs. Marwood has told Mr. Fainall what she has learned of his wife's affair with Mirabell before her marriage to Fainall.

[80] i.e., a cuckold's child. Many a child of an honest citizen was fathered by a gentleman of the town.

[81] foolish.

[82] i.e., though he had been cuckolded as many times as there are antlers of stags and deer decorating the country mansion of a deputy-lieutenant.

[83] a term in heraldry. The coat of arms of a royal bastard sometimes included a cap with two points behind, like the horns of a cuckold. Mrs. Marwood puns on the word "maintenance" since she is insinuating that, armed with this new information concerning his wife, Fainall may be in a better position to blackmail Lady Wishfort to the amount of Millamant's fortune which she controls.

[84] continue to tolerate.

part with her. My lady loves her, and will come to any composition[85] to save her reputation. Take the opportunity of breaking it, just upon the discovery of this imposture. My lady will be enraged beyond bounds, and sacrifice niece and fortune and all, at that conjuncture. And let me alone to keep her warm; if she should flag in her part, I will not fail to prompt her.

FAIN. Faith, this has an appearance.[86]

MRS. MAR. I'm sorry I hinted to my lady to endeavour a match between Millamant and Sir Wilfull; that may be an obstacle.

FAIN. Oh, for that matter leave me to manage him; I'll disable him for that. He will drink like a Dane;[87] after dinner, I'll set his hand in.[88]

MRS. MAR. Well, how do you stand affected towards your lady?

FAIN. Why, faith, I'm thinking of it. Let me see. I am married already, so that's over. My wife has played the jade with me; well, that's over too. I never loved her, or if I had, why, that would have been over too by this time. Jealous of her I cannot be, for I am certain; so there's an end of jealousy. Weary of her I am, and shall be. No, there's no end of that; no, no, that were too much to hope. Thus far concerning my repose; now for my reputation. As to my own, I married not for it, so that's out of the question. And as to my part in my wife's, why, she had parted with hers before; so bringing none to me, she can take none from me. 'Tis against all rule of play that I should lose to one who has not wherewithal to stake.

MRS. MAR. Besides, you forget marriage is honourable.

FAIN. Hum! Faith, and that's well thought on. Marriage is honourable, as you say; and if so, wherefore should cuckoldom be a discredit, being derived from so honourable a root?

---

85 agree to anything.
86 possibilities.
87 The Danes were known as heavy drinkers. See *Hamlet*, I, iv: "They clepe us drunkards . . .".
88 i.e., "I'll involve him in the plot."

MRS. MAR. Nay, I know not; if the root be honourable, why not the branches?[89]

FAIN. So, so; why, this point's clear. Well, how do we proceed?

MRS. MAR. I will contrive a letter which shall be delivered to my lady at the time when that rascal who is to act Sir Rowland is with her. It shall come as from an unknown hand, for the less I appear to know of the truth, the better I can play the incendiary. Besides, I would not have Foible provoked if I could help it, because you know she knows some passages.[90] Nay, I expect all will come out; but let the mine be sprung first, and then I care not if I am discovered.

FAIN. If the worst come to the worst, I'll turn my wife to grass,[91] I have already a deed of settlement of the best part of her estate, which I wheedled out of her; and that you shall partake at least.

MRS. MAR. I hope you are convinced that I hate Mirabell now; you'll be no more jealous?

FAIN. Jealous! No, by this kiss. Let husbands be jealous; but let the lover still believe. Or if he doubt, let it be only to endear his pleasure, and prepare the joy that follows, when he proves his mistress true. But let husbands' doubts convert to endless jealousy; or if they have belief, let it corrupt to superstition and blind credulity. I am single, and will herd no more with 'em. True, I wear the badge, but I'll disown the order. And since I take my leave of 'em, I care not if I leave 'em a common motto to their common crest.

> All husbands must or pain or shame endure;
> The wise too jealous are, fools too secure.

(Exeunt.)

---

[89] i.e., the cuckold's horns.

[90] i.e., Foible knows of Mrs. Marwood's affair with Mr. Fainall, and may divulge it. Indeed, she does, in the denouement of Act V.

[91] turn her out, as he would an animal to graze.

Preparations for "Sir R"

(Karen
Elizabeth
Anne)

Act IV

[*Scene continues*]

Enter LADY WISHFORT *and* FOIBLE

LADY WISH. Is Sir Rowland coming, sayest thou, Foible? and are things in order?

FOIB. Yes, madam, I have put wax-lights in the sconces, and placed the footmen in a row in the hall, in their best liveries, with the coachman and postillion to fill up the equipage.

LADY WISH. Have you pulvilled[1] the coachman and postillion, that they may not stink of the stable when Sir Rowland comes by?

FOIB. Yes, madam.

LADY WISH. And are the dancers and the music ready, that he may be entertained in all points with correspondence to his passion?

FOIB. All is ready, madam.

LADY WISH. And – well, and how do I look, Foible?

FOIB. Most killing well, madam.

LADY WISH. Well, and how shall I receive him? In what figure shall I give his heart the first impression? There is a great deal in the first impression. Shall I sit? No, I won't sit, I'll walk; aye, I'll walk from the door upon his entrance; and then turn full upon him. No, that will be too sudden. I'll lie, aye, I'll lie down. I'll receive him in my little dressing-room; there's a couch. Yes, yes, I'll give the first impression on a couch. I won't lie neither, but loll and lean upon one elbow; with one foot a little dangling off, jogging in a

---

[1] scented with a sweet-smelling powder.

thoughtful way. Yes, and then as soon as he appears, start, aye, start and be surprised, and rise to meet him in a pretty disorder. Yes, oh, nothing is more alluring than a levee[2] from a couch, in some confusion; it shows the foot to advantage, and furnishes with blushes and recomposing airs beyond comparison. Hark! there's a coach.

FOIB. 'Tis he, madam.

LADY WISH. Oh dear, has my nephew made his addresses to Millamant? I ordered him.

FOIB. Sir Wilfull is set in to drinking, madam, in the parlour.

LADY WISH. Ods my life, I'll send him to her. Call her down, Foible; bring her hither. I'll send him as I go. When they are together, then come to me, Foible, that I may not be too long alone with Sir Rowland.   *(Exit.)*

Enter MRS. MILLAMANT *and* MRS. FAINALL

FOIB. Madam, I stayed here to tell your ladyship that Mr. Mirabell has waited this half hour for an opportunity to talk with you, though my lady's orders were to leave you and Sir Wilfull together. Shall I tell Mr. Mirabell that you are at leisure?

MRS. MIL. No, what would the dear man have? I am thoughtful, and would amuse myself; bid him come another time.

> "There never yet was woman made,
> Nor shall, but to be curs'd."[3]
>
> *(Repeating and walking about.)*

That's hard!

MRS. FAIN. You are very fond of Sir John Suckling to-day, Millamant, and the poets.

MRS. MIL. He? Aye, and filthy verses; so I am.

FOIB. Sir Wilfull is coming, madam. Shall I send Mr. Mirabell away?

MRS. MIL. Aye, if you please, Foible, send him away, or send him

---

[2] rising.
[3] the opening lines of a poem by Sir John Suckling (1609-42), a distinguished Cavalier lyrist.

hither; just as you will, dear Foible. I think I'll see him; shall I? Aye, let the wretch come.

(Exit FOIBLE.*)*

"Thyrsis, a youth of the inspired train."[4]

(Repeating.)

Dear Fainall, entertain Sir Wilfull. Thou hast philosophy to undergo[5] a fool; thou art married and hast patience. I would confer with my own thoughts.

MRS. FAIN. I am obliged to you, that you would make me your proxy in this affair; but I have business of my own.

Enter SIR WILFULL

O Sir Wilfull, you are come at the critical instant. There's your mistress up to the ears in love and contemplation; pursue your point, now or never.

SIR WIL. Yes; my aunt will have it so. I would gladly have been encouraged with a bottle or two, because I'm somewhat wary at first, before I am acquainted. *(This while* MILLA-MANT *walks about repeating to herself.)* But I hope, after a time, I shall break my mind; that is, upon further acquaintance. So for the present, cousin, I'll take my leave. If so be you'll be so kind to make my excuse, I'll return to my company.

MRS. FAIN. Oh, fie, Sir Wilfull! What, you must not be daunted.

SIR WIL. Daunted! No, that's not it. It is not so much for that; for if so be that I set on't, I'll do't. But only for the present; 'tis sufficient till further acquaintance, that's all. Your servant.

MRS. FAIN. Nay, I'll swear you shall never lose so favourable an opportunity, if I can help it. I'll leave you together and lock the door.

(Exit.)

SIR WIL. Nay, nay, cousin. I have forgot my gloves. What d'ye do? 'Sheart, 'a has locked the door indeed, I think. Nay,

---

[4] the first line of *The Story of Phoebus and Daphne, Applied*, a poem by Edmund Waller (1606-87), a poet much admired by Dryden, and renowned for the "sweetness" of his verse. See Pope, *Essay on Criticism*, line 361; and *To Augustus*, line 267. [5] put up with.

Cousin Fainall, open the door! Pshaw, what a vixen trick is this? Nay, now 'a has seen me too. Cousin, I made bold to pass through as it were. I think this door's enchanted!

MRS. MIL. *(repeating)*

"I prithee spare me, gentle boy,
 Press me no more for that slight toy —"[6]

SIR WIL. Anan?[7] Cousin, your servant.

MRS. MIL. *(repeating)*

"That foolish trifle of a heart —"
Sir Wilfull!

SIR WIL. Yes. Your servant. No offence, I hope, cousin.

MRS. MIL. *(repeating)*

"I swear it will not do its part,
 Though thou dost thine, employ'st thy pow'r and art."
Natural, easy Suckling!

SIR WIL. Anan? Suckling? No such suckling neither, cousin, nor stripling! I thank Heaven, I'm no minor.

MRS. MIL. Ah, rustic! ruder than Gothic.[8]

SIR WIL. Well, well, I shall understand your lingo one of these days, cousin; in the meanwhile I must answer in plain English.

MRS. MIL. Have you any business with me, Sir Wilfull?

SIR WIL. Not at present, cousin. Yes, I made bold to see, to come and know if that how you were disposed to fetch a walk this evening; if so be that I might not be troublesome, I would have fought[9] a walk with you.

MRS. MIL. A walk! What then?

SIR WIL. Nay, nothing. Only for the walk's sake, that's all.

MRS. MIL. I nauseate walking; 'tis a country diversion. I loathe the country and everything that relates to it.

SIR WIL. Indeed! hah! Look ye, look ye, you do? Nay, 'tis like you

---

[6] the first two lines of a "Song" by Suckling. The three lines quoted by Millamant in her next two speeches complete the first stanza of the poem.

[7] "I beg your pardon."

[8] The Restoration and early eighteenth century considered the civilization of the Goths and "Gothic" art rude and barbarous.

[9] a provincial form of "fetched" (Perry). Although almost all recent editions read "sought", many eighteenth-century editions clearly print "fought". See O.E.D. under "fetch", where Congreve's line is cited.

and tan too!

may. Here are choice of pastimes here in town, as plays and the like; that must be confessed indeed.

MRS. MIL. *Ah, l'étourdi!*[10] I hate the town too.

SIR WIL. Dear heart, that's much. Hah! that you should hate 'em both! Hah! 'tis like you may; there are some can't relish the town, and others can't away with the country. 'Tis like you may be one of those, cousin.

MRS. MIL. Ha! ha! ha! Yes, 'tis like I may. You have nothing further to say to me?

SIR WIL. Not at present, cousin. 'Tis like when I have an opportunity to be more private, I may break my mind in some measure. I conjecture you partly guess – however, that's as time shall try; but spare to speak and spare to speed,[11] as they say.

MRS. MIL. If it is of no great importance, Sir Wilfull, you will oblige me to leave me; I have just now a little business —

SIR WIL. Enough, enough, cousin, yes, yes, all a case;[12] when you're disposed, when you're disposed. Now's as well as another time; and another time as well as now. All's one for that. Yes, yes, if your concerns call you, there's no haste; it will keep cold, as they say. Cousin, your servant. I think this door's locked.

MRS. MIL. You may go this way, sir.

SIR WIL. Your servant; then with your leave I'll return to my company.

MRS. MIL. Aye, aye; ha! ha! ha!
   "Like Phœbus sung the no less am'rous boy."[13]

Enter MIRABELL

MIR. "Like Daphne she, as lovely and as coy."[14]

Do you lock yourself up from me, to make my search more curious?[15] Or is this pretty artifice contrived, to signify that

---

[10] the silly fellow!

[11] proverbial, meaning, "If you hold your tongue, you won't get along in the world."

[12] idiomatic for "It's all the same."

[13] the third line of Waller's *Story of Phoebus and Daphne, Applied.*

[14] *Ibid.*, line 4. Mirabell completes the couplet begun by Millamant.

[15] difficult.

Mirabell v Millimant.

here the chase must end and my pursuit be crowned, for you can fly no further?

MRS. MIL. Vanity! No. I'll fly and be followed to the last moment. Though I am upon the very verge of matrimony, I expect you should solicit me as much as if I were wavering at the grate of a monastery, with one foot over the threshold. I'll be solicited to the very last, nay, and afterwards.

MIR. What, after the last?

MRS. MIL. Oh, I should think I was poor and had nothing to bestow, if I were reduced to an inglorious ease and freed from the agreeable fatigues of solicitation.

MIR. But do not you know that when favours are conferred upon instant and tedious solicitation, that they diminish in their value, and that both the giver loses the grace, and the receiver lessens his pleasure?

MRS. MIL. It may be in things of common application; but never sure in love. Oh, I hate a lover that can dare to think he draws a moment's air independent on the bounty of his mistress. There is not so impudent a thing in nature as the saucy look of an assured man, confident of success. The pedantic arrogance of a very husband has not so pragmatical[16] an air. Ah! I'll never marry, unless I am first made sure of my will and pleasure.

MIR. Would you have 'em both before marriage? Or will you be contented with the first now, and stay for the other till after grace?

MRS. MIL. Ah! don't be impertinent. My dear liberty, shall I leave thee? My faithful solitude, my darling contemplation, must I bid you then adieu? Ay-h adieu, my morning thoughts, agreeable wakings, indolent slumbers, all ye *douceurs*,[17] ye *sommeils du matin*,[18] adieu. I can't do't, 'tis more than impossible. Positively, Mirabell, I'll lie abed in a morning as long as I please.

MIR. Then I'll get up in a morning as early as I please.

My dear liberty.

[16] officious.
[17] sweet pleasures.
[18] morning sleeps.

MRS. MIL. Ah! idle creature, get up when you will. And d'ye hear, I won't be called names after I'm married; positively I won't be called names.

MIR. Names!

MRS. MIL. Aye, as wife, spouse, my dear, joy, jewel, love, sweetheart, and the rest of that nauseous cant, in which men and their wives are so fulsomely familiar; I shall never bear that. Good Mirabell, don't let us be familiar or fond, nor kiss before folks, like my Lady Fadler and Sir Francis; nor go to Hyde Park together the first Sunday in a new chariot, to provoke eyes and whispers, and then never be seen there together again, as if we were proud of one another the first week, and ashamed of one another ever after. Let us never visit together, nor go to a play together. But let us be very strange and well-bred; let us be as strange as if we had been married a great while, and as well-bred as if we were not married at all.

MIR. Have you any more conditions to offer? Hitherto your demands are pretty reasonable.

MRS. MIL. Trifles! As liberty to pay and receive visits to and from whom I please; to write and receive letters, without interrogatories[19] or wry faces on your part; to wear what I please, and choose conversation with regard only to my own taste; to have no obligation upon me to converse with wits that I don't like, because they are your acquaintance, or to be intimate with fools, because they may be your relations. Come to dinner when I please; dine in my dressing-room when I'm out of humour, without giving a reason. To have my closet inviolate; to be sole empress of my tea-table, which you must never presume to approach without first asking leave. And lastly, wherever I am, you shall always knock at the door before you come in. These articles subscribed, if I continue to endure you a little longer, I may by degrees dwindle into a wife.

MIR. Your bill of fare is something advanced in this latter ac-

[19] prying questions.

Mirabell's Provisos [handwritten in top margin]

count. Well, have I liberty to offer conditions, that when you are dwindled into a wife, I may not be beyond measure enlarged into a husband?

MRS. MIL. You have free leave. Propose your utmost; speak and spare not.

MIR. I thank you. *Imprimis*[20] then, I covenant[21] that your acquaintance be general; that you admit no sworn confidante, or intimate of your own sex; no she-friend to screen her affairs under your countenance, and tempt you to make trial of a mutual secrecy. No decoy-duck to wheedle[22] you a fop, scrambling[23] to the play in a mask; then bring you home in a pretended fright, when you think you shall be found out, and rail at me for missing the play, and disappointing the frolic which you had to pick me up and prove my constancy.

MRS. MIL. Detestable *imprimis*! I go to the play in a mask!

MIR. *Item*, I article that you continue to like your own face, as long as I shall; and while it passes current with me, that you endeavour not to new-coin it. To which end, together with all vizards for the day, I prohibit all masks for the night, made of oiled-skins and I know not what: hog's bones, hare's gall, pig-water, and the marrow of a roasted cat.[24] In short, I forbid all commerce with the gentlewoman in What-d'ye-call-it Court. *Item*, I shut my doors against all bawds with baskets, and pennyworths of muslin, china, fans, atlases,[25] etc. *Item*, when you shall be breeding —

MRS. MIL. Ah! name it not.

MIR. Which may be presumed, with a blessing on our endeavours —

MRS. MIL. Odious endeavours!

MIR. I denounce against all strait-lacing, squeezing for a shape, till you mould my boy's head like a sugar-loaf, and instead of a man child, make me father to a crooked billet.[26] Lastly,

[20] first.
[21] decree.
[22] procure.
[23] going without suitable dignity.

[24] All were ingredients in cosmetics.
[25] a kind of satin.
[26] stick.

to the dominion of the tea-table I submit, but with *proviso* that you exceed not in your province, but restrain yourself to native and simple tea-table drinks, as tea, chocolate, and coffee, as likewise to genuine and authorized tea-table talk, such as mending of fashions, spoiling reputations, railing at absent friends, and so forth; but that on no account you encroach upon the men's prerogative, and presume to drink healths, or toast fellows; for prevention of which, I banish all foreign forces, all auxiliaries to the tea-table, as orange-brandy, all aniseed, cinnamon, citron, and Barbadoes waters, together with ratafia and the most noble spirit of clary.[27] But for cowslip-wine, poppy-water, and all dormitives,[28] those I allow. These *provisos* admitted, in other things I may prove a tractable and complying husband.

MRS. MIL. O horrid *provisos*! filthy strong-waters! I toast fellows, odious men! I hate your odious *provisos*.

MIR. Then we're agreed. Shall I kiss your hand upon the contract? And here comes one to be a witness to the sealing of the deed.

Re-enter MRS. FAINALL

MRS. MIL. Fainall, what shall I do? Shall I have him? I think I must have him.

MRS. FAIN. Aye, aye, take him, take him; what should you do?

MRS. MIL. Well then – I'll take my death I'm in a horrid fright. Fainall, I shall never say it. Well – I think – I'll endure you.

MRS. FAIN. Fie! fie! have him, have him, and tell him so in plain terms; for I am sure you have a mind to him.

MRS. MIL. Are you? I think I have; and the horrid man looks as if he thought so too. Well, you ridiculous thing you, I'll have you; I won't be kissed, nor I won't be thanked. Here, kiss my hand, though. So, hold your tongue now; don't say a word.

MRS. FAIN. Mirabell, there's a necessity for your obedience; you

[27] All these "auxiliaries" were cordials made of brandy and variously flavoured.

[28] sedatives.

have neither time to talk nor stay. My mother is coming; and in my conscience, if she should see you, would fall into fits and maybe not recover, time enough to return to Sir Rowland, who, as Foible tells me, is in a fair way to succeed. Therefore spare your ecstasies for another occasion, and slip down the back-stairs, where Foible waits to consult you.

MRS. MIL. Aye, go, go. In the meantime I suppose you have said something to please me.

MIR. I am all obedience. *(Exit.)*

MRS. FAIN. Yonder Sir Wilfull's drunk, and so noisy that my mother has been forced to leave Sir Rowland to appease him; but he answers her only with singing and drinking. What they may have done by this time I know not; but Petulant and he were upon quarrelling as I came by.

MRS. MIL. Well, if Mirabell should not make a good husband, I am a lost thing; for I find I love him violently.

MRS. FAIN. So it seems; for you mind not what's said to you. If you doubt him, you had best take up with Sir Wilfull.

MRS. MIL. How can you name that superannuated lubber? foh!

Enter WITWOUD, *from drinking*

MRS. FAIN. So, is the fray made up, that you have left 'em?

WIT. Left 'em? I could stay no longer. I have laughed like ten christenings; I am tipsy with laughing. If I had stayed any longer I should have burst; I must have been let out and pieced in the sides like an unsized camlet.[29] Yes, yes, the fray is composed; my lady came in like a *noli prosequi*[30] and stopped the proceedings.

MRS. MIL. What was the dispute?

WIT. That's the jest; there was no dispute. They could neither of 'em speak for rage, and so fell a-sputtering at one another like two roasting apples.

Enter PETULANT, *drunk*

Now, Petulant? All's over, all's well? Gad, my head begins

[29] i.e., "like a piece of unstiffened satin".

[30] a legal term meaning that the plaintiff does not wish to continue the prosecution.

to whim it about.[31] Why dost thou not speak? Thou art both as drunk and as mute as a fish.

PET. Look you, Mrs. Millamant, if you can love me, dear nymph, say it, and that's the conclusion. Pass on, or pass off; that's all.

WIT. Thou hast uttered volumes, folios, in less than *decimo sexto*,[32] my dear Lacedemonian.[33] Sirrah, Petulant, thou art an epitomizer of words.[34]

PET. Witwoud, you are an annihilator of sense.

WIT. Thou art a retailer of phrases and dost deal in remnants of remnants, like a maker of pincushions; thou art in truth (metaphorically speaking) a speaker of shorthand.

PET. Thou art (without a figure) just one half of an ass, and Baldwin[35] yonder, thy half brother, is the rest. A Gemini[36] of asses split would make just four of you.

WIT. Thou dost bite, my dear mustard-seed; kiss me for that.

PET. Stand off! I'll kiss no more males. I have kissed your twin yonder in a humour of reconciliation, till he *(hiccup)* rises upon my stomach like a radish.

MRS. MIL. Eh! filthy creature! What was the quarrel?

PET. There was no quarrel; there might have been a quarrel.

WIT. If there had been words enow between 'em to have expressed provocation, they had gone together by the ears like a pair of castanets.

PET. You were the quarrel.

MRS. MIL. Me!

PET. If I have a humour to quarrel, I can make less matters conclude premises. If you are not handsome, what then, if I have a humour to prove it? If I shall have my reward, say so; if not, fight for your face the next time yourself. I'll go sleep.

WIT. Do, wrap thyself up like a wood-louse, and dream revenge;

---

[31] spin.

[32] a very tiny book; half the size of an octavo volume.

[33] Spartan. (The Spartans were known to be a very laconic people.)

[34] i.e., "You say much in few words."

[35] the name of the ass in the medieval tale *Reynard the Fox*.

[36] matched pair of twins. The constellation Gemini derives its name from the twin stars Castor and Pollux.

and hear me, if thou canst learn to write by to-morrow morning, pen me a challenge. I'll carry it for thee.

PET. Carry your mistress's monkey a spider! Go flea dogs, and read romances! I'll go to bed to my maid. *(Exit.)*

MRS. FAIN. He's horridly drunk. How came you all in this pickle?

WIT. A plot! a plot! to get rid of the knight. Your husband's advice; but he sneaked off.

Re-enter SIR WILFULL *drunk, and* LADY WISHFORT

LADY WISH. Out upon't, out upon't! At years of discretion, and comport yourself at this rantipole[37] rate!

SIR WIL. No offence, aunt.

LADY WISH. Offence? As I'm a person, I'm ashamed of you. Fogh! how you stink of wine! D'ye think my niece will ever endure such a borachio![38] you're an absolute borachio.

SIR WIL. Borachio!

LADY WISH. At a time when you should commence an amour, and put your best foot foremost —

SIR WIL. 'Sheart, an you grutch[39] me your liquor, make a bill. Give me more drink, and take my purse.

> *(sings)* "Prithee fill me the glass
> Till it laugh in my face,
> With ale that is potent and mellow;
> He that whines for a lass
> Is an ignorant ass,
> For a bumper has not its fellow."

But if you would have me marry my cousin, say the word, and I'll do't. Wilfull will do't; that's the word. Wilfull will do't; that's my crest. My motto I have forgot.

LADY WISH. My nephew's a little overtaken,[40] cousin, but 'tis with drinking your health. O' my word you are obliged to him.

---

[37] wild.

[38] Spanish for "wine-bag"; a drunkard. Cf. Shakespeare's Borachio in

Much Ado About Nothing.

[39] grudge.

[40] overcome by drink.

Sir W: very drunk

SIR WIL. *In vino veritas*,[41] aunt. If I drunk your health to-day, cousin, I am a borachio. But if you have a mind to be married, say the word, and send for the piper; Wilfull will do't. If not, dust it away, and let's have t'other round. Tony! Ods-heart, where's Tony? Tony's an honest fellow; but he spits after a bumper, and that's a fault.

> *(sings)* "We'll drink, and we'll never ha' done, boys,
>> Put the glass then around with the sun, boys;
> Let Apollo's example invite us;
>> For he's drunk every night,
>> And that makes him so bright,
> That he's able next morning to light us."

The sun's a good pimple,[42] an honest soaker; he has a cellar at your Antipodes.[43] If I travel, aunt, I touch at your Antipodes; your Antipodes are a good, rascally sort of topsy-turvy fellows. If I had a bumper, I'd stand upon my head and drink a health to 'em. A match or no match, cousin, with the hard name. Aunt, Wilfull will do't. If she has her maidenhead, let her look to't; if she has not, let her keep her own counsel in the meantime, and cry out at the nine months' end.

MRS. MIL. Your pardon, madam, I can stay no longer. Sir Wilfull grows very powerful. Egh! how he smells! I shall be overcome if I stay. Come, cousin.

> *(Exeunt* MRS. MILLAMANT *and* MRS. FAINALL.)

LADY WISH. Smells! he would poison a tallow-chandler[44] and his family! Beastly creature, I know not what to do with him. Travel, quotha! aye, travel, travel, get thee gone, get thee but far enough, to the Saracens, or the Tartars, or the Turks, for thou art not fit to live in a Christian commonwealth, thou beastly pagan!

SIR WIL. Turks, no; no Turks, aunt; your Turks are infidels,

---

[41] "In wine (there is) truth."
[42] drinking-companion.
[43] the opposite end of the world, or its inhabitants.
[44] a candle-maker.

and believe not in the grape. Your Mahometan, your Mussulman, is a dry stinkard.[45] No offence, aunt. My map says that your Turk is not so honest a man as your Christian. I cannot find by the map that your mufti[46] is orthodox; whereby it is a plain case that orthodox is a hard word, aunt, and *(hiccup)* Greek for claret.

(sings) "To drink is a Christian diversion,
    Unknown to the Turk or the Persian;
        Let Mahometan fools
        Live by heathenish rules,
    And be damn'd over tea-cups and coffee!
        But let British lads sing,
        Crown a health to the king,
    And a fig for your sultan and sophy!"[47]

Ah, Tony!

Enter FOIBLE, *and whispers* LADY WISHFORT

LADY WISH. *(aside to* FOIBLE) Sir Rowland impatient? Good lack! what shall I do with this beastly tumbril?[48] *(aloud)* Go lie down and sleep, you sot! or, as I'm a person, I'll have you bastinadoed[49] with broomsticks. Call up the wenches with broomsticks.

(Exit FOIBLE.)

SIR WIL. Ahey! Wenches, where are the wenches?

LADY WISH. Dear Cousin Witwoud, get him away, and you will bind me to you inviolably. I have an affair of moment that invades me with some precipitation. You will oblige me to all futurity.

WIT. Come, knight. Pox on him, I don't know what to say to him. Will you go to a cock-match?

---

[45] a miserable non-drinker. Mohammedans drink neither wine nor spirits.

[46] an expert in Mohammedan religious law.

[47] a former title of the Persian shah.

[48] dump-cart.

[49] beaten.

Language (Lady W.)

SIR WIL. With a wench, Tony? Is she a shake-bag,[50] Sirrah? Let me bite your cheek[51] for that.

WIT. Horrible! he has a breath like a bag-pipe! Aye, aye, come, will you march, my Salopian?[52] *Shropshireman*

SIR WIL. Lead on, little Tony; I'll follow thee, my Anthony, my Tantony. Sirrah, thou shalt be my Tantony, and I'll be thy pig.[53]

"And a fig for your sultan and sophy."

(Exit singing with WITWOUD.*)*

LADY WISH. This will never do. It will never make a match; at least before he has been abroad.

Enter WAITWELL, *disguised as* SIR ROWLAND

Dear Sir Rowland, I am confounded with confusion at the retrospection of my own rudeness! I have more pardons to ask than the Pope distributes in the Year of Jubilee.[54] But I hope, where there is likely to be so near an alliance, we may unbend the severity of decorum, and dispense with a little ceremony.

WAIT. My impatience, madam, is the effect of my transport; and till I have the possession of your adorable person, I am tantalized on the rack, and do but hang, madam, on the tenter[55] of expectation. *hook holding clon for stretching*

LADY WISH. You have excess of gallantry, Sir Rowland, and press things to a conclusion with a most prevailing vehemence. But a day or two for decency of marriage —

WAIT. For decency of funeral, madam! The delay will break my heart; or, if that should fail, I shall be poisoned. My nephew will get an inkling of my designs, and poison me — and I would willingly starve him before I die; I would gladly go out of the world with that satisfaction. That would

[50] a term in cock-fighting for a very game or sporting cock.
[51] i.e., "give you a big kiss".
[52] Shropshireman.
[53] In art and legend, the pig is associated with St. Anthony the Great.

[54] the year (approximately every twenty-fifth) in which the Pope grants general remission from the penal consequences of sin.
[55] a tenterhook.

be some comfort to me, if I could but live so long as to be revenged on that unnatural viper.

LADY WISH. Is he so unnatural, say you? Truly I would contribute much both to the saving of your life, and the accomplishment of your revenge. Not that I respect myself, though he has been a perfidious wretch to me.

WAIT. Perfidious to you!

LADY WISH. O Sir Rowland, the hours that he has died away at my feet, the tears that he has shed, the oaths that he has sworn, the palpitations that he has felt, the trances and the tremblings, the ardours and the ecstasies, the kneelings and the risings, the heart-heavings and the hand-gripings, the pangs and the pathetic regards of his protesting eyes! Oh, no memory can register!

WAIT. What, my rival! Is the rebel my rival? 'A dies.

LADY WISH. No, don't kill him at once, Sir Rowland; starve him gradually, inch by inch.

WAIT. I'll do't. In three weeks he shall be barefoot; in a month out at knees with begging an alms. He shall starve upward and upward, till he has nothing living but his head, and then go out in a stink like a candle's end upon a save-all.[56]

LADY WISH. Well, Sir Rowland, you have the way. You are no novice in the labyrinth of love; you have the clue. But as I am a person, Sir Rowland, you must not attribute my yielding to any sinister appetite, or indigestion of widowhood; nor impute my complacency to any lethargy of continence. I hope you do not think me prone to any iteration[57] of nuptials.

WAIT. Far be it from me —

LADY WISH. If you do, I protest I must recede, or think that I have made a prostitution of decorums; but in the vehemence of compassion, and to save the life of a person of so much importance —

---

[56] a device in a candle-stick to ensure that the candle will be completely burned.

[57] repetition. The sense seems to be that Lady Wishfort hopes Sir Rowland will not suspect her of a willingness to marry just any man.

WAIT. I esteem it so.

LADY WISH. Or else you wrong my condescension.

WAIT. I do not, I do not!

LADY WISH. Indeed you do.

WAIT. I do not, fair shrine of virtue!

LADY WISH. If you think the least scruple of carnality[58] was an ingredient —

WAIT. Dear madam, no. You are all camphire[59] and frankincense, all chastity and odour.

LADY WISH. Or that —

Re-enter FOIBLE

FOIBLE. Madam, the dancers are ready; and there's one with a letter, who must deliver it into your own hands.

LADY WISH. Sir Rowland, will you give me leave? Think favourably, judge candidly, and conclude you have found a person who would suffer racks in honour's cause, dear Sir Rowland, and will wait on you incessantly.[60]   *(Exit.)*

WAIT. Fie, fie! What a slavery have I undergone! Spouse, hast thou any cordial? I want spirits.

FOIB. What a washy[61] rogue art thou, to pant thus for a quarter of an hour's lying and swearing to a fine lady!

WAIT. Oh, she is the antidote to desire! Spouse, thou wilt fare the worse for't. I shall have no appetite to "iteration of nuptials" this eight-and-forty hours. By this hand I'd rather be a chair-man[62] in the dog-days[63] than act Sir Rowland till this time to-morrow!

Re-enter LADY WISHFORT, *with a letter*

LADY WISH. Call in the dancers. Sir Rowland, we'll sit, if you please, and see the entertainment. *(Dance.)* Now, with your permission, Sir Rowland, I will peruse my letter. I would open it in your presence, because I would not make you

---

[58] sensuality; lust.

[59] Camphor was believed to reduce sexual desire.

[60] immediately.

[61] weak.

[62] a sedan-chair carrier.

[63] the sultriest days of the summer, a period of about six weeks beginning in early July.

uneasy. If it should make you uneasy, I would burn it—speak if it does – but you may see, the superscription is like a woman's hand.

FOIB. *(aside to* WAITWELL*)* By Heaven! Mrs. Marwood's; I know it. My heart aches. Get it from her.

WAIT. A woman's hand? No, madam, that's no woman's hand; I see that already. That's somebody whose throat must be cut.

LADY WISH. Nay, Sir Rowland, since you give me a proof of your passion by your jealousy, I promise you I'll make a return, by a frank communication. You shall see it; we'll open it together. Look you here. *(reads)* "Madam, though unknown to you." Look you there; 'tis from nobody that I know. "I have that honour for your character, that I think myself obliged to let you know you are abused. He who pretends to be Sir Rowland is a cheat and a rascal." Oh, heavens! what's this?

FOIB. *(aside)* Unfortunate! all's ruined!

WAIT. How, how, let me see, let me see! *(reading)* "A rascal, and disguised and suborned[64] for that imposture." O villainy! O villainy! "by the contrivance of —"

LADY WISH. I shall faint, I shall die, oh!

FOIB. *(aside to* WAITWELL*)* Say 'tis your nephew's hand. Quickly, his plot, swear, swear it!

WAIT. Here's a villain! Madam, don't you perceive it? don't you see it?

LADY WISH. Too well, too well! I have seen too much.

WAIT. I told you at first I knew the hand. A woman's hand? The rascal writes a sort of a large hand, your Roman hand. I saw there was a throat to be cut presently. If he were my son, as he is my nephew, I'd pistol him!

FOIB. Oh, treachery! But are you sure, Sir Rowland, it is his writing?

WAIT. Sure? Am I here? Do I live? Do I love this pearl of India? I have twenty letters in my pocket from him in the same character.[65]

[64] bribed.   [65] handwriting.

Sir R. will send for Black Box.

LADY WISH. How!

FOIB. Oh, what luck it is, Sir Rowland, that you were present at this juncture! This was the business that brought Mr. Mirabell disguised to Madam Millamant this afternoon. I thought something was contriving, when he stole by me and would have hid his face.

LADY WISH. How, how! I heard the villain was in the house indeed; and now I remember, my niece went away abruptly, when Sir Wilfull was to have made his addresses.

FOIB. Then, then, madam, Mr. Mirabell waited for her in her chamber, but I would not tell your ladyship to discompose[66] you when you were to receive Sir Rowland.

WAIT. Enough, his date is short.

FOIB. No, good Sir Rowland, don't incur the law.

WAIT. Law? I care not for law. I can but die, and 'tis in a good cause. My lady shall be satisfied of my truth and innocence, though it cost me my life.

LADY WISH. No, dear Sir Rowland, don't fight; if you should be killed, I must never show my face; or hanged! Oh, consider my reputation, Sir Rowland! No, you shan't fight. I'll go in and examine my niece; I'll make her confess. I conjure you, Sir Rowland, by all your love, not to fight.

WAIT. I am charmed, madam; I obey. But some proof you must let me give you; I'll go for a black box, which contains the writings of my whole estate, and deliver that into your hands.

LADY WISH. Aye, dear Sir Rowland, that will be some comfort; bring the black box.

WAIT. And may I presume to bring a contract to be signed this night? May I hope so far?

LADY WISH. Bring what you will; but come alive, pray come alive. Oh, this is a happy discovery!

WAIT. Dead or alive I'll come, and married we will be in spite

---

[66] distress; upset.

of treachery; aye, and get an heir that shall defeat the last
remaining glimpse of hope in my abandoned nephew.
Come, my buxom widow.

    Ere long you shall substantial proof receive,
    That I'm an arrant knight —[67]

FOIB. *(aside)*   Or arrant[68] knave.

                        (Exeunt.)

[67] i.e., a true-knight-errant.
[68] downright.

*Between Acts Mar. has
tell Lady W. 1 plot. (P.233)*

Act V

[*Scene continues*]

Enter LADY WISHFORT *and* FOIBLE

LADY WISH. Out of my house, out of my house, thou viper! thou
serpent, that I have fostered! thou bosom traitress, that I
raised from nothing! Begone! begone! begone! go! go! That
I took from washing of old gauze and weaving of dead hair,
with a bleak blue nose, over a chafing-dish of starved embers, and dining behind a traverse rag,[1] in a shop no bigger
than a birdcage! Go, go! starve again, do, do!

FOIB. Dear madam, I'll beg your pardon on my knees.

LADY WISH. Away! out! out! Go set up for yourself again! Do,
drive a trade, do, with your three-pennyworth of small ware
flaunting upon a packthread, under a brandy-seller's bulk,[2]
or against a dead wall by a ballad-monger! Go, hang out an
old frisoneer-gorget,[3] with a yard of yellow colberteen[4]
again. Do; an old gnawed mask, two rows of pins, and a
child's fiddle; a glass necklace with the beads broken, and
a quilted nightcap with one ear. Go, go, drive a trade!
These were your commodities, you treacherous trull! this
was the merchandise you dealt in, when I took you into
my house, placed you next myself, and made you gover-
nante of my whole family! You have forgot this, have you,
now you have feathered your nest?

FOIB. No, no, dear madam. Do but hear me; have but a moment's

---

[1] a curtain or hanging that serves as
a screen.

[2] a booth where brandy is sold.

[3] a kind of wimple made of coarse

woollen cloth.

[4] a French lace of inferior quality.
The name derives from Colbert, a
minister of Louis XIV.

patience. I'll confess all. Mr. Mirabell seduced me; I am not the first that he has wheedled with his dissembling tongue. Your ladyship's own wisdom has been deluded by him; then how should I, a poor ignorant, defend myself? O madam, if you knew but what he promised me, and how he assured me your ladyship should come to no damage! Or else the wealth of the Indies should not have bribed me to conspire against so good, so sweet, so kind a lady as you have been to me.

LADY WISH. "No damage?" What, to betray me, to marry me to a cast-servingman?[5] to make me a receptacle, an hospital for a decayed pimp? "No damage?" O thou frontless[6] impudence, more than a big-bellied actress!

FOIB. Pray do but hear me, madam; he could not marry your ladyship, madam. No indeed; his marriage was to have been void in law, for he was married to me first, to secure your ladyship. He could not have bedded your ladyship; for if he had consummated with your ladyship, he must have run the risk of the law and been put upon his clergy.[7] Yes indeed; I inquired of the law in that case before I would meddle or make.[8]

LADY WISH. What, then I have been your property, have I? I have been convenient to you, it seems! While you were catering for Mirabell, I have been broker[9] for you? What, have you made a passive bawd of me? This exceeds all precedent; I am brought to fine uses, to become a botcher[10] of second-hand marriages between Abigails[11] and Andrews![12] I'll couple you! Yes, I'll baste you together, you and your Philander![13] I'll Duke's-Place[14] you, as I'm a per-

---

[5] a discharged servant.

[6] shameless.

[7] forced to plead benefit of clergy. Clergy (and, later, people who could read or write) could claim exemption from punishment imposed by a secular court.

[8] a colloquialism for "get mixed up in this business".

[9] marriage-broker.

[10] a maker or mender.

[11] a maid-servant in Beaumont and Fletcher's play *The Scornful Lady*.

[12] a man-servant in Fletcher and Massinger's *The Elder Brother*.

[13] the lover in Beaumont and Fletcher's *The Laws of Candy*.

[14] See Act I, note 11.

son! Your turtle is in custody already; you shall coo in the
same cage, if there be constable or warrant in the parish.

(Exit.)

FOIB. Oh, that ever I was born! Oh, that I was ever married! A
bride! aye, I shall be a Bridewell-bride.[15] Oh!

Enter MRS. FAINALL

MRS. FAIN. Poor Foible, what's the matter?

FOIB. O madam, my lady's gone for a constable. I shall be had
to a justice, and put to Bridewell to beat hemp. Poor Waitwell's gone to prison already.

MRS. FAIN. Have a good heart, Foible; Mirabell's gone to give
security for him. This is all Marwood's and my husband's
doing.

FOIB. Yes, yes, I know it, madam; she was in my lady's closet,
and overheard all that you said to me before dinner. She
sent the letter to my lady; and that missing effect, Mr. Fainall laid this plot to arrest Waitwell, when he pretended to
go for the papers; and in the meantime Mrs. Marwood
declared all to my lady.

MRS. FAIN. Was there no mention made of me in the letter? My
mother does not suspect my being in the confederacy? I
fancy Marwood has not told her, though she has told my
husband.

FOIB. Yes, madam; but my lady did not see that part. We stifled
the letter before she read so far. Has that mischievous devil
told Mr. Fainall of your ladyship then?

MRS. FAIN. Aye, all's out, my affair with Mirabell, everything
discovered. This is the last day of our living together; that's
my comfort.

FOIB. Indeed, madam, and so 'tis a comfort if you knew all. He
has been even with your ladyship; which I could have told
you long enough since, but I love to keep peace and quiet-
ness by my good will. I had rather bring friends together
than set 'em at distance. But Mrs. Marwood and he are
nearer related than ever their parents thought for.

[15] Bridewell was a house of correction.

MRS. FAIN. Sayest thou so, Foible? Canst thou prove this?

FOIB. I can take my oath of it, madam; so can Mrs. Mincing. We have had many a fair word from Madam Marwood, to conceal something that passed in our chamber one evening when you were at Hyde Park and we were thought to have gone a-walking; but we went up unawares, though we were sworn to secrecy too. Madam Marwood took a book and swore us upon it, but it was but a book of poems. So long as it was not a Bible oath, we may break it with a safe conscience.

MRS. FAIN. This discovery is the most opportune thing I could wish. Now, Mincing?

Enter MINCING

MIN. My lady[16] would speak with Mrs. Foible, mem. Mr. Mirabell is with her; he has set your spouse at liberty, Mrs. Foible, and would have you hide yourself in my lady's closet till my old lady's anger is abated. Oh, my old lady is in a perilous passion at something Mr. Fainall has said; he swears, and my old lady cries. There's a fearful hurricane, I vow. He says, mem, how that he'll have my lady's fortune made over to him, or he'll be divorced.

MRS. FAIN. Does your lady or Mirabell know that?

MIN. Yes, mem; they have sent me to see if Sir Wilfull be sober and to bring him to them. My lady is resolved to have him, I think, rather than lose such a vast sum as six thousand pound. Oh, come, Mrs. Foible, I hear my old lady.

MRS. FAIN. Foible, you must tell Mincing that she must prepare to vouch[17] when I call her.

FOIB. Yes, yes, madam.

MIN. O yes, mem, I'll vouch anything for your ladyship's service, be what it will.

(Exeunt MINCING *and* FOIBLE.*)*

Re-enter LADY WISHFORT, *with* MRS. MARWOOD

---

[16] i.e., Millamant.
[17] testify.

LADY WISH. O my dear friend, how can I enumerate the benefits that I have received from your goodness? To you I owe the timely discovery of the false vows of Mirabell; to you I owe the detection of the imposter, Sir Rowland. And now you are become an intercessor with my son-in-law, to save the honour of my house, and compound for the frailties of my daughter. Well, friend, you are enough to reconcile me to the bad world, or else I would retire to deserts and solitudes, and feed harmless sheep by groves and purling streams. Dear Marwood, let us leave the world, and retire by ourselves and be shepherdesses.

MRS. MAR. Let us first dispatch the affair in hand, madam. We shall have leisure to think of retirement afterwards. Here is one who is concerned in the treaty.

LADY WISH. O daughter, daughter, is it possible thou shouldst be my child, bone of my bone, and flesh of my flesh, and, as I may say, another me, and yet transgress the most minute particle of severe virtue? Is it possible you should lean aside to iniquity, who have been cast in the direct mould of virtue? I have not only been a mould but a pattern for you, and a model for you, after you were brought into the world.

MRS. FAIN. I don't understand your ladyship.

LADY WISH. Not understand? Why, have you not been naught?[18] have you not been sophisticated?[19] Not understand? Here I am ruined to compound[20] for your caprices and your cuckoldoms. I must pawn my plate and my jewels, and ruin my niece, and all little enough.

MRS. FAIN. I am wronged and abused, and so are you. 'Tis a false accusation, as false as hell, as false as your friend there, aye, or your friend's friend, my false husband.

MRS. MAR. My friend, Mrs. Fainall? Your husband my friend? What do you mean?

MRS. FAIN. I know what I mean, madam, and so do you; and so shall the world at a time convenient.

---

[18] naughty; wicked.
[19] corrupted; debauched.

[20] compensate. Lady Wishfort refers to Mr. Fainall's blackmailing tactics.

MRS. MAR. I am sorry to see you so passionate, madam. More temper[21] would look more like innocence. But I have done. I am sorry my zeal to serve your ladyship and family should admit of misconstruction, or make me liable to affronts. You will pardon me, madam, if I meddle no more with an affair in which I am not personally concerned.

LADY WISH. O dear friend, I am so ashamed that you should meet with such returns! *(to* MRS. FAINALL*)* You ought to ask pardon on your knees, ungrateful creature; she deserves more from you than all your life can accomplish. *(to* MRS. MARWOOD*)* Oh, don't leave me destitute in this perplexity! No, stick to me, my good genius.

MRS. FAIN. I tell you, madam, you're abused. Stick to you? Aye, like a leech, to suck your best blood; she'll drop off when she's full. Madam, you shan't pawn a bodkin,[22] nor part with a brass counter,[23] in composition for me. I defy 'em all. Let 'em prove their aspersions; I know my own innocence, and dare stand a trial. *(Exit.)*

LADY WISH. Why, if she should be innocent, if she should be wronged after all, ha? I don't know what to think; and, I promise you, her education has been unexceptionable.[24] I may say it; for I chiefly made it my own care to initiate her very infancy in the rudiments of virtue, and to impress upon her tender years a young odium[25] and aversion to the very sight of men. Aye, friend, she would ha' shrieked if she had but seen a man, till she was in her teens. As I'm a person 'tis true. She was never suffered to play with a male child, though but in coats; nay, her very babies[26] were of the feminine gender. Oh, she never looked a man in the face but her own father, or the chaplain, and him we made a shift[27] to put upon her for a woman, by the help of his long garments and his sleek face, till she was going in her fifteen.[28]

---

[21] temperateness.
[22] needle, or hairpin.
[23] a farthing.
[24] exemplary.

[25] dislike.
[26] dolls.
[27] devised a plan.
[28] into her fifteenth year.

MRS. MAR. 'Twas much she should be deceived so long.

LADY WISH. I warrant you, or she would never have borne to have been catechized by him; and have heard his long lectures against singing and dancing, and such debaucheries, and going to filthy plays and profane music-meetings, where the lewd trebles squeak nothing but bawdy, and the basses roar blasphemy. Oh, she would have swooned at the sight or name of an obscene play-book! And can I think, after all this, that my daughter can be naught? What, a whore? and thought it excommunication to set her foot within the door of a playhouse! O dear friend, I can't believe it, no, no! As she says, let him prove it, let him prove it.

MRS. MAR. Prove it, madam? What, and have your name prostituted in a public court? yours and your daughter's reputation worried at the bar by a pack of bawling lawyers? To be ushered in with an *Oyez*[29] of scandal, and have your case opened by an old fumbling lecher in a quoif[30] like a man-midwife; to bring your daughter's infamy to light; to be a theme for legal punsters and quibblers by the statute, and become a jest against a rule of court, where there is no precedent for a jest in any record, not even in Doomsday Book;[31] to discompose the gravity of the bench, and provoke naughty interrogatories in more naughty law Latin, while the good judge, tickled with the proceeding, simpers under a grey beard, and fidges[32] off and on his cushion as if he had swallowed cantharides,[33] or sat upon cow-itch![34]

LADY WISH. Oh, 'tis very hard!

MRS. MAR. And then to have my young revellers of the Temple[35] take notes, like prentices at a conventicle;[36] and after, talk

---

[29] the court-crier's call for silence.

[30] coif, the lawyer's white cap.

[31] a record of a survey of the lands of England made by order of William the Conqueror.

[32] fidgets.

[33] a powder made from dried beetles and used medicinally as a skin irritant.

[34] cowage, a plant which causes intense itching.

[35] the courts of law.

[36] It was customary for a Puritan master to require his apprentice to take notes of the Sunday sermon in the meeting-house (conventicle).

it over again in Commons,[37] or before drawers in an eating-house.

LADY WISH. Worse and worse!

MRS. MAR. Nay, this is nothing; if it would end here, 'twere well. But it must, after this, be consigned by the shorthand writers to the public press; and from thence be transferred to the hands, nay into the throats and lungs of hawkers,[38] with voices more licentious than the loud flounder-man's.[39] And this you must hear till you are stunned; nay, you must hear nothing else for some days.

LADY WISH. Oh, 'tis insupportable! No, no, dear friend; make it up, make it up; aye, aye, I'll compound. I'll give up all, myself and my all, my niece and her all, anything, everything for composition.

MRS. MAR. Nay, madam, I advise nothing; I only lay before you, as a friend, the inconveniencies which perhaps you have overseen. Here comes Mr. Fainall; if he will be satisfied to huddle up all in silence, I shall be glad. You must think I would rather congratulate than condole with you.

Enter FAINALL

LADY WISH. Aye, aye, I do not doubt it, dear Marwood; no, no, I do not doubt it.

FAIN. Well, madam, I have suffered myself to be overcome by the importunity of this lady, your friend, and am content you shall enjoy your own proper estate during life, on condition you oblige yourself never to marry, under such penalty as I think convenient.

LADY WISH. Never to marry?

FAIN. No more Sir Rowlands; the next imposture may not be so timely detected.

MRS. MAR. That condition, I dare answer, my lady will consent to, without difficulty; she has already but too much experienced the perfidiousness of men. Besides, madam, when we

[37] the dining-hall.
[38] pedlars.
[39] an actual flounder-seller, well known to the Londoners of the day, and noted for his "loud, but not unmusical" voice.

retire to our pastoral solitude, we shall bid adieu to all other thoughts.

LADY WISH. Aye, that's true; but in case of necessity, as of health, or some such emergency —

FAIN. Oh, if you are prescribed marriage, you shall be considered; I will only reserve to myself the power to choose for you. If your physic be wholesome, it matters not who is your apothecary. Next, my wife shall settle on me the remainder of her fortune, not made over already; and for her maintenance depend entirely on my discretion.

LADY WISH. This is most inhumanly savage, exceeding the barbarity of a Muscovite[40] husband.

FAIN. I learned it from his Czarish majesty's retinue,[41] in a winter evening's conference over brandy and pepper, amongst other secrets of matrimony and policy, as they are at present practised in the northern hemisphere. But this must be agreed unto, and that positively. Lastly, I will be endowed, in right of my wife, with that six thousand pound, which is the moiety of Mrs. Millamant's fortune in your possession; and which she has forfeited (as will appear by the last will and testament of your deceased husband, Sir Jonathan Wishfort) by her disobedience in contracting herself against your consent or knowledge, and by refusing the offered match with Sir Wilfull Witwoud, which you, like a careful aunt, had provided for her.

LADY WISH. My nephew was *non compos*,[42] and could not make his addresses.

FAIN. I come to make demands. I'll hear no objections.

LADY WISH. You will grant me time to consider?

FAIN. Yes, while the instrument[43] is drawing, to which you must set your hand till more sufficient deeds can be perfected; which I will take care shall be done with all possible speed. In the meanwhile I will go for the said instrument, and

---

[40] Russian.
[41] referring to Peter the Great's visit to England in 1697.
[42] i.e., *non compos mentis*, not in his right mind.
[43] formal agreement.

till my return you may balance this matter in your own
discretion.   *(Exit.)*

LADY WISH. This insolence is beyond all precedent, all parallel;
must I be subject to this merciless villain?

MRS. MAR. 'Tis severe indeed, madam, that you should smart for
your daughter's wantonness.

LADY WISH. 'Twas against my consent that she married this bar-
barian, but she would have him, though her year[44] was not
out. Ah! her first husband, my son Languish, would not
have carried it thus. Well, that was my choice, this is hers;
she is matched now with a witness.[45] I shall be mad! Dear
friend, is there no comfort for me? must I live to be confiscated at this rebel-rate?[46] Here come two more of my Egyp-
tian plagues[47] too.

Enter MRS. MILLAMANT *and* SIR WILFULL WITWOUD

SIR. WIL. Aunt, your servant.

LADY WISH. Out, caterpillar, call not me aunt! I know thee not!

SIR WIL. I confess I have been a little in disguise,[48] as they say.
'Sheart! and I'm sorry for't. What would you have? I hope
I committed no offence, aunt, and if I did, I am willing to
make satisfaction; and what can a man say fairer? If I have
broke anything, I'll pay for't, an it cost a pound. And so
let that content for what's past, and make no more words.
For what's to come, to pleasure you I'm willing to marry my
cousin. So pray let's all be friends; she and I are agreed
upon the matter before a witness.

LADY WISH. How's this, dear niece? Have I any comfort? Can
this be true?

MRS. MIL. I am content to be a sacrifice to your repose, madam;
and to convince you that I had no hand in the plot, as you
were misinformed, I have laid my commands on Mirabell
to come in person, and be a witness that I give my hand to

[44] period of mourning for her first
husband.

[45] colloquialism: "with a vengeance".

[46] The sense is: "Must I live to see
my property and fortune confiscated

in this piratical fashion?"

[47] referring to the plagues of Egypt
recorded in Exodus, 7ff.

[48] drunk.

this flower of knighthood; and for the contract that passed
between Mirabell and me, I have obliged him to make a
resignation of it in your ladyship's presence. He is without,
and waits your leave for admittance.

LADY WISH. Well, I'll swear I am something revived at this testi-
mony of your obedience; but I cannot admit that traitor.
I fear I cannot fortify myself to support his appearance. He
is as terrible to me as a Gorgon;[49] if I see him, I fear I shall
turn to stone, petrify incessantly.

MRS. MIL. If you disoblige him, he may resent your refusal, and
insist upon the contract still. Then 'tis the last time he will
be offensive to you.

LADY WISH. Are you sure it will be the last time? If I were sure
of that! Shall I never see him again?

MRS. MIL. Sir Wilfull, you and he are to travel together, are you
not?

SIR WIL. 'Sheart, the gentleman's a civil gentleman, aunt; let him
come in. Why, we are sworn brothers and fellow-travellers.
We are to be Pylades and Orestes,[50] he and I. He is to be
my interpreter in foreign parts. He has been overseas once
already; and with *proviso* that I marry my cousin, will cross
'em once again, only to bear me company. 'Sheart, I'll call
him in. An I set on't once, he shall come in; and see who'll
hinder him.   (*Goes to the door and hems.*)

MRS. MAR. This is precious fooling, if it would pass; but I'll
know the bottom of it.

LADY WISH. O dear Marwood, you are not going?

MRS. MAR. Not far, madam; I'll return immediately.

(*Exit.*)

Re-enter SIR WILFULL *with* MIRABELL

SIR WIL. Look up, man, I'll stand by you; 'sbud and she do
frown, she can't kill you; besides, harkee, she dare not

---

[49] any one of the three sisters in
Greek legend (Medusa was one)
whose hair was wreathed with snakes,
and whose glance turned the beholder
to stone.

[50] In Greek legend Pylades was the
loyal and trusted friend of Orestes,
son of Agamemnon and brother of
Electra.

frown desperately, because her face is none of her own. 'Sheart, an she should, her forehead would wrinkle like the coat of a cream-cheese; but mum for that, fellow-traveller.

MIR. If a deep sense of the many injuries I have offered to so good a lady, with a sincere remorse and a hearty contrition, can but obtain the least glance of compassion, I am too happy. Ah, madam, there was a time! But let it be forgotten. I confess I have deservedly forfeited the high place I once held, of sighing at your feet. Nay, kill me not, by turning from me in disdain. I come not to plead for favour; nay, not for pardon. I am a suppliant only for pity. I am going where I shall never behold you more.

SIR WIL. How, fellow-traveller! You shall go by yourself then.

MIR. Let me be pitied first, and afterwards forgotten. I ask no more.

SIR WIL. By'r lady, a very reasonable request, and will cost you nothing, aunt. Come, come, forgive and forget, aunt; why, you must, an you are a Christian.

MIR. Consider, madam, in reality you could not receive much prejudice; it was an innocent device, though I confess it had a face of guiltiness. It was at most an artifice which love contrived, and errors which love produces have ever been accounted venial. At least think it is punishment enough that I have lost what in my heart I hold most dear, that to your cruel indignation I have offered up this beauty, and with her my peace and quiet; nay, all my hopes of future comfort.

SIR WIL. An he does not move me, would I may never be o' the quorum![51] An it were not as good a deed as to drink, to give her to him again, I would I might never take shipping! Aunt, if you don't forgive quickly, I shall melt, I can tell you that. My contract went no farther than a little mouth-glue, and that's hardly dry; one doleful sigh more from my fellow-traveller, and 'tis dissolved.

LADY WISH. Well, nephew, upon your account – ah, he has a false insinuating tongue! Well, sir, I will stifle my just re-

---

[51] an indispensable member of the legal bench.

sentment at my nephew's request. I will endeavour what I can to forget, but on *proviso* that you resign the contract with my niece immediately.

MIR. It is in writing, and with papers of concern; but I have sent my servant for it, and will deliver it to you, with all acknowledgments for your transcendent goodness.

LADY WISH. *(aside)* Oh, he has witchcraft in his eyes and tongue! When I did not see him, I could have bribed a villain to his assassination; but his appearance rakes the embers which have so long lain smothered in my breast.

Re-enter FAINALL *and* MRS. MARWOOD

FAIN. Your date of deliberation, madam, is expired. Here is the instrument; are you prepared to sign?

LADY WISH. If I were prepared, I am not empowered. My niece exerts a lawful claim, having matched herself by my direction to Sir Wilfull.

FAIN. That sham is too gross to pass on me, though 'tis imposed on you, madam.

MRS. MIL. Sir, I have given my consent.

MIR. And, sir, I have resigned my pretensions.

SIR WIL. And, sir, I assert my right; and will maintain it in defiance of you, sir, and of your instrument. 'Sheart, an you talk of an instrument, sir, I have an old fox[52] by my thigh shall hack your instrument of ram vellum[53] to shreds, sir! It shall not be sufficient for a *mittimus*[54] or a tailor's measure.[55] Therefore withdraw your instrument, sir, or, by'r lady, I shall draw mine.

LADY WISH. Hold, nephew, hold!

MRS. MIL. Good Sir Wilfull, respite[56] your valour.

FAIN. Indeed? Are you provided of your guard, with your single beef-eater[57] there? But I'm prepared for you, and insist upon my first proposal. You shall submit your own estate

---

[52] sword.
[53] parchment (made from sheepskin).
[54] legal term for a warrant of commitment to prison.
[55] Tailors' measurements were recorded on parchment.
[56] control.
[57] a guard of the Tower of London.

to my management and absolutely make over my wife's to my sole use, as pursuant to the purport and tenor of this other covenant. *(to* MRS. MILLAMANT*)* I suppose, madam, your consent is not requisite in this case; nor, Mr. Mirabell, your resignation; nor, Sir Wilfull, your right. You may draw your fox if you please, sir, and make a Bear-Garden[58] flourish somewhere else; for here it will not avail. – This, my Lady Wishfort, must be subscribed, or your darling daughter's turned adrift, like a leaky hulk, to sink or swim, as she and the current of this lewd town can agree.

LADY WISH. Is there no means, no remedy to stop my ruin? Ungrateful wretch! dost thou not owe thy being, thy subsistence, to my daughter's fortune?

FAIN. I'll answer you when I have the rest of it in my possession.

MIR. *(to* LADY WISHFORT*)* But that you would not accept of a remedy from my hands – I own I have not deserved you should owe any obligation to me; or else perhaps I could advise —

LADY WISH. Oh, what? what? to save me and my child from ruin, from want, I'll forgive all that's past; nay, I'll consent to anything to come, to be delivered from this tyranny.

MIR. Aye, madam, but that is too late; my reward is intercepted. You have disposed of her who only could have made me a compensation for all my services. But be it as it may, I am resolved I'll serve you; you shall not be wronged in this savage manner.

LADY WISH. How! Dear Mr. Mirabell, can you be so generous at last? But it is not possible. Harkee, I'll break my nephew's match; you shall have my niece yet, and all her fortune, if you can but save me from this imminent danger.

MIR. Will you? I take you at your word. I ask no more. I must have leave for two criminals to appear.

LADY WISH. Aye, aye; anybody, anybody!

MIR. Foible is one, and a penitent.

---

[58] Bear-baiting was a popular amusement in the London of the day, and the gardens in which it took place were notorious for brawls and rowdy behaviour.

Re-enter MRS. FAINALL, FOIBLE, *and* MINCING

MRS. MAR. *(to* FAINALL) O my shame! *(*MIRABELL *and* LADY WISH-FORT *go to* MRS. FAINALL *and* FOIBLE.) These corrupt things are brought hither to expose me.

FAIN. If it must all come out, why let 'em know it; 'tis but the way of the world. That shall not urge me to relinquish or abate one tittle of my terms; no, I will insist the more.

FOIB. Yes indeed, madam; I'll take my Bible-oath of it.

MIN. And so will I, mem.

LADY WISH. O Marwood. Marwood, art thou false? my friend deceive me? Hast thou been a wicked accomplice with that profligate man?

MRS. MAR. Have you so much ingratitude and injustice, to give credit against your friend to the aspersions of two such mercenary trulls?

MIN. "Mercenary," mem? I scorn your words. 'Tis true we found you and Mr. Fainall in the blue garret; by the same token, you swore us to secrecy upon Messalina's poems.[59] "Mercenary?" No, if we would have been mercenary, we should have held our tongues; you would have bribed us sufficiently.

FAIN. Go, you are an insignificant thing! Well, what are you the better for this? Is this Mr. Mirabell's expedient? I'll be put off no longer. You thing, that was a wife, shall smart for this! I will not leave thee wherewithal to hide thy shame; your body shall be naked as your reputation.

MRS. FAIN. I despise you, and defy your malice! You have aspersed me wrongfully. I have proved your falsehood. Go, you and your treacherous – I will not name it, but starve together, perish!

FAIN. Not while you are worth a groat,[60] indeed, my dear. Madam, I'll be fooled no longer.

---

[59] Mincing means a volume of "miscellaneous" poems. Her mistake presents an amusing irony, since Messalina, the wife of the Roman Emperor Claudius, was notorious for her avarice, treachery, and dissoluteness.

[60] an old silver coin worth about fourpence.

Mrs Fainall had given fortune in trust to Mirabell.

LADY WISH. Ah, Mr. Mirabell, this is small comfort, the detection of this affair.

MIR. Oh, in good time. Your leave for the other offender and penitent to appear, madam.

Enter WAITWELL, *with a box of writings*

LADY WISH. O Sir Rowland! Well, rascal?

WAIT. What your ladyship pleases. I have brought the black box at last, madam.

MIR. Give it me. Madam, you remember your promise.

LADY WISH. Aye, dear sir.

MIR. Where are the gentlemen?

WAIT. At hand, sir, rubbing their eyes; just risen from sleep.

FAIN. 'Sdeath, what's this to me? I'll not wait your private concerns.

Enter PETULANT *and* WITWOUD

PET. How now? What's the matter? Whose hand's out?[61]

WIT. Heyday! what, are you all got together, like players at the end of the last act?

MIR. You may remember, gentlemen, I once requested your hands as witnesses to a certain parchment.

WIT. Aye, I do; my hand I remember. Petulant set his mark.

MIR. You wrong him, his name is fairly written, as shall appear. You do not remember, gentlemen, anything of what that parchment contained? *(Undoing the box.)*

WIT. No.

PET. Not I. I writ. I read nothing.

MIR. Very well; now you shall know. Madam, your promise.

LADY WISH. Aye, aye, sir, upon my honour.

MIR. Mr. Fainall, it is now time that you should know that your lady, while she was at her own disposal, and before you had by your insinuations wheedled her out of a pretended settlement of the greatest part of her fortune —

FAIN. Sir! pretended!

MIR. Yes, sir. I say that this lady, while a widow, having it seems

[61] "What is the trouble?"

received some cautions respecting your inconstancy and tyranny of temper, which from her own partial opinion and fondness of you she could never have suspected – she did, I say, by the wholesome advice of friends and of sages learned in the laws of this land, deliver this same as her act and deed to me in trust, and to the uses within mentioned. You may read if you please *(holding out the parchment)*, though perhaps what is written on the back may serve your occasions.

FAIN. Very likely, sir. What's here? Damnation! *(reads)* "A deed of conveyance of the whole estate real of Arabella Languish, widow, in trust to Edward Mirabell." Confusion!

MIR. Even so, sir; 'tis the way of the world, sir, of the widows of the world. I suppose this deed may bear an elder[62] date than what you have obtained from your lady?

FAIN. Perfidious fiend! then thus I'll be revenged.

(Offers to run at MRS. FAINALL.*)*

SIR WIL. Hold, sir! Now you may make your Bear-Garden flourish somewhere else, sir.

FAIN. Mirabell, you shall hear of this, sir; be sure you shall. *(to* SIR WILFULL*)* Let me pass, oaf! *(Exit.)*

MRS. FAIN. *(to* MRS. MARWOOD*)* Madam, you seem to stifle your resentment; you had better give it vent.

MRS. MAR. Yes, it shall have vent, and to your confusion; or I'll perish in the attempt. *(Exit.)*

LADY WISH. O daughter, daughter, 'tis plain thou hast inherited thy mother's prudence.

MRS. FAIN. Thank Mr. Mirabell, a cautious friend, to whose advice all is owing.

LADY WISH. Well, Mr. Mirabell, you have kept your promise, and I must perform mine. First, I pardon, for your sake, Sir Rowland there, and Foible. The next thing is to break the matter to my nephew, and how to do that —

MIR. For that, madam, give yourself no trouble; let me have your consent. Sir Wilfull is my friend; he has had compas-

---

[62] earlier.

sion upon lovers, and generously engaged a volunteer[63] in this action, for our service, and now designs to prosecute his travels.

SIR WIL. 'Sheart, aunt, I have no mind to marry. My cousin's a fine lady, and the gentleman loves her, and she loves him, and they deserve one another; my resolution is to see foreign parts. I have set on't, and when I'm set on't, I must do't. And if these two gentlemen would travel too, I think they may be spared.

PET. For my part, I say little; I think things are best off or on.[64]

WIT. Egad, I understand nothing of the matter; I'm in a maze yet, like a dog in a dancing-school.

LADY WISH. Well, sir, take her, and with her all the joy I can give you.

MRS. MIL. Why does not the man take me? Would you have me give myself to you over again?

MIR. Aye, and over and over again; *(Kisses her hand.)* for I would have you as often as possibly I can. Well, Heaven grant I love you not too well; that's all my fear.

SIR WIL. 'Sheart, you'll have time enough to toy[65] after you're married; or if you will toy now, let us have a dance in the meantime, that we who are not lovers may have some other employment besides looking on.

MIR. With all my heart, dear Sir Wilfull. What shall we do for music?

FOIB. Oh, sir, some that were provided for Sir Rowland's entertainment are yet within call.

(A dance.)

LADY WISH. As I am a person, I can hold out no longer. I have wasted my spirits so to-day already that I am ready to sink under the fatigue; and I cannot but have some fears upon me yet that my son Fainall will pursue some desperate course.

[63] i.e., "as a volunteer".
[64] one way or the other.
[65] play.

MIR. Madam, disquiet not yourself on that account; to my knowledge his circumstances are such, he must of force[66] comply. For my part, I will contribute all that in me lies to a reunion; in the meantime, madam, *(to* MRS. FAINALL*)* let me before these witnesses restore to you this deed of trust; it may be a means, well-managed, to make you live easily together.

> From hence let those be warn'd, who mean to wed,
> Lest mutual falsehood stain the bridal bed;
> For each deceiver to his cost may find,
> That marriage-frauds too oft are paid in kind.

(Exeunt omnes.)

[66] of necessity.

Epilogue

After our Epilogue this crowd dismisses,
I'm thinking how this play'll be pull'd to pieces.
But pray consider, ere you doom its fall,
How hard a thing 'twould be to please you all.
There are some critics so with spleen diseas'd,   5
They scarcely come inclining to be pleas'd;
And sure he must have more than mortal skill,
Who pleases any one against his will.
Then, all bad poets we are sure are foes,
And how their number's swell'd the town well knows;   10
In shoals I've mark'd 'em judging in the pit;
Though they're on no pretence for judgment fit,
But that they have been damn'd for want of wit.
Since when they, by their own offences taught,
Set up for spies on plays, and finding fault.   15
Others there are whose malice we'd prevent;
Such who watch plays with scurrilous intent
To mark out who by characters are meant.
And though no perfect likeness they can trace,
Yet each pretends to know the copy'd face.   20
These with false glosses[1] feed their own ill nature,
And turn to libel what was meant a satire.[2]
May such malicious fops this fortune find,
To think themselves alone the fools design'd;

---

[1] marginal notes.
[2] According to seventeenth-century pronunciation, "nature" and "satire" were good rhymes.

If any are so arrogantly vain,   25
To think they singly can support a scene,
And furnish fool enough to entertain.
For well the learn'd and the judicious know
That satire scorns to stoop so meanly low
As any one abstracted[3] fop to show.   30
For, as when painters form a matchless face,
They from each fair one catch some diff'rent grace;
And shining features in one portrait blend,
To which no single beauty must pretend;
So poets oft do in one piece expose   35
Whole *belles assemblées*[4] of coquettes and beaux.

[3] particular.
[4] fine gatherings.

The Rehearsal

GEORGE VILLIERS,
SECOND DUKE OF BUCKINGHAM

Georges Villiers, Second Duke of Buckingham

BIOGRAPHICAL DATA

(The many details of the Duke's very active public life are
here omitted.)

1628 January 30. Born in London; the second son of the first Duke of
Buckingham, the great favourite of James I and Charles I. An
older brother had died in infancy. The first duke having been
assassinated in August 1628, the second duke and his younger
brother, Lord Francis, were brought up with the children of
King Charles I.

1642 Graduated from Trinity College, Cambridge, with the degree
of M.A.

1643 With his brother he began a three- or four-year period of travel
abroad.

1648 Returned to England upon the outbreak of the Second Civil
War and engaged in the King's service. Lord Francis was killed;
the Duke escaped to Holland. His estates confiscated.

1657 Married Mary, daughter of Lord Fairfax.

1660 Upon the Restoration of Charles II, his estates were restored.
He was reputed the King's richest subject.

1662 Admitted member of the King's Privy Council.

1671 Elected chancellor of Cambridge University.

1672 Published The Rehearsal, *a parody of the popular heroic play;
it had been produced in the previous year.*

It had probably been written some years before, perhaps as
early as 1665, but the text of the 1672 edition was quite new,
and it is said that Buckingham had collaborated in its composition with Martin Clifford, Thomas Sprat, and Samuel
Butler (author of *Hudibras*). During the Duke's lifetime there
were five editions of the play. The form of *The Rehearsal* was
later imitated with great success in Fielding's farce *Tom Thumb
the Great* (1730), and in Sheridan's *The Critic* (1779).

1682 *Published his adaptation of Fletcher's play* The Chances.

1685 *Published a prose pamphlet entitled* A Short Discourse on the Reasonableness of a Man's having a Religion, *a plea for religious toleration.*

Upon the death of Charles II in this year, he retired from public life to his estates in Yorkshire.

1687 Died in the house of a Yorkshire tenant. Buried in the Chapel of Henry VII, Westminster Abbey.

His posthumous publications include: an edition by Tom Brown of the Duke's occasional verse and satire (1704) ; *The Battle of Sedgmoor* and *The Militant Couple* (1704); and an adaptation of Beaumont and Fletcher's play *Philaster*, entitled *The Restoration, or Right Will Take Place* (1714).

Dryden's portrait of Zimri is modelled upon the second Duke of Buckingham. See I *Absalom and Achitophel*, lines 544-68.

Pope's exaggerated account of the Duke's death is recorded in his *Epistles to Several Persons*, III, lines 299-314.

Prologue

SPOKEN BY MR. LACY [MR. BAYES]

We might well call this short mock-play of ours
A posy made of weeds instead of flowers;
Yet such have been presented to your noses,
And there are such, I fear, who thought 'em roses.
Would some of 'em were here to see, this night,   5
What stuff it is in which they took delight.
Here, brisk, insipid rogues, for wit, let fall
Sometimes dull sense; but oft'ner none at all:
There, strutting heroes, with a grim-fac'd train,
Shall brave the gods, in King Cambyses' vein.[1]   10
For (changing rules, of late, as if men writ
In spite of reason, nature, art, and wit)
Our poets make us laugh at tragedy,
And with their comedies they make us cry.
Now, critics, do your worst, that here are met;   15
For, like a rook,[2] I have hedg'd in my bet.[3]
If you approve, I shall assume the state
Of those high-flyers whom I imitate;[4]
And justly too, for I will teach you more
Than ever they would let you know before: 20
I will not only show the feats they do,

---

[1] The reference is to the ranting hero of Thomas Preston's *Cambises, King of Persia* (c. 1569). Cf. Shakespeare, *Henry IV*, Part 1, II, iv: "I must speak in passion, and I will do it in King Cambyses' vein." The title of Elkanah Settle's first tragedy was *Cambyses* (1671).

[2] professional gambler.

[3] bet on both sides.

[4] John Lacy was the most famous comic actor of his time. The sense of the couplet is that if the critics are foolish enough to approve the heroic rant of the play, Lacy will turn to tragic parts.

But give you all their reasons for 'em too.
Some honour may to me from hence arise;
But if, by my endeavours, you grow wise,
And what you once so prais'd shall now despise,   25
Then I'll cry out, swell'd with poetic rage,
'Tis I, John Lacy, have reform'd your stage.

Dramatis Personae

Men

MR. BAYES
JOHNSON
SMITH
PLAYERS
STAGE-KEEPER

TWO KINGS OF BRENTFORD
PRINCE PRETTYMAN
PRINCE VOLSCIUS
GENTLEMAN-USHER
PHYSICIAN
DRAWCANSIR
GENERAL
LIEUTENANT-GENERAL
CORDELIO
TOM THIMBLE

HARRY
FISHERMAN
SHIRLEY
SOL (Sun)
THUNDER
SOLDIERS
TWO HERALDS
Four CARDINALS
SERGEANTS-AT-ARMS
Three FIDDLERS

Women

AMARYLLIS
CLORIS
PARTHENOPE
PALLAS

LIGHTNING
LUNA (Moon)
ORBIS (Earth)

Attendants of Men and Women

SCENE: *Brentford*

Act I

SCENE I

Enter JOHNSON *and* SMITH

JOHNS. Honest Frank, I am glad to see thee, with all my heart. How long hast thou been in town?

SMITH. Faith, not above an hour, and if I had not met you here, I had gone to look you out; for I long to talk with you freely of all the strange new things we have heard in the country.

JOHNS. And, by my troth, I have longed as much to laugh with you at all the impertinent, dull, fantastical things we are tired out with here.

SMITH. Dull and fantastical! That's an excellent composition. Pray, what are our men of business doing?

JOHNS. I ne'er inquire after 'em. Thou knowest my humour lies another way. I love to please myself as much, and to trouble others as little as I can; and therefore do naturally avoid the company of those solemn fops, who, being incapable of reason, and insensible of wit and pleasure, are always looking grave, and troubling one another, in hopes to be thought men of business.

SMITH. Indeed I have ever observed that your grave lookers are the dullest of men.

JOHNS. Ay, and of birds and beasts too; your gravest bird is an owl, and your gravest beast is an ass.

SMITH. Well, but how dost thou pass thy time?

JOHNS. Why, as I use to do; eat and drink as well as I can, have a she-friend to be private with in the afternoon, and sometimes see a play; where there are such things, Frank, such hideous, monstrous things, that it has almost made me forswear the stage, and resolve to apply myself to the solid nonsense of your men of business, as the more ingenious pastime.

SMITH. I have heard indeed you have had lately many new plays; and our country wits commend 'em.

JOHNS. Ay, so do some of our city wits too; but they are of the new kind of wits.

SMITH. New kind! what kind is that?

JOHNS. Why, your virtuosi,[1] your civil persons, your drolls; fellows that scorn to imitate nature, but are given altogether to elevate and surprise.

SMITH. Elevate and surprise! Prithee, make me understand the meaning of that.

JOHNS. Nay, by my troth, that's a hard matter; I don't understand that myself. 'Tis a phrase they have got amongst them, to express their no-meaning by. I'll tell you, as near as I can, what it is. Let me see; 'tis fighting, loving, sleeping, rhyming, dying, dancing, singing, crying, and every thing but thinking and sense.

MR. BAYES[2] *passes over the stage*

BAYES. Your most obsequious, and most observant, very servant, Sir.

JOHNS. God so! this is an author: I'll go fetch him to you.

SMITH. No, prithee, let him alone.

JOHNS. Nay, by the Lord, I'll have him. (*Goes after him.*) Here he is; I have caught him. Pray, Sir, now, for my sake, will you do a favour to this friend of mine?

BAYES. Sir, it is not within my small capacity to do favours, but receive 'em; especially from a person that does wear the honourable title you are pleased to impose, Sir, upon this — Sweet Sir, your servant.

SMITH. Your humble servant, Sir.

JOHNS. But wilt thou do me a favour now?

---

[1] projectors: the new "wits", writers in the "new style".
[2] particularly associated with John

Dryden, poet laureate; but the name refers generally to all authors of high-flown heroic plays.

BAYES. Ay, Sir: what is it?

JOHNS. Why, to tell him the meaning of thy last play.[8]

BAYES. How, Sir, the meaning! Do you mean the plot?

JOHNS. Ay, ay, any thing.

BAYES. Faith, Sir, the intrigo's now quite out of my head; but I have a new one in my pocket, that I may say is a virgin; 't has never yet been blown upon. I must tell you one thing, 'tis all new wit, and, though I say it, a better than my last; and you know well enough how that took. In fine, it shall read, and write, and act, and plot, and show; ay, and pit, box, and gallery, egad, with any play in Europe.[4] This morning is its last rehearsal, in their habits,[5] and all that, as it is to be acted; and if you and your friend will do it but the honour to see it in its virgin attire, though perhaps it may blush, I shall not be ashamed to discover its nakedness unto you. *(Puts his hand in his pocket.)* I think it is in this pocket.

JOHNS. Sir, I confess I am not able to answer you in this new way; but if you please to lead, I shall be glad to follow you, and I hope my friend will do so too.

SMITH. Sir, I have no business so considerable as should keep me from your company.

BAYES. Yes, here it is. No, cry you mercy; this is my book of drama commonplaces,[6] the mother of many other plays.

JOHNS. Drama commonplaces! Pray, what's that?

BAYES. Why, Sir, some certain helps that we men of art have found it convenient to make use of.

SMITH. How, Sir, helps for wit?

BAYES. Ay, Sir, that's my position; and I do here aver, that no man yet the sun e'er shone upon, has parts sufficient to furnish out a stage, except it were by the help of these my rules.[7]

JOHNS. What are those rules, I pray?

---

[8] Dryden's *The Conquest of Granada* (1670-71).

[4] See "Sources of the Parody", p. 327.

[5] i.e., in costume.

[6] passages excerpted from other men's works and copied into his commonplace book, for reference in the writing of his plays.

[7] See "Sources".

BAYES. Why, Sir, my first rule is the rule of transversion, or *regula duplex*,[8] changing verse into prose, or prose into verse, alternative as you please.

SMITH. Well, but how is this done by rule, Sir?

BAYES. Why thus, Sir; nothing so easy, when understood. I take a book in my hand, either at home or elsewhere, for that's all one; if there be any wit in't, as there is no book but has some, I transverse it; that is, if it be prose, put it into verse, (but that takes up some time;) and if it be verse, put it into prose.

JOHNS. Methinks, Mr. Bayes, that putting verse into prose should be called transprosing.

BAYES. By my troth, Sir, 'tis a very good notion, and hereafter it shall be so.

SMITH. Well, Sir, and what d'ye do with it then?

BAYES. Make it my own; 'tis so changed, that no man can know it. My next rule is the rule of record, by way of table-book.[9] Pray, observe.

JOHNS. We hear you, Sir: go on.

BAYES. As thus: I come into a coffee-house, or some other place where witty men resort; I make as if I minded nothing (do you mark?); but as soon as any one speaks, pop, I slap it down, and make that, too, my own.

JOHNS. But, Mr. Bayes, are you not sometimes in danger of their making you restore, by force, what you have gotten thus by art?

BAYES. No, Sir, the world's unmindful; they never take notice of these things.

SMITH. But, pray, Mr. Bayes, among all your other rules, have you no one rule for invention?

BAYES. Yes, Sir, that's my third rule; that I have here in my pocket.

SMITH. What rule can that be, I wonder!

BAYES. Why, Sir, when I have any thing to invent, I never trouble my head about it, as other men do; but presently

[8] double rule.
[9] notebook.

turn over this book,[10] and there I have, at one view, all that Persius, Montaigne, Seneca's tragedies, Horace, Juvenal, Claudian, Pliny, Plutarch's *Lives*, and the rest, have ever thought upon this subject; and so, in a trice, by leaving out a few words, or putting in others of my own, the business is done.

JOHNS. Indeed, Mr. Bayes, this is as sure and compendious a way of wit, as ever I heard of.

BAYES. Sirs, if you make the least scruple of the efficacy of these my rules, do but come to the play-house, and you shall judge of 'em by the effects.

SMITH. We'll follow you, Sir.   (*Exeunt.*)

SCENE II

Enter three PLAYERS *on the stage*

1ST PLAYER. Have you your part perfect?

2ND PLAYER. Yes, I have it without book; but I don't understand how it is to be spoken.

3RD PLAYER. And mine is such a one, as I can't guess, for my life, what humour[11] I'm to be in, whether angry, melancholy, merry, or in love, I don't know what to make on't.

1ST PLAYER. Phoo! the author will be here presently, and he'll tell us all. You must know, this is the new way of writing, and these hard things please forty times better than the old plain way: for, look you, Sir, the grand design upon the stage is to keep the auditors in suspense; for to guess presently at the plot and the sense, tires 'em before the end of the first act. Now here, every line surprises you, and brings in new matter; and then, for scenes, clothes, and dances, we put 'em quite down, all that ever went before us; and those are the things, you know, that are essential to a play.

2ND PLAYER. Well, I am not of thy mind: but so it gets us money, 'tis no great matter.

---

[10] his commonplace book.

[11] referring to Jonson's theory of the four humours. Cf. Jonson, *Every Man in His Humour; Every Man out of His Humour.*

Enter BAYES, JOHNSON *and* SMITH

BAYES. Come, come in, gentlemen; you're very welcome. Mr. –
a[12]– ha' you your part ready?

1ST PLAYER. Yes, Sir.

BAYES. But do you understand the true humour of it?

1ST PLAYER. Ay, Sir, pretty well.

BAYES. And Amaryllis, how does she do? Does not her armour
become her?

3RD PLAYER. Oh, admirably!

BAYES. I'll tell you now a pretty conceit. What do you think I'll
make 'em call her anon, in this play?

SMITH. What, I pray?

BAYES. Why, I make 'em call her Armaryllis, because of her
armour, ha, ha, ha!

JOHNS. That will be very well indeed.

(Exeunt PLAYERS.*)*

BAYES. Ay, it's a pretty little rogue; I knew her face would set
off armour extremely: and, to tell you true, I writ that part
only for her – You must know, she is my mistress.[13]

JOHNS. Then I know another thing, little Bayes, that thou hast
had her, egad.

BAYES. No, egad, not yet; but I'm sure I shall; for I have talked
bawdy to her already.

JOHNS. Hast thou, faith? Prithee, how was that?

BAYES. Why, Sir, there is in the French tongue a certain criticism, which, by the variation of the masculine adjective instead of the feminine, makes a quite different signification
of the word: as for example, *ma vie* is my life, but if before
vie you put *mon*, instead of *ma*, you make it bawdy.[14]

JOHNS. Very true.

BAYES. Now, Sir, I having observed this, I set a trap for her the
other day in the tiring-room;[15] for this, said I, *adieu, bel*

---

[12] Mr. Bayes can seldom remember
the players' names.
[13] See "Sources".

[14] The author puns on *vie* (life) and
vit (penis).
[15] dressing-room.

esperansa de ma vie[16] (which, egad, is very pretty), to which she answered, I vow, almost as prettily, every jot; for she said, *songes à ma vie, Monsieur*.[17] Whereupon I presently snapped this upon her, *Non, non, Madam – Songes vous à mon*,[18] by gad, and named the thing directly to her.

SMITH. This is one of the richest stories, Mr. Bayes, that ever I heard of.

BAYES. Ay, let me alone; egad, when I get to 'em, I'll nick 'em, I warrant you. But I'm a little nice; for, you must know, at this time I am kept by another woman in the city.

SMITH. How, kept! For what?

BAYES. Why, for a *beau garson*;[19] I am, i'fackins.[20]

SMITH. Nay, then, we shall never have done.

BAYES. And the rogue is so fond of me, Mr. Johnson, that, I vow to gad, I know not what to do with myself.

JOHNS. Do with thyself! No, I wonder how thou canst make a shift to hold out at this rate.

BAYES. Oh, devil! I can toil like a horse; only sometimes it makes me melancholy; and then, I vow to gad, for a whole day together I am not able to say you one good thing, if it were to save my life.

SMITH. That we do verily believe, Mr. Bayes.

BAYES. And that's the only thing, egad, which mads me in my amours; for I'll tell you, as a friend, Mr. Johnson, my acquaintances, I hear, begin to give it out that I am dull – Now I am the farthest from it in the whole world, egad; but only, forsooth, they think I am so, because I can say nothing.

JOHNS. Phoo, pox! that's ill-naturedly done of 'em.

BAYES. Ay, gad, there's no trusting o' these rogues – But – a – come, let's sit down. Look you, Sirs, the chief hinge of this play, upon which the whole plot moves and turns, and that causes the variety of all the several accidents, which, you

[16] "Farewell, fair hope of my life." Mrs. Reeves had played the part of Esperanza in Dryden's *Conquest of Granada*.

[17] "Dream of my life, sir."

[18] "No, no, madam – dream of my" (the word *vit* is omitted). Here, as elsewhere in the passage, Mr. Bayes's French is poor.

[19] "a fine boy"; here, a gigolo.

[20] "i'faith".

know, are the things in nature that make up the grand
refinement of a play, is, that I suppose two kings of the
same place,[21] as for example, at Brentford:[22] for I love to
write familiarly. Now the people having the same relations
to 'em both, the same affections, the same duty, the same
obedience, and all that, are divided among themselves in
point of *devoir*[23] and interest, how to behave themselves
equally between 'em, these kings differing sometimes in
particular, though, in the main they agree – I know not
whether I make myself well understood.

JOHNS. I did not observe you, Sir. Pray, say that again.

BAYES. Why, look you, Sir (nay, I beseech you, be a little curious[24] in taking notice of this, or else you'll never understand my notion of the thing), the people being embarrassed
by their equal ties to both, and the sovereigns concerned in
a reciprocal regard, as well to their own interest, as the good
of the people, they make a certain kind of a – you understand me – upon which, there do arise several disputes, tur-
moils, heart-burnings, and all that – In fine, you'll apprehend it better when you see it.   *(Exit to call the Players.)*

SMITH. I find the author will be very much obliged to the
players, if they can make any sense out of this.

Re-enter BAYES

BAYES. Now, gentlemen, I would fain ask your opinion of one
thing; I have made a prologue and an epilogue,[25] which may
both serve for either,[26] that is, the prologue for the epilogue,
or the epilogue for the prologue (do you mark?); nay, they
may both serve too, egad, for any other play as well as this.

SMITH. Very well; that's indeed artificial.[27]

BAYES. And I would fain ask your judgements, now, which of
them would do best for the prologue. For, you must know,

---

[21] See "Sources".

[22] a market town a few miles from
London.

[23] duty.

[24] careful.

[25] Dryden was famous for the prologues and epilogues to his own
plays, as well as those he frequently
wrote for the plays of others.

[26] See "Sources".

[27] artfully done; well contrived.

there is in nature but two ways of making very good prologues. The one is by civility, by insinuation, good language,
and all that, to – a – in a manner, steal your plaudit from
the courtesy of the auditors: the other, by making use of
some certain personal things, which may keep a hank[28]
upon such censuring persons as cannot otherways, egad, in
nature, be hindered from being too free with their tongues;
to which end, my first prologue is, that I come out in a long
black veil, and a great, huge hangman behind me, with a
furred cap and his sword drawn; and there tell 'em plainly
that if, out of good nature, they will not like my play, egad,
I'll e'en kneel down, and he shall cut my head off. Whereupon they all clapping – a —

SMITH. Ay, but suppose they don't.

BAYES. Suppose! Sir, you may suppose what you please; I have
nothing to do with your suppose, Sir; nor am not at all
mortified at it; not at all, Sir; egad, not one jot, Sir. "Suppose," quoth-a! – ha, ha, ha!   (*Walks away.*)

JOHNS. Phoo! prithee, Bayes, don't mind what he says; he's a
fellow newly come out of the country; he knows nothing
of what's the relish here, of the town.[29]

BAYES. If I writ, Sir, to please the country, I should have followed the old plain way; but I write for some persons of
quality, and peculiar friends of mine, that understand what
flame and power in writing is; and they do me the right,
Sir, to approve of what I do.

JOHNS. Ay, ay, they will clap, I warrant you; never fear it.

BAYES. I'm sure the design's good; that cannot be denied. And
then for language, egad, I defy 'em all in nature to mend it.
Besides, Sir, I have printed above a hundred sheets of paper,
to insinuate the plot into the boxes;[30] and withal, have
appointed two or three dozen of my friends to be ready in
the pit, who, I'm sure, will clap, and so the rest, you know,
must follow; and then, pray, Sir, what becomes of your

[28] a restraining hand.
[29] i.e., he is ignorant of the sophisticated taste and manners of the city.
[30] See "Sources".

"suppose"? Ha, ha, ha!

JOHNS. Nay, if the business be so well laid, it cannot miss.

BAYES. I think so, Sir; and therefore would choose this to be the prologue. For if I could engage 'em to clap before they see the play, you know 'twould be so much the better, because then they were engaged: for let a man write never so well, there are, now-a-days, a sort of persons[81] they call critics, that, egad, have no more wit in 'em than so many hobby-horses; but they'll laugh you, Sir, and find fault, and censure things that, egad, I'm sure they are not able to do themselves – a sort of envious persons that emulate the glories of persons of parts, and think to build their fame by calumniating of persons that, egad, to my knowledge, of all persons in the world are, in nature, the persons that do as much despite all that as – a – In fine, I'll say no more of 'em.

JOHNS. Nay, you have said enough of 'em, in all conscience; I'm sure more than they'll e'er be able to answer.

BAYES. Why, I'll tell you, Sir, sincerely, and *bona fide*,[82] were it not for the sake of some ingenious persons and choice female spirits[83] that have a value for me, I would see 'em all hanged, egad, before I would e'er more set pen to paper, but let 'em live in ignorance, like ingrates.

JOHNS. Ay, marry, that were a way to be revenged of 'em indeed; and if I were in your place now, I would do so.

BAYES. No, Sir; there are certain ties upon me that I cannot be disengaged from;[84] otherwise I would. But, pray, Sir, how do you like my hangman?

SMITH. By my troth, Sir, I should like him very well.

BAYES. But how do you like it, Sir? (for I see you can judge.) Would you have it for a prologue, or the epilogue?

JOHNS. Faith, Sir, 'tis so good, let it e'en serve for both.

BAYES. No, no, that won't do. Besides, I have made another.

---

[81] See "Sources".

[82] in good faith.

[83] possibly a reference to Lady Castle-maine, the King's mistress, who had extended her patronage to *The Wild Gallant*.

[84] See "Sources".

JOHNS. What other, Sir?

BAYES. Why, Sir, my other is thunder and lightning.

JOHNS. That's greater; I'd rather stick to that.

BAYES. Do you think so? I'll tell you then; though there have been many witty prologues written of late, yet I think you'll say this is a *non pareillo*:[35] I'm sure nobody has hit upon it yet. For here, Sir, I make my prologue to be dialogue;[36] and as in my first, you see, I strive to oblige the auditors by civility, by good nature, good language, and all that; so in this, by the other way, *in terrorem*,[37] I choose for the persons Thunder and Lightning. Do you apprehend the conceit?

JOHNS. Phoo, pox! then you have it cocksure. They'll be hanged before they'll dare to affront an author that has 'em at that lock.[38]

BAYES. I have made, too, one of the most delicate, dainty similes in the whole world, egad, if I knew but how to apply it.

SMITH. Let's hear it, I pray you.

BAYES. 'Tis an allusion to love.

> So boar and sow, when any storm is nigh,
> Snuff up, and smell it gath'ring in the sky;
> Boar beckons sow to trot in chestnut groves,
> And there consummate their unfinish'd loves.
> Pensive, in mud, they wallow all alone,
> And snore and gruntle to each other's moan.[39]

How do you like it now, ha?

JOHNS. Faith, 'tis extraordinary fine, and very applicable to thunder and lightning, methinks, because it speaks of a storm.

BAYES. Egad, and so it does, now I think on't. Mr. Johnson, I thank you; and I'll put it in *profecto*.[40] Come out, Thunder and Lightning.

---

[35] *non-pareil*; unequalled.

[36] Dryden had written parts of the prologues to *The Wild Gallant* and *The Rival Ladies* (1663) in dialogue.

[37] to secure effects of terror.

[38] a term in wrestling.

[39] See "Sources".

[40] by all means, certainly.

Enter THUNDER *and* LIGHTNING.

THUN. I am the bold Thunder.[41]

BAYES. Mr. Cartwright,[42] prithee, speak that a little louder, and with a hoarse voice. "I am the bold Thunder." Pshaw! speak it me in a voice that thunders it out indeed. *I am the bold Thunder.*

THUN. I am the bold thunder.

LIGHT. The brisk Lightning, I.

BAYES. Nay, but you must be quick and nimble – "The brisk Lightning, I." That's my meaning.

THUN. I am the bravest Hector of the sky.

LIGHT. And I, fair Helen, that made Hector die.

THUN. I strike men down.

LIGHT. I fire the town.

THUN. Let the critics take heed how they grumble,
For then I begin for to rumble.

LIGHT. Let the ladies allow us their graces,[43]
Or I'll blast all the paint on their faces,
And dry up their peter[44] to soot.

THUN. Let the critics look to't.

LIGHT. Let the ladies look to't.

THUN. For Thunder will do't.

LIGHT. For Lightning will shoot.

THUN. I'll give you dash for dash.

LIGHT. I'll give you flash for flash.
Gallants, I'll singe your feather.

THUN. I'll thunder you together.

BOTH. Look to't, look to't; we'll do't, we'll do't; look to't, we'll do't. *(twice or thrice repeated)*

(Exeunt ambo.[45])

BAYES. There's no more. 'Tis but a flash of a prologue – a droll.[46]

---

[41] See "Sources".
[42] a distinguished actor of the age (d. 1686).
[43] See "Sources".
[44] a cosmetic.
[45] both.
[46] a brief comic scene usually ending in a dance.

SMITH. Yes, 'tis short indeed, but very terrible.

BAYES. Ay, when the simile's in, it will do to a miracle, egad. Come, come, begin the play.

Enter FIRST PLAYER

1ST PLAYER. Sir, Mr. Ivory[47] is not come yet, but he'll be here presently; he's but two doors off.

BAYES. Come then, gentlemen, let's go out and take a pipe of tobacco.

(Exeunt.)

[47] See "Sources".

Act II

SCENE I

BAYES, JOHNSON, *and* SMITH

BAYES. Now, Sir, because I'll do nothing here that ever was done before, instead of beginning with a scene that discovers something of the plot, I begin this play with a whisper.[1]

SMITH. Umph! very new, indeed.

BAYES. Come, take your seats. Begin, Sirs.

Enter GENTLEMAN-USHER *and* PHYSICIAN

PHYS. Sir, by your habit, I should guess you to be the Gentleman-Usher of this sumptuous place.

USHER. And by your gait and fashion, I should almost suspect you rule the healths of both our noble Kings, under the notion of Physician.

PHYS. You hit my function right.

USHER. And you mine.

PHYS. Then let's embrace.

USHER. Come.

PHYS. Come.

JOHNS. Pray, Sir, who are those so very civil persons?

BAYES. Why, Sir, the Gentleman-Usher and Physician of the two Kings of Brentford.

JOHNS. But, pray then, how comes it to pass that they know one another no better?

BAYES. Phoo! that's for the better carrying on of the plot.

JOHNS. Very well.

PHYS. Sir, to conclude —

[1] See "Sources of the Parody", p. 327.

SMITH. What, before he begins?

BAYES. No, Sir, you must know they had been talking of this a pretty while without.

SMITH. Where? In the tiring-room?

BAYES. Why, ay, Sir – He's so dull – Come, speak again.

    PHYS. Sir, to conclude, the place you fill has more than amply exacted the talents of a wary pilot; and all these threat'ning storms, which, like impregnate clouds, hover o'er our heads, will (when they once are grasped but by the eye of reason) melt into fruitful showers of blessings on the people.

BAYES. Pray, mark that allegory! Is not that good?

JOHNS. Yes, that grasping of a storm with the eye is admirable.

    PHYS. But yet some rumours great are stirring; and if Lorenzo should prove false (which none but the great gods can tell), you then perhaps would find that —

                                 (Whispers.)

BAYES. Now he whispers.

    USHER. Alone, do you say?

    PHYS. No; attended with the noble —   *(Whispers.)*

BAYES. Again.

    USHER. Who, he in grey?

    PHYS. Yes; and at the head of —   *(Whispers.)*

BAYES. Pray, mark.

    USHER. Then, Sir, most certain 'twill in time appear.
        These are the reasons that have mov'd him to't:
        First, he —   *(Whispers.)*

BAYES. Now the other whispers.

    USHER. Secondly, they —   *(Whispers.)*

BAYES. At it still.

    USHER. Thirdly, and lastly, both he and they — *(Whispers.)*

BAYES. Now they both whisper.

                    (Exeunt whispering.)

    Now, gentlemen, pray, tell me true, and without flattery, is not this a very odd beginning of a play?

JOHNS. In troth, I think it is, Sir. But why two Kings of the same place?

BAYES. Why? because it's new; and that's it I aim at. I despise your Jonson and Beaumont,[2] that borrowed all they writ from nature: I am for fetching it purely out of my own fancy, I.

SMITH. But what think you, Sir, of Sir John Suckling?[3]

BAYES. By Gad, I am a better poet than he.

SMITH. Well, Sir; but pray, why all this whispering?

BAYES. Why, Sir (besides that it is new, as I told you before), because they are supposed to be politicians; and matters of state ought not to be divulged.

SMITH. But then, Sir, why —

BAYES. Sir, if you'll but respite your curiosity till the end of the fifth act, you'll find it a piece of patience not ill recompensed.   (Goes to the door.)

JOHNS. How dost thou like this, Frank? Is it not just as I told thee?

SMITH. Why, I never did before this see anything in nature, and all that (as Mr. Bayes says), so foolish, but I could give some guess at what moved the fop to do it: but this, I confess, does go beyond my reach.

JOHNS. It is all alike; Mr. Wintershul[4] has informed me of this play already. And I'll tell thee, Frank, thou shalt not see one scene here worth one farthing, or like anything thou canst imagine has ever been the practice of the world. And then, when he comes to what he calls "good language", it is, as I told thee, very fantastical, most abominably dull, and not one word to the purpose.

SMITH. It does surprise me, I'm sure, very much.

JOHNS. Ay, but it won't do so long. By that time thou hast seen a play or two that I'll show thee, thou wilt be pretty well acquainted with this new kind of foppery.

SMITH. Pox on't, but there's no pleasure in him: he's too gross a fool to be laughed at.

---

[2] Ben Jonson and Francis Beaumont, whose famous partner was John Fletcher. Dryden was a great admirer of the work of these earlier dramatists of the seventeenth century.

[3] Cavalier lyrist and dramatist (1609-42).

[4] an actor (d. 1679) equally celebrated for his comic and tragic parts.

Enter BAYES

JOHNS. I'll swear, Mr. Bayes, you have done this scene most admirably: though I must tell you, Sir, it is a very difficult matter to pen a whisper well.

BAYES. Ay, gentlemen, when you come to write yourselves, o' my word, you'll find it so.

JOHNS. Have a care of what you say, Mr. Bayes, for Mr. Smith, there, I assure you, has written a great many fine things already.

BAYES. Has he, i'fackins? Why then, pray, Sir, how do you do when you write?

SMITH. Faith, Sir, for the most part, I am in pretty good health.

BAYES. Ay, but I mean, what do you do when you write?

SMITH. I take pen, ink, and paper, and sit down.

BAYES. Now I write standing, that's one thing; and then another thing is, with what do you prepare yourself?

SMITH. Prepare myself! What the devil does the fool mean?

BAYES. Why, I'll tell you now what I do. If I am to write familiar things, as sonnets to Armida,[5] and the like, I make use of stewed prunes[6] only; but when I have a grand design in hand, I ever take physic, and let blood: for, when you would have pure swiftness of thought, and fiery flights of fancy, you must have a care of the pensive part. In fine, you must purge the belly.

SMITH. By my troth, Sir, this is a most admirable receipt for writing.

BAYES. Ay, 'tis my secret; and, in good earnest, I think one of the best I have.

SMITH. In good faith, Sir, and that may very well be.

BAYES. May be, Sir! Egad, I'm sure on't. *Experto crede Roberto.*[7] But I must give you this caution by the way: be sure you never take snuff when you write.[8]

SMITH. Why so, Sir?

---

[5] See "Sources".

[6] For Dryden's fondness for stewed plums see his letter to Tonson (August, 1693).

[7] i.e., "believe Robert; he's an authority". Probably an ironic reference to Sir Robert Howard.

[8] See "Sources".

BAYES. Why, it spoiled me once, egad, one of the sparkishest[9] plays in all England. But a friend of mine, at Gresham-college,[10] has promised to help me to some spirit of brains; and, egad, that shall do my business.

SCENE II

Enter the two Kings hand in hand

BAYES. Oh, these are now the two Kings of Brentford. Take notice of their style; 'twas never yet upon the stage; but if you like it, I could make a shift, perhaps, to show you a whole play, writ all just so.

1ST KING. Did you observe their whisper, brother King?

2ND KING. I did, and heard, besides, a grave bird sing,
   That they intend, sweetheart, to play us pranks.

BAYES. This is now familiar; because they are both persons of the same quality.

SMITH. 'Sdeath! this would make a man spew.

1ST KING. If that design appears,
   I'll lug 'em by the ears,
   Until I make 'em crack.

2ND KING. And so will I, i'fack.

1ST KING. You must begin, *mon foy*.[11]

2ND KING. Sweet Sir, *pardonnes moy*.[12]

BAYES. Mark that; I make 'em both speak French, to show their breeding.

JOHNS. Oh, 'tis extraordinary fine!

2ND KING. Then, spite of Fate, we'll thus combined stand,
   And, like two brothers, walk still hand in hand.

        (Exeunt Reges.)

JOHNS. This is a very majestic scene, indeed.

BAYES. Ay, 'tis a crust, a lasting crust for your rogue-critics, egad; I would fain see the proudest of 'em all but dare to nibble at this; egad, if they do, this shall rub their gums for 'em,

---

[9] wittiest, sprightliest.

[10] i.e., a member of the Royal Society.

[11] deliberately incorrect for *ma foi*;

i.e., i'faith.

[12] "pardon me".

I promise you. It was I, you must know, that have written a whole play just in this very same style; it was never acted yet.

JOHNS. How so?

BAYES. Egad, I can hardly tell you for laughing – ha, ha, ha! it is so pleasant a story – ha, ha, ha!

SMITH. What is't?

BAYES. Egad, the players refused to act it – ha, ha, ha!

SMITH. That's impossible!

BAYES. Egad, they did it, Sir; point blank refused it, egad. Ha, ha, ha!

JOHNS. Fie, that was rude!

BAYES. Rude! ay, egad, they are the rudest, uncivilest persons, and all that, in the whole world, egad. Egad, there's no living with 'em. I have written, Mr. Johnson, I do verily believe, a whole cart-load of things, every whit as good as this; and yet, I vow to gad, these insolent rascals have turned 'em all back upon my hands again.

JOHNS. Strange fellows, indeed!

SMITH. But pray, Mr. Bayes, how came these two Kings to know of this whisper? For, as I remember, they were not present at it.

BAYES. No; but that's the actors' fault, and not mine; for the two Kings should (a pox take 'em!) have popped both their heads in at the door, just as the other went off.

SMITH. That, indeed, would ha' done it.

BAYES. Done it! ay, egad, these fellows are able to spoil the best things in Christendom. I'll tell you, Mr. Johnson, I vow to gad, I have been so highly disobliged by the peremptoriness of these fellows, that I'm resolved hereafter to bend my thoughts wholly for the service of the Nursery,[13] and mump[14] your proud players, egad. So, now Prince Pretty-man comes in, and falls asleep making love to his mistress; which, you know, was a grand intrigue in a late play, written by a very honest gentleman, a knight.[15]

---

[13] a training school for actors. Cf. Dryden, *MacFlecknoe*, line 74.

[14] overreach, cheat.

[15] See "Sources".

SCENE III

Enter PRINCE PRETTYMAN

PRETTY. How strange a captive am I grown of late!
Shall I accuse my love, or blame my fate?
My love, I cannot; that is too divine:
And against fate what mortal dares repine?

Enter CLORIS

But here she comes.
Sure 'tis some blazing comet! is it not?

(Lies down.)

BAYES. Blazing comet! Mark that; egad, very fine.

PRETTY. But I am so surprised with sleep, I cannot speak the
rest. *(Sleeps.)*

BAYES. Does not that, now, surprise you, to fall asleep in the
nick? His spirits exhale with the heat of his passion, and all
that, and, swop, falls asleep, as you see. Now, here she must
make a simile.

SMITH. Where's the necessity of that, Mr. Bayes?

BAYES. Because she's surprised. That's a general rule; you must
ever make a simile when you are surprised; 'tis the new way
of writing.[16]

CLORIS. As some tall pine, which we on Aetna find
T'have stood the rage of many a boist'rous wind,
Feeling without, that flames within do play,
Which would consume his root and sap away;
He spreads his worsted arms unto the skies,
Silently grieves, all pale, repines and dies;
So, shrouded up, your bright eye disappears.
Break forth, bright scorching sun, and dry my
tears.[17] *(Exit.)*

JOHNS. Mr. Bayes, methinks this simile wants a little application, too.

[16] Dryden consistently observes this
rule in his dramatic practice. In *The
Indian Emperor*, IV, iv, the heroine's
surprise is expressed in an extended
simile.
[17] See "Sources".

BAYES. No, faith; for it alludes to passion, to consuming, to dying, and all that, which, you know, are the natural effects of an amour. But I'm afraid this scene has made you sad; for, I must confess, when I writ it, I wept myself.

SMITH. No, truly, Sir, my spirits are almost exhaled too, and I am likelier to fall asleep.

PRINCE PRETTYMAN *starts up, and says*

PRETTY. It is resolved!   (*Exit.*)

BAYES. That's all.

SMITH. Mr. Bayes, may one be so bold as to ask you a question now, and you not be angry?

BAYES. Oh, Lord, Sir, you may ask me any thing! what you please; I vow to gad, you do me a great deal of honour; you do not know me if you say that, Sir.

SMITH. Then pray, Sir, what is it that this Prince here has resolved in his sleep?

BAYES. Why, I must confess, that question is well enough asked for one that is not acquainted with this new way of writing. But you must know, Sir, that to out-do all my fellow-writers, whereas they keep their intrigo secret till the very last scene before the dance, I now, Sir, (do you mark me) – a —

SMITH. Begin the play and end it, without ever opening the plot at all.

BAYES. I do so; that's the very plain truth on't. Ha, ha, ha! I do, egad. If they cannot find it out themselves, e'en let 'em alone for Bayes, I warrant you. But here, now, is a scene of business. Pray observe it; for I dare say, you'll think it no unwise discourse this, nor ill argued. To tell you true, 'tis a discourse I over-heard once betwixt two grand, sober, governing persons.

SCENE IV

Enter GENTLEMAN-USHER *and* PHYSICIAN

USHER. Come, Sir, let's state the matter of fact, and lay our heads together.[18]

[18] See "Sources".

PHYS. Right, lay our heads together. I love to be merry, sometimes; but when a knotty point comes, I lay my head close to it, with a snuff-box in my hand; and then I fegue[19] it away, i'faith.

BAYES. I do just so, egad, always.

USHER. The grand question is, whether they heard us whisper; which I divide thus —

PHYS. Yes, it must be divided so, indeed.

SMITH. That's very complaisant, I swear, Mr. Bayes, to be of another man's opinion, before he knows what it is.

BAYES. Nay, I bring in none here but well-bred persons, I assure you.

USHER. I divided the question into when they heard, what they heard, and whether they heard or no.

JOHNS. Most admirably divided, I swear!

USHER. As to the when, you say just now; so that is answered. Then, as for what. Why, that answers itself; for what could they hear, but what we talked of? So that naturally and of necessity we come to the last question, *videlicet*,[20] whether they heard or no?

SMITH. This is a very wise scene, Mr. Bayes.

BAYES. Ay, you have it right; they are both politicians.

USHER. Pray, then, to proceed in method, let me ask you that question.

PHYS. No, you'll answer better; pray let me ask it you.

USHER. Your will must be a law.

PHYS. Come, then, what is't I must ask?

SMITH. This politician, I perceive, Mr. Bayes, has somewhat a short memory.

BAYES. Why, Sir, you must know, that t'other is the main politician, and this is but his pupil.

USHER. You must ask me whether they heard us whisper.

PHYS. Well, I do so.

USHER. Say it then.

SMITH. Hey-day! here's the bravest work that ever I saw.

---

[19] beat, drive.
[20] namely.

JOHNS. This is mighty methodical.

BAYES. Ay, Sir, that's the way; 'tis the way of art; there is no other way, egad, in business.

    PHYS. Did they hear us whisper?

      USHER. Why, truly, I can't tell; there is much to be said upon the word *whisper*. To whisper in Latin is *susurrare*, which is as much as to say, to speak softly; now, if they heard us speak softly, they heard us whisper; but then comes in the *quomodo*,[21] the how; how did they hear us whisper? Why, as to that, there are two ways: the one by chance or accident; the other on purpose; that is, with design to hear us whisper.

    PHYS. Nay, if they heard us that way, I'll never give 'em physic more.

      USHER. Nor I e'er more will walk abroad before 'em.

BAYES. Pray, mark this; for a great deal depends upon it towards the latter end of the play.

SMITH. I suppose that's the reason why you brought in this scene, Mr. Bayes.

BAYES. Partly, it was, Sir; but, I must confess, I was not unwilling, besides, to show the world a pattern here, how men should talk of business.

JOHNS. You have done it exceeding well indeed.

BAYES. Yes, I think this will do.

    PHYS. Well, if they heard us whisper, they'll turn us out, and nobody else will take us.

SMITH. Not for politicians, I dare answer for it.

    PHYS. Let's then no more ourselves in vain bemoan:
      We are not safe until we them unthrone.

      USHER. 'Tis right.
        And since occasion now seems debonair
        I'll seize on this, and you shall take that chair.
            (They draw their swords, and sit down
            in the two great chairs upon the Stage.)

BAYES. There's now an odd surprise! the whole state's turned

[21] in what way.

quite topsy-turvy,[22] without any pother or stir in the whole world, egad.

JOHNS. A very silent change of government, truly, as ever I heard of.

BAYES. It is so: and yet you shall see me bring 'em in again by and by in as odd a way every jot.

(The usurpers march out, flourishing their swords.)

Enter SHIRLEY[23]

SHIRLEY. Hey ho! hey ho! what a change is here! Hey day! hey day! I know not what to do, nor what to say![24]

(Exit.)

JOHNS. Mr. Bayes, in my opinion now, that gentleman might have said a little more upon this occasion.

BAYES. No, Sir, not at all; for I underwrit his part on purpose to set off the rest.

JOHNS. Cry you mercy, Sir.

SMITH. But, pray, Sir, how came they to depose the Kings so easily?

BAYES. Why, Sir, you must know, they long had a design to do it before; but never could put it in practice till now; and to tell you true, that's one reason why I made 'em whisper so at first.

SMITH. Oh, very well! now I'm fully satisfied.

BAYES. And then, to show you, Sir, it was not done so very easily neither, in this next scene you shall see some fighting.

SMITH. Oh, ho! so then you make the struggle to be after the business is done.

BAYES. Ay.

SMITH. Oh, I conceive[25] you! That, I swear, is very natural.

---

[22] See "Sources".
[23] a noted dancer of the day.

[24] See "Sources".
[25] understand.

SCENE V

Enter four men at one door, and four at another, with their swords drawn

1ST SOLDIER. Stand. Who goes there?

2ND SOLDIER. A friend.

1ST SOLDIER. What friend?

2ND SOLDIER. A friend to the house.

1ST SOLDIER. Fall on.

(They all kill one another. Music strikes.)

BAYES. *(to the music)* Hold, hold! *(It ceaseth.)* – Now here's an odd surprise; all these dead men you shall see rise up presently, at a certain note that I have made in *Effaut flat*,[26] and fall a-dancing. Do you hear, dead men? Remember your note in *Effaut flat* – *(to the music)* Play on. Now, now, now! *(The music play his note, and the dead men rise, but cannot get in order.)* Oh, Lord! Oh, Lord! Out, out, out! Did ever men spoil a good thing so? No figure, no ear, no time, nothing! Udzookers, you dance worse than the angels in *Harry the Eight*,[27] or the fat spirits in *The Tempest*,[28] egad.

1ST SOLDIER. Why, Sir, 'tis impossible to do anything in time to this tune.

BAYES. Oh, Lord! Oh, Lord! impossible! Why, gentlemen, if there be any faith in a person that's a Christian, I sat up two whole nights in composing this air, and adapting it for the business: for if you observe, there are two several designs in this tune; it begins swift, and ends slow. You talk of time, and time; you shall see me do't. Look you now; here I am dead. *(Lies down flat on his face.)* Now mark my note *Effaut flat*. Strike up, music. Now! *(As he rises up has-*

---

[26] F-flat; the correct designation would be E.

[27] Davenant's version (1663) of the Shakespeare play. In IV, ii, the angels appear in the vision of Queen Katharine.

[28] See "Sources".

tily, he falls down again.) Ah, gadzookers, I have broke
my nose.[29]

JOHNS. By my troth, Mr. Bayes, this is a very unfortunate note
of yours, in *Effaut.*

BAYES. A plague of this damned stage, with your nails and your
tenter-hooks, that a gentleman can't come to teach you to
act but he must break his nose, and his face, and the devil
and all. Pray, Sir, can you help me to a wet piece of brown
paper?

SMITH. No, indeed, Sir; I don't usually carry any about me.

2ND SOLDIER. Sir, I'll go get you some within presently.

BAYES. Go, go, then, I follow you. Pray, dance out the dance,
and I'll be with you in a moment. Remember, you dance
like horsemen. *(Exit.)*

SMITH. Like horsemen! What a plague can that be?

(They dance the dance, but can make nothing of it.)

1ST SOLDIER. A devil! let's try this no longer; play my dance that
Mr. Bayes found fault with so.

(Dance, and exeunt.)

SMITH. What can this fool be doing all this while about his nose?

JOHNS. Prithee, let's go see. *(Exeunt.)*

---

[29] a satiric reference to Sir William
Davenant, the author of *The Siege
of Rhodes* (1661), who lost his nose
in the course of an illness.

Act III

SCENE I

BAYES, *with a paper on his nose, and the two Gentlemen*

BAYES. Now, Sirs, this I do because my fancy in this play is to end every act with a dance.

SMITH. Faith, that fancy is very good; but I should hardly have broke my nose for it, though.

JOHNS. That fancy, I suppose, is new too.

BAYES. Sir, all my fancies are so. I tread upon no man's heels, but make my flight upon my own wings, I assure you. Now, here comes in a scene of sheer wit without any mixture in the whole world, egad, between Prince Prettyman and his tailor.[1] It might properly enough be called a prize of wit; for you shall see 'em come in one upon another snip-snap, hit for hit, as fast as can be. First one speaks, then presently the other's upon him, slap, with a repartee, then he at him again, dash, with a new conceit; and so eternally, eternally, egad, till they go quite off the stage.

(Goes to call the Players.)

SMITH. What a plague does this fop mean, by his snip-snap, hit for hit, and dash.

JOHNS. Mean! why he never meant any thing in's life; what dost talk of meaning for?

Enter BAYES

BAYES. Why don't you come in?

Enter PRINCE PRETTYMAN *and* TOM THIMBLE

This scene will make you die with laughing, if it be well

---

[1] See "Sources of the Parody", p. 327.

acted, for 'tis as full of drollery as ever it can hold. 'Tis like an orange stuffed with cloves, as for conceit.

PRETTY. But, prithee, Tom Thimble, why wilt thou needs marry? If nine tailors make but one man,[2] and one woman cannot be satisfied with nine men; what work art thou cutting out here for thyself, trow?

BAYES. Good.

TOM. Why, an't please your highness, if I can't make up all the work I cut out, I shan't want[3] journeymen enow to help me, I warrant you.

BAYES. Good again.

PRETTY. I am afraid thy journeymen, though, Tom, won't work by the day, but by the night.

BAYES. Good still.

TOM. However, if my wife sits but cross-legged, as I do, there will be no great danger: not half so much as when I trusted you, Sir, for your coronation-suit.

BAYES. Very good, i'faith.

PRETTY. Why, the times then lived upon trust; it was the fashion. You would not be out of time, at such a time as that, sure: a tailor, you know, must never be out of fashion.

BAYES. Right.

TOM. I'm sure, Sir, I made your clothes in the Court fashion, for you never paid me yet.

BAYES. There's a bob for the Court.[4]

PRETTY. Why, Tom, thou art a sharp rogue when thou art angry, I see. Thou pay'st me now, methinks.

BAYES. There's pay upon pay? As good as ever was written, egad.

TOM. Ay, Sir, in your own coin; you give me nothing but words.

BAYES. Admirable, before Gad!

PRETTY. Well, Tom, I hope shortly I shall have another coin for thee; for now the wars are coming on, I shall grow to be a man of metal.[5]

---

[2] an old proverb.
[3] lack.

[4] a joke at the expense of the Court.
[5] pun on "mettle".

BAYES. Oh, you did not do that half enough.

JOHNS. Methinks he does it admirably.

BAYES. Ay, pretty well; but he does not hit me in't;[6] he does not top his part.[7]

    TOM. That's the way to be stamped yourself, Sir. I shall see you come home, like an angel for the king's evil,[8] with a hole bored through you.   *(Exeunt.)*

BAYES. Ha, there he has hit it up to the hilts, egad! How do you like it now, gentlemen? Is not this pure wit?

SMITH. 'Tis snip-snap, Sir, as you say; but, methinks, not pleasant nor to the purpose; for the play does not go on.

BAYES. Play does not go on! I don't know what you mean; why, is not this part of the play?

SMITH. Yes, but the plot stands still.

BAYES. Plot stand still! Why, what a devil is the plot good for but to bring in fine things?

SMITH. Oh, I did not know that before.

BAYES. No, I think you did not, nor many things more that I am master of. Now, Sir, egad, this is the bane of all us writers: let us soar but never so little above the common pitch, egad, all's spoiled, for the vulgar never understand it. They can never conceive you, Sir, the excellency of these things.

JOHNS. 'Tis a sad fate, I must confess; but you write on still for all that.

BAYES. Write on! Ay, egad, I warrant you. 'Tis not their talk shall stop me; if they catch me at that lock, I'll give 'em leave to hang me. As long as I know my things are good, what care I what they say?[9] What, are they gone, without singing my last new song? 'Sbud,[10] would it were in their bellies. I'll tell you, Mr. Johnson, if I have any skill in these matters, I vow to gad this song is peremptorily[11] the very best that ever yet was written. You must know it was

---

[6] i.e., he does not impress me with it.

[7] See "Sources".

[8] The sovereign's touch was believed to cure scrofula, a disease known as "the King's evil". At the ceremony of "touching", the king hung an "angel" (a gold coin worth about ten shillings) about the patient's neck.

[9] See "Sources".

[10] an oath: "God's blood".

[11] without question.

made by Tom Thimble's first wife, after she was dead.

SMITH. How, Sir! after she was dead?

BAYES. Aye, Sir, after she was dead. Why, what have you to say to that?

JOHNS. Say! why nothing: he were a devil that had anything to say to that.

BAYES. Right.

SMITH. How did she come to die, pray, Sir?

BAYES. Phoo! that's no matter; by a fall. But here's the conceit: that upon his knowing she was killed by an accident, he supposes, with a sigh, that she died for love of him.

JOHNS. Ay, ay, that's well enough; let's hear it, Mr. Bayes.

BAYES. 'Tis to the tune of *Farewell, fair Armida; on seas, and in battles, in bullets*, and all that.

(Song)

In swords, pikes, and bullets, 'tis safer to be,
Than in a strong castle remoted from thee:
My death's bruise pray think you gave me, though a fall
Did give it me more, from the top of a wall;
For then if the moat on her mud would first lay,
And after, before you my body convey,
The blue on my breast when you happen to see,
You'll say, with a sigh, there's a true blue for me.[12]

Ha, rogues! when I am merry, I write these things as fast as hops, egad; for, you must know, I am as pleasant a debauchee as ever you saw; I am, i'faith.

SMITH. But, Mr. Bayes, how comes this song in here? for, methinks, there is no great occasion for it.

BAYES. Alack, Sir, you know nothing; you must ever interlard your plays with songs, ghosts and dances,[13] if you mean to — a —

JOHNS. Pit, box, and gallery,[14] Mr. Bayes.

[12] See "Sources".
[13] Such "interlarding" is common in Dryden's plays.
[14] See p. 261, line 10.

BAYES. Egad, and you have nicked it. Hark you, Mr. Johnson, you know I don't flatter; egad you have a great deal of wit.

JOHNS. Oh, Lord, Sir, you do me too much honour.

BAYES. Nay, nay, come, come, Mr. Johnson, i'faith this must not be said amongst us that have it. I know you have wit by the judgement you make of this play, for that's the measure I go by; my play is my touchstone. When a man tells me such a one is a person of parts, "Is he so?" say I; what do I do, but bring him presently to see this play; if he likes it, I know what to think of him; if not, "your most humble servant, Sir." I'll no more of him, upon my word, I thank you. I am *clara voyant*,[15] egad. Now here we go to our business.

SCENE II

Enter the two Usurpers hand in hand

USHER. But what's become of Volscius the great?
     His presence has not grac'd our courts of late.

PHYS. I fear some ill, from emulation sprung,
     Has from us that illustrious hero wrung.

BAYES. Is not that majestical?

SMITH. Yes, but who a devil is that Volscius?

BAYES. Why, that's a prince I make in love with Parthenope.

SMITH. I thank you, Sir.

Enter CORDELIO

CORD. My lieges, news from Volscius the prince.

USHER. His news is welcome, whatsoe'er it be.[16]

SMITH. How, Sir! do you mean whether it be good or bad?

BAYES. Nay, pray, Sir, have a little patience; gadzookers, you'll spoil all my play. Why, Sir, 'tis impossible to answer every impertinent question you ask.

SMITH. Cry you mercy, Sir.

CORD. His highness, Sirs, commanded me to tell you,

---

[15] clairvoyant.
[16] See "Sources".

> That the fair person whom you both do know,
> Despairing of forgiveness for her fault,
> In a deep sorrow, twice she did attempt
> Upon her precious life; but, by the care
> Of standers-by, prevented was.

SMITH. 'Sheart,[17] what stuff's here?

CORD.   At last,
> Volscius the great this dire resolve embrac'd:
> His servants he into the country sent,
> And he himself to Piccadilly went:
> Where he's inform'd by letters that she's dead.

USHER. Dead! Is that possible? Dead!

PHYS. Oh, ye gods!   (*Exeunt.*)

BAYES. There's a smart expression of a passion: "Oh, ye gods!" That's one of my bold strokes, egad.

SMITH. Yes; but who is the fair person that's dead?

BAYES. That you shall know anon, Sir.

SMITH. Nay, if we know it at all, 'tis well enough.

BAYES. Perhaps you may find too, by-and-by, for all this, that she's not dead neither.

SMITH. Marry, that's good news indeed; I am glad of that with all my heart.

BAYES. Now here's the man brought in, that is supposed to have killed her.

> (*A great shout within.*)

SCENE III

Enter AMARYLLIS, *with a book in her hand,*
and Attendants

AMAR. What shout triumphant's that?

Enter a SOLDIER

SOLDIER. Shy maid, upon the river-brink,
> Near Twick'nam town, the false assassinate
> Is ta'en.

---

[17] "God's heart".

AMAR. Thanks to the powers above for this deliverance.
    I hope its slow beginning will portend
    A forward exit to all future end.

BAYES. Pish, there you are out; "to all future end!" No, no – "to all future *end*!" You must lay the accent upon *end*, or else you lose the conceit.

SMITH. I see you are very perfect in these matters.

BAYES. Ay, Sir, I have been long enough at it, one would think, to know something.

    Enter SOLDIERS, *dragging in an old* FISHERMAN

AMAR. Villain, what monster did corrupt thy mind
    T'attack the noblest soul of human kind?
    Tell me who set thee on.

FISHER. Prince Prettyman.

AMAR. To kill whom?

FISHER. Prince Prettyman.

AMAR. What, did Prince Prettyman hire you to kill Prince Prettyman?

FISHER. No, Prince Volscius.

AMAR. To kill whom?

FISHER. Prince Volscius.

AMAR. What, did Prince Volscius hire you to kill Prince Volscius?

FISHER. No, Prince Prettyman.

AMAR. So! Drag him hence,
    'Till torture of the rack produce his sense.[18]

                              (Exeunt.)

BAYES. Mark how I make the horror of his guilt confound his intellects, for he's out at one and t'other; and that's the design of this scene.

SMITH. I see, Sir, you have a several design for every scene.

BAYES. Ay, that's my way of writing; and so, Sir, I can dispatch you a whole play, before another man, egad, can make an end of his plot.

---

[18] See "Sources".

SCENE IV

So, now enter Prince Prettyman in a rage. Where the devil is he? Why, Prettyman! Why, when,[19] I say? Oh, fie, fie, fie, fie! all's marred, I vow to gad, quite marred.

Enter PRINCE PRETTYMAN

Phoo, pox! you are come too late, Sir; now you may go out again if you please. I vow to gad, Mr. – a – I would not give a button for my play, now you have done this.

PRETTY. What, Sir!

BAYES. What, Sir! 'slife, Sir, you should have come out in choler, rous[20] upon the stage, just as the other went off. Must a man be eternally telling you of these things?

JOHNS. Sure this must be some very notable matter that he's so angry at.

SMITH. I am not of your opinion.

BAYES. Pish! Come, let's hear your part, Sir.

PRETTY. Bring in my father: why d'ye keep him from me?
Although a fisherman, he is my father.
Was ever son yet brought to this distress,
To be, for being a son, made fatherless?
Ah! you just gods, rob me not of a father:
The being of a son take from me rather.[21]   *(Exit.)*

SMITH. Well, Ned, what think you now?

JOHNS. A devil, this is worst of all. Mr. Bayes, pray what's the meaning of this scene?

BAYES. Oh, cry you mercy, Sir: I protest I had forgot to tell you. Why, Sir, you must know that long before the beginning of this play this Prince was taken by a fisherman.

SMITH. How, Sir! taken prisoner?

BAYES. Taken prisoner! Oh, Lord, what a question's there! Did ever any man ask such a question? Gadzookers, he has put the plot quite out of my head with this damned question! What was I going to say?

---

[19] i.e., "when are you coming?" with impatience.

[20] with a bounce or a bang.

[21] See "Sources".

JOHNS. Nay, the Lord knows: I cannot imagine.

BAYES. Stay, let me see; taken; oh, 'tis true. Why, Sir, as I was going to say, his highness here, the Prince, was taken in a cradle by a fisherman, and brought up as his child.

SMITH. Indeed!

BAYES. Nay, prithee hold thy peace. And so, Sir, this murder being committed by the river-side, the fisherman, upon suspicion, was seized, and thereupon the Prince grew angry.

SMITH. So, so; now 'tis very plain.

JOHNS. But, Mr. Bayes, is not this some disparagement to a Prince, to pass for a fisherman's son? Have a care of that, I pray.

BAYES. No, no, not at all; for 'tis but for a while; I shall fetch him off again presently, you shall see.

Enter PRETTYMAN *and* THIMBLE

PRETTY. By all the gods, I'll set the world on fire,
        Rather than let 'em ravish hence my sire.[22]

TOM. Brave Prettyman, it is at length reveal'd,
        That he is not thy sire who thee conceal'd.

BAYES. Lo[23] you now, there he's off again.

JOHNS. Admirably done, i'faith!

BAYES. Ay, now the plot thickens very much upon us.

PRETTY. What oracle this darkness can evince?
        Sometimes a fisher's son, sometimes a prince.
        It is a secret, great as is the world,
        In which I, like the soul, am toss'd and hurl'd.
        The blackest ink of fate sure was my lot,
        And when she writ my name, she made a blot.

                                                    (*Exit.*)

BAYES. There's a blustering verse for you now.

SMITH. Yes, Sir; but why is he so mightily troubled to find he is not a fisherman's son?

BAYES. Phoo! that is not because he has a mind to be his son, but for fear he should be thought to be nobody's son at all.

[22] See "Sources".

[23] a contraction of "look".

SMITH. Nay, that would trouble a man indeed.
BAYES. So, let me see.

SCENE V

BAYES. *(reads)* "Enter Prince Volscius going out of town."
SMITH. I thought he had gone to Piccadilly.[24]
BAYES. Yes, he gave it out so, but that was only to cover his design.
JOHNS. What design?
BAYES. Why, to head the army that lies concealed for him in Knightsbridge.
JOHNS. I see here's a great deal of plot, Mr. Bayes.
BAYES. Yes, now it begins to break; but we shall have a world of more business anon.

> *Enter* PRINCE VOLSCIUS, CLORIS, AMARYLLIS, *and* HARRY
> *with a riding-cloak and boots*[25]

AMAR. Sir, you are cruel thus to leave the town,
    And to retire to country solitude.
CLORIS. We hop'd this summer that we should at least
    Have held the honour of your company.
BAYES. "Held the honour of your company!" prettily expressed: "held the honour of your company!" gadzookers, these fellows will never take notice of any thing.
JOHNS. I assure you, Sir, I admire it extremely; I don't know what he does.
BAYES. Ay, ay, he's a little envious; but 'tis no great matter. Come.
AMAR. Pray, let us two this single boon obtain,
    That you will here with poor us still remain![26]
    Before your horses come, pronounce our fate;
    For then, alas! I fear 'twill be too late.
BAYES. Sad!
VOLS. Harry, my boots; for I'll go range among

---

[24] Cf. III, ii.
[25] See "Sources".
[26] See "Sources".

My blades encamp'd, and quit this urban throng.[27]

SMITH. But pray, Mr. Bayes, is not this a little difficult, that you were saying e'en now, to keep an army thus concealed in Knightsbridge?

BAYES. In Knightsbridge! Stay.

JOHNS. No, not if the inn-keepers be his friends.

BAYES. His friends! ay, Sir, his intimate acquaintance; or else indeed I grant it could not be.

SMITH. Yes, faith, so it might be very easy.

BAYES. Nay, if I do not make all things easy, egad I'll give you leave to hang me. Now you would think that he's going out of town; but you shall see how prettily I have contrived to stop him presently.

SMITH. By my troth, Sir, you have so amazed me, that I know not what to think.

Enter PARTHENOPE

VOLS. Bless me! how frail are all my best resolves!
    How in a moment is my purpose changed!
    Too soon I thought myself secure from love.[28]
    Fair Madam, give me leave to ask her name
    Who does so gently rob me of my fame:
    For I should meet the army out of town,
    And if I fail, must hazard my renown.

PARTH. My mother, Sir, sells ale by the town-walls;
    And me her dear Parthenope she calls.

BAYES. Now, that's the Parthenope I told you of.

JOHNS. Ay, ay, egad, you are very right.

VOLS. Can vulgar vestments high-born beauty shroud?
    Thou bring'st the morning pictur'd in a cloud.[29]

BAYES. "The morning pictured in a cloud!" Ah, gadzookers, what a conceit is there!

PARTH. Give you good even, Sir.   (*Exit.*)

VOLS. Oh, inauspicious stars! that I was born
    To sudden love, and to more sudden scorn.

[27] See "Sources".   [29] See "Sources".
[28] See "Sources".

AMAR *and* CLORIS. How! Prince Volscius in love! Ha, ha,
ha![30]   *(Exeunt laughing.)*

SMITH. Sure, Mr. Bayes, we have lost some jest here, that they
laugh at so.

BAYES. Why, did you not observe? He first resolves to go out of
town; and then, as he's pulling on his boots, falls in love
with her; ha, ha, ha!

SMITH. Well, and where lies the jest of that?

BAYES. Ha? *(Turns to JOHNSON.)*

JOHNS. Why, in the boots; where should the jest lie?

BAYES. Egad, you are in the right; it does lie in the boots –
(Turns to SMITH.) Your friend and I know where a good jest
lies, though you don't, Sir.

SMITH. Much good do't you, Sir.

BAYES. Here now, Mr. Johnson, you shall see a combat betwixt
love and honour. An ancient author has made a whole play
on it;[31] but I have dispatched it all in this scene.

> *(VOLSCIUS sits down to pull on his boots: BAYES
> stands by and overacts the part as he speaks it.)*

VOLS. How has my passion made me Cupid's scoff!
>   This hasty boot is on, the other off,
>   And sullen lies, with amorous design
>   To quit loud fame, and make that beauty mine.

SMITH. Prithee, mark what pains Mr. Bayes takes to act this
speech himself!

JOHNS. Yes, the fool, I see, is mightily transported with it.

VOLS.[32] My legs, the emblem of my various thought,
>   Shew to what sad distraction I am brought:
>   Sometimes with stubborn honour, like this boot,
>   My mind is guarded, and resolv'd to do't:
>   Sometimes again, that very mind, by love
>   Disarmed, like this other leg does prove.
>   Shall I to Honour or to Love give way?
>   "Go on," cries Honour; tender Love says, "Nay."[33]

---

[30] See "Sources".

[31] Davenant's heroic play *Love and
Honour* (acted in 1634, published in
1649, and revived in 1661).

[32] See "Sources".

[33] See "Sources".

Honour aloud commands, "Pluck both boots on";
But softer Love does whisper, "Put on none."
What shall I do? What conduct shall I find
To lead me through this twilight of my mind?
For as bright day, with black approach of night
Contending, makes a doubtful puzzling light;
So does my honour and my love together
Puzzle me so. I can resolve for neither.

> *(Goes out hopping with one boot*
> *on, and the other off.)*

JOHNS. By my troth, Sir, this is as difficult a combat as ever I saw,
and as equal; for 'tis determined on neither side.

BAYES. Ay, is't not now, egad, ha? For to go off hip-hop, hip-hop,
upon this occasion, is a thousand times better than any conclusion in the world, egad.

JOHNS. Indeed, Mr. Bayes, that hip-hop, in this place, as you say,
does a very great deal.

BAYES. Oh, all in all, Sir; they are these little things that mar,
or set you off a play; as I remember once in a play of mine,
I set off a scene, egad, beyond expectation, only with a
petticoat and the belly-ache.[34]

SMITH. Pray, how was that, Sir?

BAYES. Why, Sir, I contrived a petticoat[35] to be brought in upon
a chair (nobody knew how) into a prince's chamber, whose
father was not to see it, that came in by chance.

JOHNS. God's-my-life, that was a notable contrivance indeed.

SMITH. Ay, but Mr. Bayes, how could you contrive the belly-
ache?

BAYES. The easiest i' th' world, egad; I'll tell you how: I made
the prince sit down upon the petticoat, no more than so,
and pretended to his father that he had just then got the
belly-ache; whereupon his father went out to call a physician, and his man ran away with the petticoat.

SMITH. Well, and what followed upon that?

BAYES. Nothing; no earthly thing, I vow to gad.

---

[34] See "Sources".
[35] i.e., a girl, concealed by a petticoat.

JOHNS. O' my word, Mr. Bayes, there you hit it.

BAYES. Yes, it gave a world of content. And then I paid 'em away besides; for I made 'em all talk bawdy, ha, ha, ha, beastly, downright bawdry upon the stage, egad, ha, ha, ha; but with an infinite deal of wit, that I must say.

JOHNS. That, we know well enough, can never fail you.

BAYES. No, egad, can't it. Come, bring in the dance.

(Exit to call the Players.)

SMITH. Now, the devil take thee for a silly, confident, unnatural, fulsome rogue.

Enter BAYES *and* PLAYERS

BAYES. Pray dance well before these gentlemen; you are commonly so lazy, but you should be light and easy, tah, tah, tah. *(All the while they dance,* BAYES *puts 'em out with teaching 'em.)* Well, gentlemen, you will see this dance, if I am not deceived, take very well upon the stage, when they are perfect in their motions, and all that.

SMITH. I don't know how 'twill take, Sir; but I am sure you sweat hard for't.

BAYES. Ay, Sir, it costs me more pains and trouble to do these things than almost the things are worth.

SMITH. By my troth, I think so, Sir.

BAYES. Not for the things themselves, for I could write you, Sir, forty of 'em in a day; but, egad, these players are such dull persons that, if a man be not by 'em upon every point and at every turn, egad, they'll mistake you, Sir, and spoil all.

Enter a PLAYER

What, is the funeral ready?

PLAYER. Yes, Sir.

BAYES. And is the lance filled with wine?

PLAYER. Sir, 'tis just now a-doing.

BAYES. Stay then, I'll do it myself.

SMITH. Come, let's go with him.

BAYES. A match. But, Mr. Johnson, egad, I am not like other persons; they care not what becomes of their things, so they can but get money for 'em. Now, egad, when I write, if it be not just as it should be in every circumstance, to every particular, egad, I am no more able to endure it; I am not myself, I'm out of my wits, and all that; I'm the strangest person in the whole world. For what care I for money? I write for fame and reputation.

(Exeunt.)

Act IV

SCENE I

BAYES *and the two gentlemen*

BAYES. Gentlemen, because I would not have any two things alike in this play, the last act beginning with a witty scene of mirth, I make this to begin with a funeral.

SMITH. And is that all your reason for it, Mr. Bayes?

BAYES. No, Sir, I have a precedent for it besides; a person of honour, and a scholar, brought in his funeral just so;[1] and he was one (let me tell you) that knew as well what belonged to a funeral as any man in England, egad.

JOHNS. Nay, if that be so, you are safe.

BAYES. Egad, but I have another device, a frolic which I think yet better than all this, not for the plot or characters (for in my heroic plays, I make no difference as to those matters) but for another contrivance.

SMITH. What is that, I pray?

BAYES. Why, I have designed a conquest that cannot possibly, egad, be acted in less than a whole week.[2] And I'll speak a bold word, it shall drum, trumpet, shout, and battle,[3] egad, with any the most warlike tragedy we have, either ancient or modern.

JOHNS. Ay, marry, Sir, there you say something.

SMITH. And pray, Sir, how have you ordered this same frolic of yours?

BAYES. Faith, Sir, by the rule of romance;[4] for example, they divided their things into three, four, five, six, seven, eight,

---

[1] See "Sources of the Parody", p. 327. [3] See "Sources".
[2] See "Sources". [4] See "Sources".

or as many tomes as they please. Now I would very fain
know what should hinder me from doing the same with
my things if I please?

JOHNS. Nay, if you should not be master of your own works, 'tis
very hard.

BAYES. That is my sense. And then, Sir, this contrivance of mine
has something of the reason of a play in it too; for as every
one makes you five acts to one play, what do me I, but
make five plays to one plot, by which means the auditors
have every day a new thing.

JOHNS. Most admirably good, i'faith! and must certainly take,
because it is not tedious.

BAYES. Ay, Sir, I know that; there's the main point. And then,
upon Saturday, to make a close of all (for I ever begin upon
a Monday), I make you, Sir, a sixth play, that sums up the
whole matter to 'em, and all that, for fear they should have
forgot it.

JOHNS. That consideration, Mr. Bayes, indeed, I think, will be
very necessary.

SMITH. And when comes in your share, pray, Sir?

BAYES. The third week.[5]

JOHNS. I vow, you'll get a world of money.

BAYES. Why, faith, a man must live; and if you don't thus pitch
upon some new device, egad, you'll never do't; for this age
(take it o' my word) is somewhat hard to please. But there
is one pretty odd passage in the last of these plays, which
may be executed two several ways, wherein I'd have your
opinion, gentlemen.

JOHNS. What is't, Sir?

BAYES. Why, Sir, I make a male person to be in love with a
female.

SMITH. Do you mean that, Mr. Bayes, for a new thing?

BAYES. Yes, Sir, as I have ordered it. You shall hear: he having
passionately loved her through my five whole plays, finding
at last that she consents to his love, just after that his mother

[5] It was customary for the author to
receive the profits of the third day's
performance of his play. Mr. Bayes
claims those of the third week.

had appeared to him like a ghost,[6] he kills himself. That's one way. The other is, that she coming at last to love him with as violent a passion as he loved her, she kills herself.[7] Now, my question is, which of these two persons should suffer upon this occasion?

JOHNS. By my troth, it is a very hard case to decide.

BAYES. The hardest in the world, egad; and has puzzled this pate very much. What say you, Mr. Smith?

SMITH. Why, truly, Mr. Bayes, if it might stand with your justice now, I would spare 'em both.

BAYES. Egad, and I think – ha! – Why, then, I'll make him hinder her from killing herself. Ay, it shall be so. Come, come, bring in the funeral.

Enter a Funeral, with the two Usurpers and Attendants

Lay it down there; no, no, here, Sir. So, now speak.

USHER. Set down the funeral pile, and let our grief
   Receive from its embraces some relief.

PHYS. Was't not unjust to ravish hence her breath,
   And in life's stead to leave us nought but death?
   The world discovers now its emptiness,
   And by her loss demonstrates we have less.

BAYES. Is not this good language now? Is not that elevate? 'Tis my *non ultra*,[8] egad; you must know they were both in love with her.

SMITH. With her! with whom?

BAYES. Why, this is Lardella's funeral.

SMITH. Lardella! Ay, who is she?

BAYES. Why, Sir, the sister of Drawcansir; a lady that was drowned at sea, and had a wave for her winding-sheet.[9]

USHER. Lardella, Oh, Lardella! from above
   Behold the tragic issues of our love:
   Pity us, sinking under grief and pain,
   For thy being cast away upon the main.

BAYES. Look you now, you see I told you true.

---

[6] See "Sources".
[7] See "Sources".

[8] i.e., my very best.
[9] See "Sources".

SMITH. Ay, Sir, and I thank you for it very kindly.

BAYES. Ay, egad, but you will not have patience; honest Mr. –
a – you will not have patience.

JOHNS. Pray, Mr. Bayes, who is that Drawcansir?[10]

BAYES. Why, Sir, a fierce hero, that frights his mistress, snubs up
kings, baffles armies, and does what he will, without regard
to numbers, good manners, or justice.

JOHNS. A very pretty character.

SMITH. But, Mr. Bayes, I thought your heroes had ever been
men of great humanity and justice.

BAYES. Yes, they have been so; but, for my part, I prefer that one
quality of singly beating of whole armies above all your
moral virtues put together, egad. You shall see him come in
presently. *(to the Players)* Zookers! why don't you read the
paper?

PHYS. Oh, cry you mercy! *(Goes to take the paper.)*

BAYES. Pish! Nay, you are such a fumbler – Come, I'll read it
myself. *(Takes a Paper from off the coffin.)* – Stay; it's an
ill hand; I must use my spectacles. This, now, is a copy of
verses, which I make Lardella compose just as she is dying,
with design to have it pinned upon her coffin, and so read
by one of the usurpers, who is her cousin.

SMITH. A very shrewd design that, upon my word, Mr. Bayes.

BAYES. And what do you think now I fancy her to make love
like, here, in this paper?

SMITH. Like a woman: what should she make love like?

BAYES. O' my word, you are out, though, Sir; egad, you are.

SMITH. What then? like a man?

BAYES. No, Sir, like a humble-bee.[11]

SMITH. I confess, that I should not have fancied.

BAYES. It may be so, Sir; but it is, though, in order to the opinion of some of your ancient philosophers, who held the
transmigration of the soul.

SMITH. Very fine.

BAYES. I'll read the title. "To my dear coz, King Phys."

[10] See "Sources".
[11] an old form of "bumble-bee".

SMITH. That's a little too familiar with a king, though, Sir, by
your favour, for a humble-bee.

BAYES. Mr. Smith, in other things I grant your knowledge may
be above me; but as for poetry, give me leave to say, I
understand that better. It has been longer my practice; it
has, indeed, Sir.

SMITH. Your servant, Sir.

BAYES. Pray, mark it. *(reads)*

> Since death my earthly part will thus remove,
> I'll come a humble-bee to your chaste love.
> With silent wings I'll follow you, dear coz;
> Or else before you in the sun-beams buzz.
> And when to melancholy groves you come,
> An airy ghost you'll know me by my hum;
> For sound, being air, a ghost does well become.

SMITH. *(after a pause)* Admirable!

BAYES. At night, into your bosom I will creep,
> And buzz but softly, if you chance to sleep;
> Yet in your dreams I will pass sweeping by,
> And then both hum and buzz before your eye.

JOHNS. By my troth, that's a very great promise.

SMITH. Yes, and a most extraordinary comfort to boot.

BAYES. Your bed of love from dangers I will free;
> But most, from love of any future bee.
> And when with pity your heart-strings shall crack,
> With empty arms I'll bear you on my back.

SMITH. A pick-a-pack, a pick-a-pack.

BAYES. Ay, egad; but is not that *tuant*[12] now, ha? Is it not *tuant*?
Here's the end.

> Then at your birth of immortality,
> Like any winged archer hence I'll fly,
> And teach you your first flutt'ring in the sky.[13]

JOHNS. Oh, rare! this is the most natural refined fancy that ever
I heard, I'll swear.

BAYES. Yes, I think, for a dead person, it is a good way enough

[12] "killing"; i.e., marvellously good.
[13] See "Sources".

of making love; for, being divested of her terrestrial part, and all that, she is only capable of these little, pretty, amorous designs that are innocent, and yet passionate. Come, draw your swords.

PHYS. Come, sword, come sheath thyself within this breast,
      Which only in Lardella's tomb can rest.

USHER. Come, dagger, come, and penetrate this heart,
      Which cannot from Lardella's love depart,

   Enter PALLAS

PALLAS. Hold, stop your murd'ring hands
      At Pallas's commands;
      For the supposed dead, Oh, Kings!
      Forbear to act such deadly things.
      Lardella lives; I did but try
      If princes for their loves could die.
      Such celestial constancy
      Shall by the gods rewarded be:
      And from these fun'ral obsequies,
      A nuptial banquet shall arise.
      (The coffin opens, and a banquet is discovered.)

BAYES. So, take away the coffin. Now it's out. This is the very funeral of the fair person which Volscius sent word was dead; and Pallas, you see, has turned it into a banquet.

SMITH. Well, but where is this banquet?

BAYES. Nay, look you, Sir, we must first have a dance, for joy that Lardella is not dead. Pray, Sir, give me leave to bring in my things properly at least.

SMITH. That, indeed, I had forgot. I ask your pardon.

BAYES. Oh, d'ye so, Sir? I am glad you will confess yourself once in an error, Mr. Smith.

          (Dance)

USHER. Resplendent Pallas, we in thee do find
      The fiercest beauty and a fiercer mind:
      And since to thee Lardella's life we owe,
      We'll supple statues in thy temple grow.

PHYS. Well, since alive Lardella's found,
    Let in full bowls her health go round.

          (The two Usurpers take each of them
          a bowl in their hands.)

USHER. But where's the wine?

PALLAS. That shall be mine.

    Lo! from this conquering lance
    Does flow the purest wine of France:

        (Fills the bowls out of her lance.)

    And to appease your hunger, I
    Have in my helmet brought a pie;
    Lastly, to bear a part with these,
    Behold a buckler made of cheese.[14]

          (Vanish PALLAS.)

BAYES. There's the banquet. Are you satisfied now, Sir?

JOHNS. By my troth, now, that is new, and more than I expected.

BAYES. Yes, I knew this would please you; for the chief art in poetry is to elevate your expectation, and then bring you off some extraordinary way.

    Enter DRAWCANSIR

PHYS. What man is this that dares disturb our feast?

DRAW. He that dares drink, and for that drink dares die;
    And, knowing this, dares yet drink on, am I.[15]

JOHNS. That is, Mr. Bayes, as much as to say, that though he would rather die than not drink, yet he would fain drink for all that too.

BAYES. Right; that's the conceit on't.

JOHNS. 'Tis a marvellous good one, I swear.

BAYES. Now, there are some critics that have advised me to put out the second *dare*, and print *must* in the place on't; but, egad, I think 'tis better thus a great deal.

JOHNS. Whoo! a thousand times.

BAYES. Go on, then.

    USHER. Sir, if you please, we should be glad to know

---

[14] See "Sources".
[15] See "Sources".

>How long you here will stay, how soon you'll go?

BAYES. Is not that now like a well-bred person, egad? So modest, so gentl![16]

SMITH. Oh, very like.

>DRAW. You shall not know how long I here will stay;
>But you shall know I'll take your bowls away.[17]
>
>>*(Snatches the bowls out of the Kings'*
>>*hands, and drinks 'em off.)*

SMITH. But, Mr. Bayes, is that, too, modest and gent?

BAYES. No, egad, Sir; but it's great.

>USHER. Though, brother, this grum stranger be a clown,
>He'll leave us, sure, a little to gulp down.

>DRAW. Whoe'er to gulp one drop of this dares think,
>I'll stare away his very power to drink.[18]
>
>>*(The two Kings sneak off the*
>>*stage, with their attendants.)*
>
>I drink, I huff, I strut, look big and stare;
>And all this I can do, because I dare.[19]   *(Exit.)*

SMITH. I suppose, Mr. Bayes, this is the fierce hero you spoke of.

BAYES. Yes, but this is nothing: you shall see him, in the last act, win above a dozen battles, one after another, egad, as fast as they can possibly come upon the stage.

JOHNS. That will be a fight worth seeing, indeed.

SMITH. But, pray, Mr. Bayes, why do you make the Kings let him use 'em so scurvily?

BAYES. Phoo! that is to raise the character of Drawcansir.

JOHNS. O' my word, that was well thought on.

BAYES. Now, Sirs, I'll show you a scene indeed, or rather, indeed, the scene of scenes. 'Tis an heroic scene.

SMITH. And, pray, Sir, what's your design in this scene?

BAYES. Why, Sir, my design is Roman clothes,[20] gilded truncheons, forced conceit, smooth verse, and a rant; in fine, if this scene do not take, egad, I'll write no more. Come, come in, Mr. – a – nay, come in as many as you can – Gentlemen, I

---

[16] gentlemanly.
[17] See "Sources".
[18] See "Sources".

[19] See "Sources".
[20] See "Sources".

must desire you to remove a little, for I must fill the stage.

SMITH. Why fill the stage?

BAYES. Oh, Sir, because your heroic verse never sounds well, but when the stage is full.

SCENE II

Enter PRINCE PRETTYMAN *and* PRINCE VOLSCIUS

Nay, hold, hold; pray, by your leave a little. Look you, Sir, the drift of this scene is somewhat more than ordinary; for I make 'em both fall out, because they are not in love with the same woman.

SMITH. Not in love! You mean, I suppose, because they are in love, Mr. Bayes?

BAYES. No, Sir, I say, not in love; there's a new conceit for you! – Now, speak.

PRETTY. Since fate, Prince Volscius, now has found the way
For our so long'd-for meeting here this day,
Lend thy attention to my grand concern.

VOLS. I gladly would that story from thee learn;
But thou to love dost, Prettyman, incline;
Yet love in thy breast is not love in mine.

BAYES. Antithesis! thine and mine.

PRETTY. Since love itself's the same, why should it be
Diff'ring in you from what it is in me?

BAYES. Reasoning! egad, I love reasoning in verse.[21]

VOLS. Love takes, chameleon-like, a various dye
From every plant on which itself does lie.

BAYES. Simile!

PRETTY. Let not thy love the course of nature fright:
Nature does most in harmony delight.

VOLS. How weak a deity would nature prove,
Contending with the pow'rful god of love!

BAYES. There's a great verse!

VOLS. If incense thou wilt offer at the shrine

[21] See "Sources" (ref. 279).

Of mighty love, burn it to none but mine.
Her rosy lips eternal sweets exhale,
And her bright flames make all flames else look pale.

BAYES. Egad, that is right.

PRETTY. Perhaps dull incense may thy love suffice,
But mine must be ador'd with sacrifice.
All hearts turn ashes, which her eyes control:
The body they consume, as well as soul.

VOLS. My love has yet a power more divine;
Victims her altars burn not, but refine.
Amidst the flames they ne'er give up the ghost,
But, with her looks, revive still as they roast.
In spite of pain and death they're kept alive:
Her fiery eyes make 'em in fire survive.[22]

BAYES. That is as well, egad, as I can do.

VOLS. Let my Parthenope at length prevail.

BAYES. Civil, egad.

PRETTY. I'll sooner have a passion for a whale,
In whose vast bulk, though store of oil doth lie,
We find more shape, more beauty, in a fly.

SMITH. That's uncivil, egad.

BAYES. Yes; but as far a fetched fancy, though, egad, as e'er you
saw.

VOLS. Soft, Prettyman, let not thy vain pretence
Of perfect love defame love's excellence.
Parthenope is, sure, as far above
All other loves, as above all his love.

BAYES. Ah! egad, that strikes me!

PRETTY. To blame my Cloris, gods would not pretend.

BAYES. Now mark.

VOLS. Were all gods join'd they could not hope to mend
My better choice; for fair Parthenope
Gods would, themselves, ungod themselves to see.[23]

BAYES. Now the rant's a-coming.

[22] See "Sources".
[23] See "Sources".

PRETTY. Durst any of the gods be so uncivil,
     I'd make that god subscribe himself a devil.[24]
BAYES. Ah, gadzookers, that's well writ!
              (Scratching his head, his peruke falls off.)
VOLS. Could'st thou that god from heav'n to earth translate,
     He could not fear to want a heav'nly state;
     Parthenope, on earth, can heav'n create.
PRETTY. Cloris does heav'n itself so far excel,
     She can transcend the joys of heav'n in hell.
BAYES. There's a bold flight for you now! 'Sdeath, I have lost
my peruke. Well, gentlemen, this is what I never yet saw
any one could write but myself. Here's true spirit and flame
all through, egad – So, so; pray, clear the stage.
              (He puts 'em off the stage.)
JOHNS. I wonder how the coxcomb has got the knack of writing
smooth verse thus.
SMITH. Why, there's no need of brain for this; 'tis but scanning;
the labour's in the finger. But where's the sense of it?
JOHNS. Oh, for that he desires to be excused! He is too proud a
man to creep servilely after sense,[25] I assure you. But pray,
Mr. Bayes, why is this scene all in verse?
BAYES. Oh, Sir, the subject is too great for prose.[26]
SMITH. Well said, i'faith! I'll give thee a pot of ale for that
answer; 'tis well worth it.
BAYES. Come, with all my heart. "I'll make that god subscribe
himself a devil." That single line, egad, is worth all that my
brother poets ever writ – Let down the curtain.
                     (Exeunt.)

[24] See "Sources".
[25] See "Sources".
[26] See "Sources".

Act V

Enter BAYES *and the two Gentlemen*

BAYES. Now, gentlemen, I will be bold to say I'll show you the greatest scene that ever England saw: I mean not for words, for those I do not value, but for state, show, and magnificence. In fine, I'll justify it to be as grand to the eye, every whit, egad, as that great scene in *Harry the Eight,*[1] and grander too, egad; for instead of two bishops, I bring in here four cardinals.[2]

> *The curtain is drawn up, the two usurping Kings appear in state, with the* FOUR CARDINALS, PRINCE PRETTY-MAN, PRINCE VOLSCIUS, AMARYLLIS, CLORIS, PARTHENOPE, *etc. Before them,* HERALDS *and* SERGEANTS-AT-ARMS, *with maces.*

SMITH. Mr. Bayes, pray, what is the reason that two of the Cardinals are in hats, and the other in caps?

BAYES. Why, Sir, because – By gad, I won't tell you. Your country-friend, Sir, grows so troublesome —

USHER. Now, Sir, to the business of the day.

PHYS. Speak, Volscius.

VOLS. Dread Sovereign Lords, my zeal to you must not invade my duty to your son; let me intreat that great Prince Prettyman first do speak, whose high preeminence in all things that do bear the name of good may justly claim that privilege.

BAYES. Here it begins to unfold; you may perceive, now, that he is his son.

[1] See Act II, note 27.
[2] See "Sources of the Parody", p. 327.

JOHNS. Yes, Sir, and we are very much beholden to you for that
discovery.

PRETTY. Royal father, upon my knees I beg,
That the illustrious Volscius first be heard.

VOLS. That preference is only due to Amaryllis, Sir.

BAYES. I'll make her speak very well by-and-by, you shall see.

AMAR. Invincible Sovereigns —   *(Soft music.)*

USHER. But stay, what sound is this invades our ears?[3]

PHYS. Sure 'tis the music of the moving spheres!

PRETTY. Behold, with wonder, yonder comes from far
A godlike cloud and a triumphant car.
In which our two right Kings sit, one by one,
With virgins' vests,[4] and laurel-garlands on.

USHER. Then brother Phys', 'tis time we should begone.

*(The two Usurpers steal out of
the throne, and go away.)*

BAYES. Look you now, did not I tell you that this would be as
easy a change as the other?

SMITH. Yes, faith, you did so; though I confess I could not believe you; but you have brought it about, I see.

*The two right Kings of Brentford descend in the clouds,
singing, in white garments; and three Fiddlers sitting
before them, in green*

BAYES. Now, because the two right Kings descend from above,
I make 'em sing to the tune and style of our modern spirits.[5]

1ST KING. Haste, brother King, we are sent from above.

2ND KING. Let us move, let us move,
Move to remove the fate
Of Brentford's long united state.[6]

1ST KING. Tarra, tan-tarra, full east and by south.

2ND KING. We sail with thunder in our mouth.
In scorching noon-day, whilst the traveller stays;
Busy, busy, busy, busy we bustle along,

---

[8] See "Sources".   [5] See "Sources".
[4] i.e., in white. See stage direction   [6] See "Sources".
nine lines on.

Mounted upon warm Phoebus[7] his rays
Through the heav'nly throng,
Hasting to those
Who will feast us at night with a pig's pettitoes.[8]

1ST KING. And we'll fall with our pate
In an olio[9] of hate.

2ND KING. But now supper's done, the servitors try,
Like soldiers, to storm a whole half-moon pie.

1ST KING. They gather, they gather hot custards in spoons.
But alas! I must leave these half-moons,
And repair to my trusty dragoons.[10]

2ND KING. Oh, stay! for you need not as yet go astray;
The tide, like a friend, has brought ships in our
way,
And on their high ropes we will play.
Like maggots in filberts, we'll snug[11] in our shell;
We'll frisk in our shell,
We'll firk[12] in our shell,
And farewell.

1ST KING. But the ladies have all inclination to dance,
And the green frogs croak out a Coranto[13] of
France.

BAYES. Is not that pretty now? The fiddlers are all in green.

SMITH. Ay, but they play no Coranto.

JOHNS. No, but they play a tune that's a great deal better.

BAYES. "No Coranto," quoth-a! That's a good one, with all my
heart. Come, sing on.

2ND KING. Now mortals that hear
How we tilt and career[14]
With wonder will fear
The event of such things as shall never appear.

1ST KING. Stay you to fulfil what the gods have decreed.

---

[7] Apollo, the sun-god.
[8] pigs' feet, a delicacy.
[9] mixture, potpourri.
[10] See "Sources".
[11] snuggle.

[12] be frisky; dance a jig.
[13] a brisk dance; from Fr. *courant*, running.
[14] run along.

2ND KING. Then call me to help you, if there shall be need.

1ST KING. So firmly resolv'd is a true Brentford King,
       To save the distress'd, and help to 'em bring,
       That e'er a full pot of good ale you can swallow,
       He's here with a whoop, and gone with a holla.
              (BAYES *fillips*[15] *his finger, and sings after 'em.*)

BAYES. "He's here with a whoop, and gone with a holla." This, Sir, you must know, I thought once to have brought in with a conjurer.[16]

JOHNS. Ay, that would have been better.

BAYES. No, faith, not when you consider it; for thus 'tis more compendious, and does the thing every whit as well.

SMITH. Thing! What thing?

BAYES. Why bring 'em down again into the throne, Sir; what thing would you have?

SMITH. Well, but methinks the sense of this song is not very plain.

BAYES. Plain! Why, did you ever hear any people in clouds speak plain? They must be all for flight of fancy at its full range, without the least check or control upon it. When once you tie up spirits and people in clouds to speak plain, you spoil all.

SMITH. Bless me, what a monster's this!

              (*The two Kings 'light out of the clouds,*
                       and step into the thrones.)

1ST KING. Come, now to serious counsel we'll advance.

2ND KING. I do agree; but first, let's have a dance.[17]

BAYES. Right! you did that very well, Mr. Cartwright. "But first, let's have a dance." Pray, remember that: be sure you do it always just so, for it must be done as if it were the effect of thought and premeditation. "But first, let's have a dance." Pray, remember that.

SMITH. Well, I can hold no longer; I must gag this rogue; there's no enduring of him.

---

[15] flips, snaps.
[16] See "Sources".

[17] Dances were frequent in the heroic play.

JOHNS. No, prithee, make use of thy patience a little longer; let's see the end of him now.

(Dance a grand dance.)

BAYES. This, now, is an ancient dance, of right belonging to the Kings of Brentford; but since derived, with a little alteration, to the Inns of Court.

An alarm; enter two HERALDS

1ST KING. What saucy groom molests our privacies?

1ST HERALD. The army's at the door, and, in disguise,
Desires a word with both your Majesties.

2ND HERALD. Having from Knightsbridge hither marched
by stealth.

2ND KING. Bid 'em attend awhile and drink our health.

SMITH. How, Mr. Bayes? The army in disguise?

BAYES. Ay, Sir, for fear the usurpers might discover them that went out but just now.

SMITH. Why, what if they had discovered them?

BAYES. Why, then they had broke the design.

1ST KING. Here, take five guineas for those warlike men.

2ND KING. And here's five more; that makes the sum just ten.

1ST HERALD. We have not seen so much the Lord knows
when. *(Exeunt* HERALDS.*)*

1ST KING. Speak on, brave Amaryllis.

AMAR. Invincible Sovereigns, blame not my modesty,
If at this grand conjuncture —

(Drums beat behind the stage.)

1ST KING. What dreadful noise is this that comes and goes?

Enter a SOLDIER *with his sword drawn*

SOLDIER. Haste hence, great Sirs, your royal persons save,
For the event of war no mortal knows:
The army, wrangling for the gold you gave,
First fell to words, and then to handy-blows.[18]

(Exit.)

[18] See "Sources".

BAYES. Is not that now a pretty kind of a stanza and a handsome come-off?

 2ND KING. Oh, dangerous estate of sovereign power!
    Obnoxious to the change of every hour.

 1ST KING. Let us for shelter in our cabinet stay:
    Perhaps these threat'ning storms may pass away.
             (Exeunt.)

JOHNS. But, Mr. Bayes, did not you promise us, just now, to make Amaryllis speak very well?

BAYES. Ay, and so she would have done, but that they hindered her.

SMITH. How, Sir! whether you would or no?

BAYES. Ay, Sir; the plot lay so, that, I vow to gad, it was not to be avoided.

SMITH. Marry, that was hard.

JOHNS. But, pray, who hindered her?

BAYES. Why, the battle, Sir, that's just coming in at door. And I'll tell you now a strange thing; though I don't pretend to do more than other men, egad, I'll give you both a whole week to guess how I'll represent this battle.

SMITH. I had rather be bound to fight your battle, I assure you, Sir.

BAYES. Whoo! there's it now – Fight a battle! there's the common error. I knew presently where I should have you. Why, pray, Sir, do but tell me this one thing: Can you think it a decent thing, in a battle before ladies, to have men run their swords through one another, and all that?

JOHNS. No, faith, 'tis not civil.

BAYES. Right; on the other side, to have a long relation of squadrons here, and squadrons there – what is it but dull prolixity?

JOHNS. Excellently reasoned, by my troth!

BAYES. Wherefore, Sir, to avoid both those indecorums, I sum up my whole battle in the representation of two persons only, no more; and yet so lively that, I vow to gad you would swear ten thousand men were at it, really engaged. Do you mark me?

SMITH. Yes, Sir; but I think I should hardly swear, though, for all that.

BAYES. By my troth, Sir, but you would, though, when you see it; for I make 'em both come out in armour, *cap-a-pie*,[19] with their swords drawn, and hung with a scarlet ribbon at their wrists, which, you know, represents fighting enough.

JOHNS. Ay, ay, so much that, if I were in your place, I would make 'em go out again, without ever speaking one word.

BAYES. No, there you are out; for I make each of 'em hold a lute in his hand.

SMITH. How, Sir, instead of a buckler?

BAYES. Oh, Lord! Oh, Lord! instead of a buckler? Pray, Sir, do you ask no more questions. I make 'em, Sir, play the battle *in recitativo*.[20] And here's the conceit. Just at the very same instant that one sings, the other, Sir, recovers you his sword, and puts himself in a warlike posture; so that you have at once your ear entertained with music and good language, and your eye satisfied with the garb and accoutrements of war.

SMITH. I confess, Sir, you stupefy me.

BAYES. You shall see.

JOHNS. But, Mr. Bayes, might not we have a little fighting? For I love those plays where they cut and slash one another upon the stage for a whole hour together.

BAYES. Why, then, to tell you true, I have contrived it both ways; but you shall have my *recitativo* first.

JOHNS. Ay, now you are right; there is nothing then can be objected against it.

BAYES. True; and so, egad, I'll make it, too, a tragedy in a trice.[21]

> *Enter at several doors the* GENERAL *and* LIEUTENANT-GENERAL, *armed* cap-a-pie, *with each of them a lute in his hand, and his sword drawn and hung with a scarlet ribbon at his wrist*

[19] from head to foot.
[20] See "Sources".
[21] See "Sources".

LIEUT. Villain, thou liest!

GEN. Arm, arm, Gonsalvo, arm;[22] what ho!
　　The lie no flesh can brook, I trow.

LIEUT. Advance from Acton with the musqueteers.[23]

GEN. Draw down the Chelsea cuirassiers.

LIEUT. The band you boast of, Chelsea cuirassiers,
　　　　Shall, in my Putney pikes, now meet their peers.

GEN. Chiswickians, aged, and renown'd in fight,
　　Join with the Hammersmith brigade.

LIEUT. You'll find my Mortlake boys will do them right,
　　　　Unless by Fulham numbers overlaid.

GEN. Let the left-wing of Twick'nam foot advance,
　　And line that eastern hedge.

LIEUT. The horse I raised in Petty-France,
　　　　Shall try their chance,
　　　　And scour the meadows, overgrown with sedge.

GEN. Stand! Give the word.

LIEUT. Bright sword.

GEN. That may be thine,
　　But 'tis not mine.

LIEUT. Give fire, give fire, at once give fire,
　　　　And let those recreant troops perceive mine ire.

GEN. Pursue, pursue; they flee
　　That first did give the lie.　　　　　　　　*(Exeunt.)*

BAYES. This now, is not improper, I think, because the spectators know all these towns, and may easily conceive them to be within the dominions of the two kings of Brentford.

JOHNS. Most exceeding well designed!

BAYES. How do you think I have contrived to give a stop to this battle?

SMITH. How?

BAYES. By an eclipse; which, let me tell you, is a kind of fancy that was yet never so much as thought of but by myself and one person more that shall be nameless.[24]

Enter LIEUTENANT-GENERAL

LIEUT. What midnight darkness does invade the day,
And snatch the victor from his conquer'd prey?
Is the sun weary of this bloody sight,
And winks upon us with the eye of light?
'Tis an eclipse! This was unkind, Oh, moon,
To clap between me and the sun so soon.
Foolish eclipse! thou this in vain hast done;
My brighter honour had eclips'd the sun,
But now behold eclipses two in one.   *(Exit.)*

JOHNS. This is an admirable representation of a battle, as ever I saw.

BAYES. Ay, Sir: but how would you fancy now to represent an eclipse?

SMITH. Why, that's to be supposed.

BAYES. Supposed! Ay, you are ever at your "suppose"; ha, ha, ha! Why, you may as well suppose the whole play. No, it must come in upon the stage, that's certain: but in some odd way that may delight, amuse, and all that. I have a conceit for't that I am sure is new and, I believe, to the purpose.

JOHNS. How's that?

BAYES. Why, the truth is, I took the first hint of this out of a dialogue between Phoebus and Aurora,[25] in *The Slighted Maid*, which, by my troth, was very pretty; but I think you'll confess this is a little better.

JOHNS. No doubt on't, Mr. Bayes, a great deal better.

(BAYES hugs JOHNSON, then turns to SMITH.)

BAYES. Ah, dear rogue! But – a – Sir, you have heard, I suppose, that your eclipse of the moon is nothing else but an interposition of the earth between the sun and moon; as likewise your eclipse of the sun is caused by an interlocation of the moon betwixt the earth and the sun?

SMITH. I have heard some such thing indeed.

BAYES. Well, sir, then what do me I, but make the earth, sun, and moon, come out upon the stage, and dance the hey.[26]

[25] the sun and the dawn.
[26] a country dance.

Hum! and of necessity by the very nature of this dance, the earth must be sometimes between the sun and the moon, and the moon between the earth and sun: and there you have both your eclipses, by demonstration.

JOHNS. That must needs be very fine, truly.

BAYES. Yes, it has fancy in't. And then, Sir, that there may be something in't too of a joke, I bring 'em in all singing, and make the moon sell the earth a bargain.[27] Come, come out, Eclipse, to the tune of *Tom Tyler*.[28]

> *Enter* LUNA

LUNA. Orbis, Oh, Orbis![29]
>> Come to me, thou little rogue, Orbis.

> *Enter* ORBIS

ORBIS. Who calls Terra Firma, pray?
LUNA. Luna, that ne'er shines by day.
ORBIS. What means Luna in a veil?
LUNA. Luna means to show her tail.

BAYES. There's the bargain.[30]

> *Enter* SOL, *to the tune of* Robin Hood

SOL. Fye, sister, fye! thou mak'st me muse,
>> Derry, derry down.
>> To see the Orb abuse.
LUNA. I hope his anger 'twill not move;
>> Since I show'd it out of love,
>> Hey down, derry down.
ORBIS. Where shall I thy true love know,
>> Thou pretty, pretty moon?
LUNA. To-morrow soon, e'er it be noon,
>> On mount Vesuvio.[31]   *(Bis.)*
SOL. Then I will shine.   *(to the tune of* Trenchmore)

---

[27] to answer a question in an unexpected and often obscene way. Cf. Dryden, *MacFlecknoe*, line 181.

[28] Like "Robin Hood" and "Trenchmore" mentioned below, "Tom Tyler" was a popular tune for country dances.

[29] See "Sources".

[30] i.e., the obscenity.

[31] See "Sources".

ORBIS. And I will be fine.

LUNA. And I will drink nothing but Lipary wine.[82]

OMNES. And we, etc.

(As they dance the hey, BAYES speaks.)

BAYES. Now the earth's before the moon; now the moon's before the sun; there's the eclipse again.

SMITH. He's mightily taken with this, I see.

JOHNS. Ay, 'tis so extraordinary, how can he choose?

BAYES. So, now, vanish eclipse, and enter t'other battle, and fight. Here now, if I am not mistaken, you will see fighting enough.

A battle is fought between foot and great hobby-horses. At last DRAWCANSIR comes in, and kills 'em all on both sides. All this while the battle is fighting, BAYES is telling 'em when to shout, and shouts with 'em

DRAW. Others may boast a single man to kill,
But I the blood of thousands daily spill.[83]
Let petty kings the names of parties know;
Where'er I come, I slay both friend and foe.
The swiftest horsemen my swift rage controls,
And from their bodies drives their trembling souls.
If they had wings, and to the gods could fly,
I would pursue, and beat 'em through the sky;
And make proud Jove, with all his thunder, see
This single arm more dreadful is than he. *(Exit.)*

BAYES. There's a brave fellow for you now, Sirs. You may talk of your Hector and Achilles,[84] and I know not who; but I defy all your histories, and your romances too, to show me one such conqueror as this Drawcansir.

JOHNS. I swear, I think you may.

SMITH. But, Mr. Bayes, how shall all these dead men go off? for I see none alive to help 'em.[85]

BAYES. Go off, why, as they came on; upon their legs. How should they go off? Why, do you think the people here don't know

[82] See "Sources".
[83] See "Sources".
[84] See "Sources".
[85] See "Sources".

they are not dead? He's mighty ignorant, poor man! Your
friend here is very silly, Mr. Johnson, egad he is. Ha, ha, ha!
Come, Sir, I'll show you how they shall go off. Rise, rise,
Sirs, and go about your business. There's "go off" for you
now. Ha, ha, ha! Mr. Ivory, a word. Gentlemen, I'll be with
you presently. *(Exit.)*

JOHNS. Will you so? Then we'll be gone.

SMITH. Ay, prithee let's go, that we may preserve our hearing.
One battle more will take mine quite away. *(Exeunt.)*

Enter BAYES *and* PLAYERS

BAYES. Where are the gentlemen?

1ST PLAYER. They are gone, Sir.

BAYES. Gone! 'sdeath! this last act is best of all! I'll go fetch 'em
again. *(Exit.)*

1ST PLAYER. What shall we do, now he's gone away?

2ND PLAYER. Why, so much the better; then let's go to dinner.[36]

3RD PLAYER. Stay, here's a foul piece of paper of his.[37] Let's see
what 'tis.

4TH PLAYER. Ay, ay, come, let's hear it.

3RD PLAYER. *(reads)* "*The Argument of the Fifth Act*: Cloris at
length, being sensible of Prince Prettyman's passion, consents to marry him; but just as they are going to church,
Prince Prettyman meeting by chance with old Joan, the
chandler's widow, and remembering it was she that first
brought him acquainted with Cloris, out of a high point of
honour breaks off his match with Cloris and marries old
Joan. Upon which, Cloris, in despair, drowns herself, and
Prince Prettyman discontentedly walks by the riverside."
This will never do; 'tis just like the rest. Come, let's be gone.

MOST OF THE PLAYERS. Ay, pox on't, let's go away. *(Exeunt.)*

Enter BAYES

BAYES. A plague on 'em both for me, they have made me sweat

---

[36] The rehearsal of Mr. Bayes's play
has taken place in the morning.
Dinner was at noon, and the performance at three or three-thirty in the
afternoon.
[37] Mr. Bayes's original manuscript.

to run after 'em. A couple of senseless rascals that had rather go to dinner than see this play out, with a pox to 'em. What comfort has a man to write for such dull rogues? Come, Mr. – a – where are you, Sir? Come away, quick, quick.

Enter STAGE KEEPER

STAGE KEEPER. Sir, they are gone to dinner.

BAYES. Yes, I know the gentlemen are gone; but I ask for the players.

STAGE KEEPER. Why, an't please your worship, Sir, the players are gone to dinner, too.

BAYES. How! are the players gone to dinner? 'Tis impossible! The players gone to dinner! Egad, if they are, I'll make 'em know what it is to injure a person that does 'em the honour to write for 'em, and all that. A company of proud, conceited, humourous, cross-grained persons, and all that. Egad, I'll make 'em the most contemptible, despicable, inconsiderable persons, and all that, in the whole world, for this trick. Egad, I'll be revenged on 'em; I'll sell this play to the other house.[38]

STAGE KEEPER. Nay, good Sir, don't take away the book; you'll disappoint the company that comes to see it acted here this afternoon.

BAYES. That's all one, I must reserve this comfort to myself. My play and I shall go together; we will not part, indeed, Sir.

STAGE KEEPER. But what will the town say, Sir!

BAYES. The town! Why, what care I for the town? Egad, the town has used me as scurvily as the players have done; but I'll be revenged on them too; for I'll lampoon 'em all. And since they will not admit of my plays, they shall know what a satirist I am. And so farewell to this stage, egad, for ever.

(Exit BAYES.*)*

Enter PLAYERS

1ST PLAYER. Come then, let's set up bills for another play.

[38] the rival theatre.

2ND PLAYER. Ay, ay; we shall lose nothing by this, I warrant you.

1ST PLAYER. I am of your opinion. But before we go, let's see Haynes[39] and Shirley practise the last dance; for that may serve us another time.

2ND PLAYER. I'll call 'em in: I think they are but in the tiring-room.

(The Dance done.)

1ST PLAYER. Come, come; let's go away to dinner.

(Exeunt.)

[39] A celebrated comic actor and dancer, Joseph Haines (d. 1701) succeeded Lacy in the part of Mr. Bayes.

Epilogue

The play is at an end; but where's the plot?
That circumstance our poet Bayes forgot.
And we can boast, though 'tis a plotting age,
No place is freer from it than the stage.
The ancients plotted though, and strove to please   5
With sense that might be understood with ease;
They every scene with so much wit did store,
That who brought any in, went out with more.
But this new way of wit does so surprise,
Men lose their wits in wond'ring where it lies.   10
If it be true that monstrous births presage
The following mischiefs that afflict the age,
And sad disasters to the state proclaim,
Plays without head or tail may do the same.
Wherefore for ours, and for the kingdom's peace,   15
May this prodigious way of writing cease.
Let's have at least once in our lives a time
When we may hear some reason, not all rhyme.
We have these ten years felt its influence;
Pray, let this prove a year of prose and sense.   20

Sources of the Parody in "The Rehearsal"

261 "it shall read . . . in Europe"

"The usual language of the Honourable Edward Howard, Esq., at the rehearsal of his plays" (*Key*, 1704). Edward Howard was one of four of Dryden's brothers-in-law who wrote for the theatre.

"no man . . . my rules"

He who writ this, not without pain and thought,
From French and English theatres has brought
Th' exactest rules by which a play is wrought.
The unity of action, place, and time;
The scenes unbroken; and a mingled chime
Of Jonson's humour with Corneille's rhyme.

DRYDEN, Prologue to *The Maiden Queen* (*Key*)

264 "she is my mistress"

"The part of Amaryllis was acted by Mrs. Ann Reeves, who, at that time, was kept by Mr. Bayes." (*Key*). Biographers of Dryden have been unable to find evidence to substantiate this charge.

266 "two kings of the same place"

According to the *Key*, there are three possible references: (i) the rival brothers in *The Conquest of Granada*; (ii) the two kings in *The United Kingdoms* by Henry Howard, Dryden's brother-in-law; (iii) Charles II and his brother, James, Duke of York, later James II.

"I have made a prologue . . . for either"

"See the two Prologues to *The Maiden Queen*." (*Key*).

267 "I have printed . . . the boxes"

"There were printed papers given the audience before the acting *The Indian Emperor*, telling them that it was the sequel of *The Indian Queen*, part of which play was written by Mr. Bayes, etc." (*Key*). The former play was by Dryden; in the latter Dryden had collaborated with his brother-in-law Sir Robert Howard.

268 "persons"

Mr. Bayes's repeated use of *persons, egad, I vow to gad, and all that*, is "the constant style of Failer" (*Key*) in Dryden's play *The Wild Gallant* (1663).

"certain ties . . . disengaged from"

"He contracted with the King's Company of actors in the year 1668, for a whole share, to write them four plays a year." (*Key*).

269 "So boar and sow . . . other's moan."

Cf. 2 *The Conquest of Granada*, I, ii:

So two kind turtles, when a storm is nigh,
Look up, and see it gath'ring in the sky;
Each calls his mate to shelter in the groves,
Leaving in murmurs their unfinish'd loves.
Perch'd on some drooping branch, they sit alone,
And coo, and hearken to each other's moan. (*Key*)

270 "I am the bold Thunder."

Cf. Stapylton, *The Slighted Maid*, III:

EVENING. I am an evening dark as night. (*Key*)

Dryden's low opinion of the Stapylton play is recorded in his essay *A Parallel of Poetry and Painting* (1695).

"Let the ladies . . . graces"

Cf. *The Slighted Maid*, III:

Let the men 'ware the ditches,
Maids, look to their breeches,
We'll scratch them with briars and thistles. (*Key*)

271 "Mr. Ivory"

"Abraham Ivory had formerly been a considerable actor of women's parts; but afterwards stupefied himself so far with drinking strong waters that, before the first acting of this farce, he was fit for nothing but to go of errands, for which, and mere charity, the company allowed him a weekly salary." (*Key*).

272 "I begin this play with a whisper"

"See [Mrs. Aphra Behn's] *The Amorous Prince* [1671] where you will find all the chief commands and directions are given in whispers." (*Key*). Dryden and other dramatists abused the stage-whisper.

275 "sonnets to Armida"

The reference is to *A Song* ("Farewell, fair Armeda, my joy and my grief"), published anonymously in various collections of Restoration poems, and subsequently attributed to Dryden, largely on the strength of this statement in *The Rehearsal*. In the *Key* Dryden's *Song* is described as "the latter part of a song written by Mr. Bayes on the death of Captain Digby, son of George, Earl of Bristol, who was a passionate admirer of the Duchess Dowager of Richmond, called by the author Armida: he lost his life in a sea fight against the Dutch, on the 28th of May, 1672." This connection has never been confirmed. See 288 below.

"never take snuff when you write"

Dryden "was a great taker of snuff, and made most of it himself" (*Key*).

277 "a late play . . . a knight"

The reference is obscure. It may refer, as the *Key* suggests, to a similar situation in Sir William Berkeley's play *The Lost Lady* (1639); or, more likely, as Bishop Percy's later key suggests, to Sir Richard Fanshawe's paraphrase of a Spanish play, entitled *To Love only for Love's Sake* (1670).

278 "As some tall pine . . . my tears."

> Cf. 1 *The Conquest of Granada*, V, iii:
>
>> As some fair tulip, by a storm oppress'd,
>> Shrinks up, and folds its silken arms to rest;
>> And bending to the blast, all pale and dead,
>> Hears from within the wind sing round its head:
>> So shrouded up your beauty disappears;
>> Unveil, my love, and lay aside your fears.
>> The storm, that caus'd your fright, is past and gone. (*Key*)

279 "let's . . . lay our heads together"

> Their dialogue burlesques Dryden's delight in good argument in his plays and in his verse. Cf. IV, ii: "BAYES. . . . egad, I love reasoning in verse." See also Dryden, *A Defence of an Essay of Dramatic Poesy* (1668): "They cannot be good poets, who are not accustomed to argue well."

282 "the whole state's turned quite topsy-turvy"

> "Such easy turns of state are frequent in our modern plays, where we see princes dethroned and governments changed by very feeble means and on slight occasions." (*Key*). The author of the *Key* goes on to cite parallels between Dryden's *Marriage à la Mode* (1671) and *The Rehearsal*, of which the greatest similarity is between Dryden's Leonidas, "sometimes a king's son, sometimes a shepherd's", and Prince Prettyman, "sometimes a fisher's son, sometimes a prince". There may be also a reference to Dryden's *Conquest of Granada*, in which the kingship seesaws between the claims of two rival brothers.

> "I know not . . . what to say!"
>
> Cf. Sir William Killigrew, *Ormasdes, or Love and Friendship* (1664), V, i:
>
>> ORMASDES. I know not what to say nor what to think.
>
> Cf. also the same author's *Pandora* (1662), V, i:
>
>> PANDORA. I know not what to do nor what to say. (*Key*)
>
> Numerous other parallels exist.

PAGE

283 "the fat spirits in *The Tempest*"

In the Davenant-Dryden version (1667) of the Shakespeare play (III, iii), the stage direction *"Enter eight fat spirits"* appears in the 1701 edition. It was later deleted, but Scott-Saintsbury retained it (III, 160).

285 "Prince Prettyman and his tailor"

The scene that follows parodies a scene in Dryden's *The Wild Gallant* (I, i) between Failer and Bibber, his tailor.

287 "he does not top his part"

"A great word with Mr. Edward Howard" (*Key*).

"what care I what they say?"

"Referring to Mr. Dryden's obstinate adherence to some things in his plays, in opposition to the sound judgment of all unprejudiced critics." (Note to edition of 1775, quoted in Noyes's edition of the play.)

288 "In swords, pikes . . . for me."

The lines parodied here are those of Dryden's *Song*, stanza 2. See 275 above.

> On seas and in battles, through bullets and fire,
> The danger is less than in hopeless desire;
> My death's wound you gave me, though far off I bear
> My fall from your sight, not to cost you a tear.
> But if the kind flood on a wave would convey,
> And under your window my body would lay,
> When the wound on my breast you happen to see,
> You'll say with a sigh, "It was given by me." (*Key*)

289 "His news is welcome, whatsoe'er it be."

Cf. Aphra Behn, *The Amorous Prince*, III, ii:

> ALBERTO. Curtius, I've something to deliver to your ear.
> CURTIUS. Anything from Alberto is welcome. (*Key*)

291 " 'Till torture of the rack . . . sense."

The Arber edition cites Stapylton's *The Slighted Maid*, III, as the source of the scene between Amaryllis and the fisherman. It would seem more likely a burlesque of a scene in Dryden's *Marriage à la Mode*, I, in which Polydamas cross-examines Hermogenes, a shepherd. In the course of the dialogue Polydamas threatens the shepherd with the rack.

292 "Although a fisherman . . . rather."

Cf. *Marriage à la Mode*, III, i:

> LEONIDAS. I never shall forget what nature owes,
>> Nor be asham'd to pay it; though my father
>> Be not a king, I know him brave and honest,
>> And well deserving of a worthier son.

The fortunes of Leonidas are consistently burlesqued in those of Prince Prettyman.

293 "By all the gods . . . sire."

In this and the following speech of Prettyman, the author parodies the exaggerated rhetoric that was a general characteristic of the heroic play.

294 *"Enter . . . with a riding-cloak and boots"*

The scene that follows plainly burlesques *The English Monsieur*, IV, ii, a comedy by James Howard, another brother-in-law of Dryden. In that scene, Comely, "In a riding garb", is about to leave the city, which he finds wearisome and dull, for the country. Ladies of the town try to dissuade him, but he is resolved, until his eye falls on Elsbeth Pritty (like Parthenope here, a country girl), who changes his mind.

"you will here . . . remain"

Cf. Dryden, *The Indian Emperor*, V, ii: "And leaves poor me defenceless here alone."

295 "I'll go range . . . throng"

Cf. *The English Monsieur*, IV, ii:

PAGE

> Let my horses be brought ready to the door, for I'll go out of
> town this evening.
>> Into the country I'll with speed,
>> With hounds and hawks my fancy feed. . . .
>> Now I'll away; a country life
>> Shall be my mistress and my wife. (*Key*)

"I thought myself secure from love"
Cf. *The English Monsieur*, IV, ii:

> What sudden fate hath changed my mind! I feel my heart so
> restless now as if it ne'er knew rest. Sure I'm in love.

Cf. also 1 *The Conquest of Granada*, III, i:

>> I'm all over love:
> Nay, I am love.

"Thou bring'st . . . cloud."
Cf. Davenant, 1 *The Siege of Rhodes*, II:

> I bring the morning pictur'd in a cloud. (*Key*)

296 "Prince Volscius in love! Ha, ha, ha!"
Cf. *The English Monsieur*, IV, ii:

> What, Mr. Comely in love? . . . (*They laugh a great while.*)
> (*Key*)

"My legs . . . for neither."
Volscius's delightful burlesque soliloquy on his boots parodies
the interminable debates between love and honour in heroic
drama.

" 'Go on' . . . 'Nay'."
Cf. 1 *The Siege of Rhodes*, III:

> But honour says, "Not so."

Cf. also Fanshawe, *To Love only for Love's Sake*, III:

> Love and Honour pull two ways,
> And I stand doubtful which to take:
> "To Arabia," Honour says,
> Love says, "No, thy stay here make."

297 "a petticoat and the bellyache"
Cf. Dryden, *The Assignation, or Love in a Nunnery* (1672), **IV**,
i (*Key*).

300 "his funeral just so"
The United Kingdoms (see 266 above) begins with a funeral.

"cannot possibly, egad, be acted . . . week"
The reference is to Dryden's *Conquest of Granada*, in two parts,
each of which is a full-length play.

"drum . . . battle"
Cf. Dryden, *Essay of Heroic Plays*, prefixed to 1 *The Conquest
of Granada*: "my frequent use of drums and trumpets, and my
representations of battles".

"the rule of romance"
The interminable French romances, whose grandiloquence (and
length) are reflected in the heroic plays of Davenant, Dryden,
and others.

302 "his mother . . . ghost"
In 2 *The Conquest of Granada*, IV, iii, the ghost of the hero's
mother appears to him.

"she kills herself"
Probably a reference to 2 *The Conquest of Granada*, IV, iii, in
which the heroine finally returns the love of the hero, and
then threatens to stab herself.

"a wave for her winding-sheet"
Shroud. Cf. 2 *The Conquest of Granada*, IV, iii:

> On seas I bore thee, and on seas I died,
> I died; and for a winding-sheet, a wave
> I had, and all the ocean for my grave. (*Key*)

303 "Drawcansir"
A burlesque of Almanzor, hero of *The Conquest of Granada*.
Dryden defends his "epic" characterization in the dedication

PAGE

of the play to the Duke of York, and writes a further defence in the *Essay of Heroic Plays*.

304 "Then at your birth . . . sky."

The eighteen poetic lines read by Mr. Bayes are a parody of a speech in Dryden's *Tyrannic Love* (1669), III, i:

> BERENICE. My earthly part —
>> Which is my tyrant's right, death will remove;
>> I'll come all soul and spirit to your love.
>> With silent steps I'll follow you all day;
>> Or else, before you, in the sunbeams play.
>> I'll lead you thence to melancholy groves,
>> And there repeat the scenes of our past loves.
>> At night I will within your curtains peep;
>> With empty arms embrace you while you sleep.
>> In gentle dreams I often will be by,
>> And sweep along before your closing eye.
>> All dangers from your bed I will remove,
>> But guard it most from any future love.
>> And when at last in pity you will die,
>> I'll watch your birth of immortality:
>> Then, turtle-like, I'll to my mate repair,
>> And teach you your first flight in open air. (*Key*)

See also 1 *The Conquest of Granada*, IV, ii.

306 "from this conquering lance . . . cheese"

Cf. Thomas Porter, *The Villain* (1663), III, i: "where the host furnishes his guests with a collation out of his clothes: a capon from his helmet, a tansey out of the lining of his cap, cream out of his scabbard, etc." (*Key*).

"He that dares drink . . . am I."

Cf. 2 *The Conquest of Granada*, IV, iii:

> ALMAHIDE. Who dares to interrupt my private walk?
> ALMANZOR. He who dares love, and for that love must die,
>> And, knowing this, dares yet love on, am I. (*Key*)

307 "You shall not know . . . away."

    Cf. 1 *The Conquest of Granada*, V, iii:

        ALMANZOR. I would not now, if thou wouldst beg me, stay;
                But I will take my Alm[ah]ide away. (*Key*)

"Whoe'er to gulp . . . drink."

    Cf. *ibid*:

        ALMANZOR. Thou dar'st not marry her while I'm in sight:
                With a bent brow thy priest and thee I'll fright;
                And in that scene
                Which all thy hopes and wishes should content,
                The thought of me shall make thee impotent.
                                        (*Key*)

"And all this . . . dare."

    Cf. 2 *The Conquest of Granada*, II, iii:

        ALMANZOR. Spite of myself I'll stay, fight, love, despair;
                And I can do all this because I dare. (*Key*)

"Roman clothes"

A reference to Ben Jonson's *Catiline,* revived in 1668.

309 "My love . . . survive."

The speeches of Volscius recall the high-flown style of the heroic
plays of the Earl of Orrery, especially *Mustapha*, II, i.

"Gods would . . . to see."

    Cf. Dryden, *Tyrannic Love*, II, i:

        MAXIMIN. Thou liest. There's not a god inhabits there,
                But for this Christian would all heaven forswear.
                Ev'n Jove would try new shapes her love to win,
                And in new birds and unknown beasts would sin;
                At least, if Jove could love like Maximin. (*Key*)

310 "Durst . . . a devil."

A parody of the extravagant rant of Dryden's hero, Maximin,
in *Tyrannic Love*. Cf.:

> Some god now, if he dares, relate what's past:
> Say but he's dead, that god shall mortal be. (I, i)

> Provoke my rage no farther, lest I be
> Reveng'd at once upon the gods and thee. (*ibid.*)

> What had the gods to do with me or mine? (V, i) (*Key*)

"creep servilely after sense"
Cf. Dryden, Prologue to *Tyrannic Love*:

> Poets, like lovers, should be bold, and dare;
> They spoil their business with an over-care;
> And he who servilely creeps after sense
> Is safe, but ne'er will reach an excellence. (*Key*)

"the subject is too great for prose"
Cf. Dryden's defence of rhymed tragedies in the *Essay of Heroic Plays*: "All the arguments which are formed against it can amount to no more than this, that it is not so near conversation as prose, and therefore not so natural. But it is very clear to all who understand poetry that serious plays ought not to imitate conversation too nearly." Cf. also the argument of Neander in Dryden's *Essay of Dramatic Poesy* (1668).

311 "two bishops ... four cardinals"
In the Davenant version of Shakespeare's *Henry VIII*, II, iv, there are four bishops and two cardinals.

312 "what sound is this invades our ears?"
Cf. Davenant, 1 *The Siege of Rhodes*, I:

> What various noises do mine ears invade?
> And have a concert of confusion made? (*Key*)

Cf. also Howard-Dryden, *The Indian Queen*, I, i:

> What noise is this invades my ear?

"our modern spirits"
Nakar and Damilcar, the two spirits raised by Nigrinus, a conjurer, in *Tyrannic Love*, IV, i.

"Let us move . . . united state."

Cf. *Tyrannic Love*, IV, i:

> NAKAR. Hark, my Damilcar, we are call'd below.
> DAMIL. Let us go, let us go;
> Go to relieve the care
> Of longing lovers in despair, etc. (*Key*)

The remainder of the song of the two kings here is a close parody of the equally lengthy song of Nakar and Damilcar in *Tyrannic Love*.

313 "But alas! . . . dragoons."

Cf. *Tyrannic Love*, IV, i:

> I must leave thee, my fair,
> And to my light-horsemen repair.

314 "a conjurer"

A reference to Nigrinus in *Tyrannic Love*, IV, i (*Key*). Cf. also the role of Ismeron in *The Indian Queen*, III, ii.

315 "The army . . . handy-blows."

Cf. 2 *The Conquest of Granada*, I, ii:

> BOABDELIN. What new misfortunes do these cries presage? . . .
> 2 MESSENGER. Haste all you can their fury to assuage:
> You are not safe from their rebellious rage.
> 3 MESSENGER. This minute, if you grant not their desire,
> They'll seize your person, and your palace fire.
> (*Key*)

317 "in recitativo"

"There needs nothing more to explain the meaning of the battle than the perusal of the first part of *The Siege of Rhodes*, which was performed in *Recitative* music by seven persons only: and the passage out of *Play-House to be Let* [IV, iii and iv, by Sir William Davenant]." (*Key*).

Recitativo: a term meaning rapid musical dialogue in opera; or a part-spoken, part-sung section preceding a great aria.

"a tragedy in a trice"
"*Aglaura* [by Sir John Suckling] and *The Vestal Virgin* [by Sir Robert Howard] are so contrived by a little alteration towards the latter end of them, that they have been acted both ways, either as tragedies or comedies." (*Key*).

318 "Arm, arm, Gonsalvo, arm"
Cf. 1 *The Siege of Rhodes*, I: "Arm, arm, Valerius, arm." (*Key*)

"Acton with the musqueteers"
The numerous geographical adjectives used in the ensuing dialogue of the two generals parody the use of proper nouns and, in places, exotic place-names in much of the heroic drama of the time. All the places here — Acton, Chelsea, Putney, Chiswick, Hammersmith, etc. — are close to the City of London and are recognizable today in the names of London boroughs and suburbs. Davenant's *Siege of Rhodes* is the source of most of the heroics parodied here, but other authors followed a similar practice.

"one . . . that shall be nameless"
Sir Robert Stapylton, in *The Slighted Maid.*

320 "Orbis, Oh, Orbis!"
The dialogue that follows between Luna (the moon), Orbis (the earth), and Sol (the sun) is a parody of the dialogue between Phoebus and Aurora in Stapylton's *The Slighted Maid*, V, i.

"mount Vesuvio"
In *The Slighted Maid* Phoebus speaks of "burning mount Vesuvio".

321 "Lipary wine"
A wine imported from the Lipari islands, north of Sicily. Cf. *The Slighted Maid*, V, i: "Drink, drink, Wine, Lippari-wine."

"Others may boast . . . spill."
True to the spirit of the hero of the heroic play and, especially,

of Dryden's Almanzor. Cf. 1 *The Conquest of Granada*, III, i:

ALMANZOR. Thou, single, art not worth my answering.
But take what friends, what armies thou canst
bring;
What worlds; and, when you are united all,
Then I will thunder in your ears, "She shall!"

"Achilles"
Cf. Dryden, *Essay of Heroic Plays*: "The first image I had of him
[Almanzor] was from the Achilles of Homer. . . . "

"how shall . . . help 'em"
In the Restoration theatre, the heroes (who died in front of the
curtain) were usually carried off. Cf. Epilogue to *Tyrannic Love*.
"Valeria (played by Nell Gwynne), daughter to Maximin, having killed herself for the love of Porphyrius, when she was to
be carried off by the bearers, strikes one of them a box on the
ear, and speaks thus:

Hold! are you mad? you damn'd confounded dog,
I am to rise and speak the epilogue." (*Key*)

She then turned to the audience and said:

I come, kind gentlemen, strange news to tell ye:
I am the ghost of poor, departed Nelly. . . .

Selected Bibliography

BAUDELAIRE, P. C., "On the Essence of Laughter" in *The Mirror of Art*, New York, Doubleday and Co., 1956.

BERGSON, Henri, "Laughter" in *Comedy*, New York, Doubleday and Co., 1956.

CONGREVE, William, *Comedies by William Congreve*, ed. Bonamy Dobrée, London, Oxford University Press, 1925.

——, *The Complete Works of William Congreve*, ed. Montague Summers, 4 vols., London, Nonesuch Press, 1923.

——, *The Works of Congreve*, ed. F. W. Bateson, London, P. Davies, 1930.

COOK, Albert, *The Dark Voyage and the Golden Mean*, Cambridge, Harvard University Press, 1949.

DOBRÉE, Bonamy, *Restoration Comedy, 1660-1720*, London, Oxford University Press, 1924.

FRYE, H. Northrop, *Anatomy of Criticism*, Princeton, Princeton University Press, 1957.

FUJIMURA, T. H., *The Restoration Comedy of Wit*, Princeton, Princeton University Press, 1952.

HAZLITT, William, *Lectures on the English Comic Writers*, Everyman's Library, London, J. M. Dent and Sons, 1921.

HOLLAND, N. N., *The First Modern Comedies*, Cambridge, Harvard University Press, 1959.

LAMB, Charles, "On the Artificial Comedy of the Last Century" in *Essays of Elia*, 1823.

LYNCH, K.M., *The Social Mode of Restoration Comedy*, New York, The Macmillan Co., 1926.

MACAULAY, T. B., "Leigh Hunt's *Comic Dramatists of the Restoration*" in *Historical Essays*, 1843.

MEREDITH, George, "The Spirit of English Comedy" in *Comedy*, New York, Doubleday and Co., 1956.

MIGNON, Elizabeth, *Crabbed Age and Youth*, Durham, Duke University Press, 1947.

MUESCHKE, Paul and Miriam, *A New View of Congreve's "Way of the World"*, Ann Arbor, University of Michigan Press, 1958.

NICOLL, Allardyce, *A History of Restoration Drama, 1660-1700*, Cambridge, Cambridge University Press, 1928.

PALMER, John, *The Comedy of Manners*, London, G. Bell, 1913.

PERRY, Henry T. E., *The Comic Spirit in Restoration Drama*, New Haven, Yale University Press, 1925.

POTTS, L. J., *Comedy*, London, Hutchinson's University Library, 1949.

SHERBURN, George, "Restoration Drama" in *A Literary History of England*, ed. A. C. Baugh, New York, Appleton-Century-Crofts, 1948, pp. 748-79.

STYAN, J. L., *The Dark Comedy*, Cambridge, Cambridge University Press, 1962.

SWABEY, M. C., *Comic Laughter: A Philosophical Survey*, New Haven, Yale University Press, 1961.

SYPHER, Wylie, Introduction, and Appendix: "The Meanings of Comedy" in *Comedy*, New York, Doubleday and Co., 1956.

UNDERWOOD, Dale, *Etherege and the Seventeenth-Century Comedy of Manners*, New Haven, Yale University Press, 1957.

VILLIERS, George, second Duke of Buckingham, *The Rehearsal*, ed. Edward Arber, London, English Reprints, 1869 (Reprinted, London, 1909).

WILCOX, John, *The Relation of Molière to Restoration Comedy*, New York, Columbia University Press, 1938.

WYCHERLEY, William, *The Complete Works of William Wycherley*, ed. Montague Summers, 4 vols., London, Nonesuch Press, 1924.